Globalizatio

This book analyzes how increases in international trade, finance, and production have altered voter decisions, political party positions, and the types of public issues that parties focus on in postindustrial democracies. Although many studies interrogate whether internationalization matters in regard to policy outcomes and how globalization relates to mass protest, few examine globalization and mass politics more generally. This book argues that, by reducing the room in which to maneuver in policy making, globalization reduces the importance of economics-based issues while increasing the electoral importance of noneconomic issues. The argument is tested on original and existing data sources. Timothy Hellwig demonstrates that rather than reduce its scope, economic globalization shifts the bases of mass politics.

Timothy Hellwig is an associate professor of political science and the director of the Institute for European Studies at Indiana University Bloomington. His work has been published in several peer-reviewed journals, including the *American Journal of Political Science*, the *British Journal of Political Science*, *Comparative Political Studies*, and the *Journal of Politics*. He has previously served as a researcher at the International Foundation for Election Systems, with the faculty at the University of Houston, and as a visiting researcher at the University of Essex and at Gothenburg University.

Cambridge Studies in Comparative Politics

Books in the Series

Ben W. Ansell, *From the Ballot to the Blackboard: The Redistributive Political Economy of Education*
Leonardo R. Arriola, *Multi-Ethnic Coalitions in Africa: Business Financing of Opposition Election Campaigns*
David Austen-Smith, Jeffry A. Frieden, Miriam A. Golden, Karl Ove Moene, and Adam Przeworski, eds., *Selected Works of Michael Wallerstein: The Political Economy of Inequality, Unions, and Social Democracy*
Andy Baker, *The Market and the Masses in Latin America: Policy Reform and Consumption in Liberalizing Economies*
Lisa Baldez, *Why Women Protest: Women's Movements in Chile*
Stefano Bartolini, *The Political Mobilization of the European Left, 1860–1980: The Class Cleavage*
Robert Bates, *When Things Fell Apart: State Failure in Late-Century Africa*
Mark Beissinger, *Nationalist Mobilization and the Collapse of the Soviet State*
Nancy Bermeo, ed., *Unemployment in the New Europe*

(*continued after the index*)

Globalization and Mass Politics

Retaining the Room to Maneuver

TIMOTHY HELLWIG

Indiana University Bloomington

CAMBRIDGE
UNIVERSITY PRESS

CAMBRIDGE
UNIVERSITY PRESS

32 Avenue of the Americas, New York NY 10013-2473, USA

Cambridge University Press is part of the University of Cambridge.

It furthers the University's mission by disseminating knowledge in the pursuit of education, learning and research at the highest international levels of excellence.

www.cambridge.org
Information on this title: www.cambridge.org/9781107427723

First published 2015
First paperback edition 2016

A catalogue record for this publication is available from the British Library

Library of Congress Cataloguing in Publication data
Hellwig, Timothy, 1972–
Globalization and mass politics : retaining the room to maneuver / Timothy Hellwig, Indiana University Bloomington.
pages cm. – (Cambridge studies in comparative politics)
ISBN 978-1-107-07507-8
1. Globalization – Political aspects. 2. Globalization – Economic aspects. 3. Economics – Political aspects. 4. Political participation. 5. Representative government and representation. 6. Voting research. I. Title.
JZ1320.H45 2015
324–dc23 2014020984

ISBN 978-1-107-07507-8 Hardback
ISBN 978-1-107-42772-3 Paperback

To Tana

Contents

Figures

Tables

Acknowledgments

This book has been a work in progress for some time. The reasons for the long gestation period are several and include access to research funding, waiting on data releases, time diverted to other responsibilities, and, of course, more than a few trips down dead ends. But this manuscript would remain a work in progress if it were not for the generosity of many individuals. It is a pleasure to acknowledge them here.

John Freeman and Ray Duch deserve top billing. John shared my interest in the room to maneuver and how it matters for democracy and markets in capitalist economies. I thank John for always making time to provide comments and for never shying from constructive feedback. Ray was also an early supporter of the project. Much of my thinking about the voter's calculus comes from conversations with Ray and from reading his work. Ray also guided me through the world of international survey research. John and Ray share a common belief in the value of rigorous scientific research. I'm not sure this book lives up to their standards, but I hope it is somewhere in the ballpark.

I've been fortunate to have many other colleagues and friends weigh in on this project, some by reading chapter drafts, some by way of back-and-forth exchanges of ideas. These many individuals include Jim Adams, Isabella Alcañiz, Chris Anderson, Andy Baker, Clem Brooks, Lawrence Broz, Ernesto Calvo, Nick Clark, Lawrence Ezrow, Lucy Goodhart, Peter Gourevitch, Stephan Haggard, Sara Hobolt, Nate Jensen, Mark Kayser, Jason Kuo, Mike Lewis-Beck, René Lindstädt, Dani Marinova, Patricia McManus, Richard Nadeau, Megumi Naoi, David Samuels, Phil Shively, Matt Singer, Nils Steiner, Rune Stubager, Erik Tillman, Jack Vowles, Stefanie Walter, Guy Whitten, and Chris Wlezien. Special thanks to Matt Singer for organizing a panel on the manuscript at the 2012 Midwest Political Science meetings in Chicago, to Lawrence Broz for inviting me to present much of the manuscript at UCSD, and to Mike Lewis-Beck for letting me tag along on his European travels. Ian Anson, Eva Coffey,

Dani Marinova, Kirk Harris, and Anna Mikulska also deserve thanks for their research assistance.

This book reports evidence from a wide range of empirical analyses pitched at the micro, macro, and elite levels. I am indebted to several individuals and institutions for assisting me in the collection and analyses of these data. I am extremely grateful for funding from the U.S. National Science Foundation, grants SES-0819570 and SES-0241824. Without this funding, the public opinion and expert survey data used in Chapters 5, 6, and 7, as well as the original interview evidence, would not exist. Christophe Jourdain at the Institut Français d'Opinion Publique (IFOP) deserves much credit for – and displayed great patience in – shepherding the mass surveys from drawing board to dataset. Jack Vowles and Georgios Xezonakis were my partners in devising and implementing the expert survey. Thanks too to Jack for including those items in the 2008 NZES. Chapter 5 draws in part on analysis of a special component of the 2009 European Election Study on performance evaluations; I thank the principal investigators on this project, Susan Banducci, Sara Hobolt, and James Tilley, for releasing these data. And I am grateful to Carine Marcé, Rune Stubager, and Henrik Oscarsson for their assistance in obtaining data from Taylor Nelson Sofres, the Danish National Election Study, and the Swedish National Election Study, respectively. Thanks to David Sanders at the University of Essex and Henrik Oscarsson at Gothenburg University for serving as hosts during research trips abroad.

Select parts of the manuscript have appeared elsewhere, in various forms. Chapter 3 includes arguments and evidence published in the *Journal of Politics* as "Balancing Demands: The World Economy and the Composition of Policy Preferences" (vol. 76:1). Data analyses reported in Chapter 6 have appeared in part in *The Sociological Quarterly* under the title "The Structure of Issue Voting in Postindustrial Democracies" (vol. 55:4). And Chapter 8 on party shifts draws on joint work with Lawrence Ezrow appearing in *International Studies Quarterly* ("Responding to Voters or Responding to Markets? Political Parties and Public Opinion in an Era of Globalization," vol. 58:4). I am grateful for permission to reproduce this material here. I also thank the individuals at Cambridge University Press, Lew Bateman and Shaun Vigil, for taking an interest in the project and for shepherding it through to publication.

Finally, and most importantly, I thank my family for their support in this and all my pursuits. I thank my parents for their interest and support over the years. I thank Claire and Owen for putting up with my absences and giving me reason to get away from the keyboard. And I especially thank Tana for being my partner through this and other adventures, through thick and thin. I dedicate this book to her.

1

Globalization and Democracy in Advanced Industrial Societies

In the fall of 2008, the U.S. economy was in a poor state. Some might say it was on life support. Brought to the fore by skyrocketing Wall Street bonuses, income disparities between the rich and the poor had reached levels not seen since the 1930s. Income growth had fallen to 1 percent. Unemployment, after holding steady at around 5 percent, was steadily creeping upward. Unsurprisingly, polls taken in advance of November's presidential election identified economic issues as the most important for a majority of the electorate. Conventional wisdom has it that, under such circumstances, voters voice their disdain by ousting the political party of the incumbent, in this case the Republicans. This prediction indeed came to pass as the Democrats and Barack Obama handily defeated the Republican candidate in the presidential election.

It would be a mistake, however, to assume that the "Great Recession" of 2007–2009 produced, in some mechanical way, a victory for the Democrats. To inflict punishment on the incumbent party for overseeing a poor economy, voters must first attribute at least partial responsibility to government officials – if not for the severity of the downturn then for the effectiveness of the policy response. In 2008, many voters did just that, but many also did not. According to one public opinion poll just ahead of the vote, many Americans in fact doubted their government's ability to affect economic outcomes. When asked about the federal government's ability to manage the economy effectively, more than half of the respondents were of the belief that the government had the power to do so. A sizeable minority, however, questioned this capacity; 40 percent maintained that the government's ability to steer the economy was limited, on account of U.S. ties to the global economy (Pew Research Center 2008). In light of the conventional understanding of economics and elections (Tufte 1978), the differences among Americans' views on the capacity of the government to manage the economy are noteworthy.

TABLE 1.1. *Room-to-maneuver perceptions and vote choice, 2008 U.S. presidential election*

	All respondents (N=1,485)	Gov't still has power to fix economy (N=814)		Gov't cannot fix economy because of global economy (N=573)	
	All	All	Non-partisans	All	Non-partisans
McCain-Palin	46	43	39	50	52
Obama-Biden	54	57	61	50	48
Margin	*+8 Obama-Biden*	*+14 Obama-Biden*	*+22 Obama-Biden*	*0 even*	*+4 McCain-Palin*

Chi-square (all respondents) = 4.23, p-value = 0.04.

Note: Cells report percent who intend to vote for the Republican ticket of John McCain and Sarah Palin and those who intend to vote for the Democratic ticket of Barack Obama and Joseph Biden in the 2008 election according to whether they believe "the federal government cannot fix the economy so easily these days because the United States is part of a global economy" or that "the government still has the power to fix the economy." "Don't know" responses and intentions to vote for other candidates are excluded.

Source: Pew Research Center for the People and the Press Early October 2008 Political and Economic Survey.

Of even greater interest is how these views mattered for voter decisions. The poll predicted 46 percent of the popular vote for the Republican ticket of John McCain and Sarah Palin and 54 percent for Democrats Obama and Joseph Biden, for a margin of nearly 8 percent for the latter.[1] However, as Table 1.1 shows, for those Americans who believed in the room to maneuver – that is, who thought the government could still fix the economy – the Democrats' advantage was nearly twice as large. Yet those who said the government could no longer fix the economy were split equally in support of the Democratic and Republican tickets. This effect is not a function of partisan disposition; a look at independents yields an even sharper competency-based effect on voter support. Obama, it appears, owed much of his popular vote advantage to the long-held perception that governments can manage the economy, and he may not have won the election if more Americans believed that globalization's room-to-maneuver constraints were such that it made no difference which individual was pulling the policy levers as president.

This anecdote illustrates a potential implication of globalization for how voters decide. It is notable that the example hails not from some small

[1] This turned out to be an accurate prediction. The popular vote in November was 53 to 46 percent in favor of Obama-Biden.

export-driven economy of northern Europe but from the country with the world's largest domestic economy. As we will see in the examples that follow, these effects are as great or greater in democracies with smaller domestic markets and deeper ties to world markets. The September 2009 German election offers a case in point. According to some yardsticks, the Federal Republic that year had weathered the worst economic performance since the end of World War II. We would not expect such a state of affairs to bode well for Chancellor Angela Merkel and her Christian Democratic Union Party. However, counter the conventional wisdom that incumbents are rewarded for good times and punished in times of distress, the election yielded a solid victory for Merkel and the Christian Democrats. Indeed, the party emerged from the vote in a better position – from a standpoint of advocating for its preferred policies – than they had been in going into it.[2]

Or consider the Finnish election of April 2011. The Finnish case offers an illustration of the relationship between policy performance and election outcomes in a small open economy when, in terms of policy performance, the economic situation was relatively stable. Indeed, in 2010, Finland's economic growth was a respectable 3.4 percent, comfortably above the 2 percent average across the seventeen-member Eurozone. And by the first quarter of 2011, the jobless rate had dipped below 8 percent while the Eurozone average remained above 10 percent. The run-up to the election, however, was not about Finland's ability to weather the storm economically; rather, party disagreements over financial support for worse-off EU member states, such as Portugal and Greece, dominated campaign discussions. This discourse, which de-emphasized Finland's performance and focused on the country's position in the wider European economy, may account for why the incumbent Center Party (KESK) was not rewarded for comparably sound economic management but instead experienced a drop of support on the order of 16 seats in the 200-seat *Eduskunta*, falling from the largest party in the legislature to fourth in size. The populist True Finns and their charismatic leader, Timo Soini, reaped the benefits with thirty-nine seats, well above the five the party previously held.

These examples highlight many of the questions raised in this book. In today's open economies, how do voters assign credit and blame for observed outcomes? Do they attribute responsibility to the government of the day? Or do ties to the economy beyond borders absolve national politicians from being held to accounts? If capitalism on a global scale requires governments to act in line with the preferences of foreign producers and investors, then what remains of the government's policy room to maneuver? Does globalization matter for how electors choose their representatives? How does reliance on

[2] Prior to the 2009 vote, the Christian Democrats were in an uncomfortable partnership with the Social Democrats. After the election, the party was able to form a government with the Free Democratic Party, its preferred partner.

the movement of goods, services, and people across borders shape the incentives of political elites? When it comes to globalization, do leaders follow the preferences of the masses or are politicians allowed free reign? Ultimately, what effect does globalization have on political representation and popular sovereignty?

The consequences of market integration have been widely discussed by scholars, journalists, and the public at large. The lion's share of scholarly attention in political economy is concerned with how political institutions, economic organizations, and producer groups exacerbate, filter, redirect, and otherwise affect how cross-border economic ties influence domestic politics. Politics, in this sense, takes the form of *policy outputs*, such as the size of social safety nets or tax policy convergence, and the resulting *policy outcomes*, such as economic inequality or insecurity. These foci have a long and respected lineage in the study of political economy. Early work in open-economy macroeconomics predicted how policy regimes and capital movements condition domestic policy autonomy (Mundell 1960; Cohen 1965). Also influential were comparative studies on how the policy effects of governments' policy strategies were facilitated or stymied by particular structures of administrative capitalism (Katzenstein 1985; Hall 1986; Zysman 1983). More recently, work in the "varieties of capitalism" tradition, which emphasizes producer and vocational-training systems, has made an imprint on scholarly thinking about the domestic effects of the world economy (Hall and Soskice 2001; Jensen 2011a).

Attention to policy outputs and outcomes, however, has come at the expense of understanding whether and how wide-ranging trends in the movement of goods, services, people, and especially capital affect decisions of political actors. Little attention is accorded to globalization's effects on politics viewed through the lens of voters, parties, and the quality of electoral democracy. As Kayser (2007, 341) notes, "the sheer volume of literature ... has made it easy to overlook an important fact: Very little of it addresses the effect of economic globalization on actual politics, understood more narrowly as electoral politics."

This is where this book comes in. Unlike most studies on the political economy of advanced capitalism, the protagonists in this story are not the aggregated entities of governments, interest groups, and macro-political organizations, per se. The emphasis instead is on individuals in their roles as citizens and political elites in their roles as representatives. This book is about how globalization alters the self-interested behavior of citizens and their representatives. This "mass politics" reorientation is informed more by insights from the study of public opinion and of party competition than it is by the study of the partisan make-up of governments or domestic political institutions. I elaborate on this point in the next section. First, however, this introductory chapter describes the current landscape in the study of economic globalization and domestic politics.

1.1. The Global Economy and Domestic Politics: The State of Affairs

Broadly construed, scholarship on the political implications of economic globalization may be put into one of two lines of argument.[3] The first of these emphasizes the efficiency gains from market integration. This argument states that, by privileging the free movement of capital for investment, employment, and growth, globalization has created a "race-to-the-bottom" in social protections. According to this *efficiency thesis*, social-democratic solutions are unattainable in a world where rules are shaped by impersonal and unaccountable financial markets. To attract capital, national policies inevitably converge on to a neoliberal mix, characterized by spending cuts, lower taxes, balanced budgets, and a general weakening of the state's productive and redistributive capacity. Observers have drawn on this logic to paint an uncertain future for independent national policies (e.g. Greider 1999; Korpi and Palme 2003; Mishra 1999; Moses 2000). The essence of the argument is captured by Steinmo (2002, 839): "Internationalization increases the availability of the exit option accorded mobile asset holders, [forcing] policymakers to compete for transnationally fluid investment via tax reductions. The result ... is that all nation-states must redesign their tax systems – and most probably reduce tax burdens – to effectively compete in the new world economy."

Although many studies from the late 1990s and early 2000s discredited this perspective for lacking an understanding of the diversities in policy responses, subsequent empirical investigations have provided some vindication for earlier globalization pessimists. Drawing on evidence from this later period – a time characterized by trans-border capital market integration of a greater order of magnitude than times previous – researchers show that the relationship between economic globalization and public spending has qualitatively changed over time. Consistent with efficiency arguments, this connection has become negative in recent years (Busemeyer 2009; Jahn 2006; Plümper et al. 2005).

Evidence of globalization's constraining effects notwithstanding, many students of advanced capitalist economies would take issue with the pessimistic conclusions of the efficiency thesis. These scholars emphasize the resiliency of national policy solutions in the face of common exogenous shocks. This more positive revisionist view owes much to research examining the industrial economies' distinct policy responses in the wake of the 1970s oil crises (Cameron 1978; Katzenstein 1985; Ruggie 1982; Zysman 1983). Out of this tradition, many have become proponents of what might be called a *divergent paths* or

[3] The discussion in this section pertains to politics in advanced industrial societies. Scholars debate the extent to which these arguments apply to middle- and low-income countries (e.g., Rudra 2002; Wibbels 2006).

compensation thesis. According to this perspective, the structure of domestic politics prominently shapes policy responses to common exogenous shocks. Among the advanced capitalist economies, certain countries have willingly rolled back social protections and alleviated tax burdens so as to engage in world markets. Such is the case in the Anglo-American democracies. In many other countries, however, governments have come to terms with the exigencies of world markets by redoubling efforts to compensate those who lose out from liberalization.

The latter path has been characterized in terms of the bargain of embedded liberalism. The bargain's logic may be traced to *The Great Transformation* (1944). In it, Karl Polanyi identifies periods in western history, culminating in the collapse of democracy during the interwar period, when the economy alternatively became embedded in and dis-embedded from society. In the post-war era, governments in democracies were required to strike a bargain with the public whereby the latter supported liberal policies vis-à-vis the world economy in exchange for policies targeted at those who would lose out from globalization. The embedded liberalism bargain thus offers an explanation why the most open economies tend also to have the most extensive forms of social protection. In many cases, such as the small open states of northwest Europe, the data show that globalization does not result in the withering away of popular social safety nets.

Proponents of this compensation thesis identify a set of factors integral to the maintenance of distinct national policies. Some point to particular, path-dependent trajectories, stemming from pre-World War II bargains between capital and labor and between various producer groups, which insulate states from transnational pressures (Pierson 2001). Others focus on how domestic institutions or welfare-production regimes diffuse global economic forces (Franzese 2002; Swank 2002) or combine with partisan politics to produce specific policy outcomes (Garrett 1998). It is argued, for example, that democracies with corporatist forms of interest intermediation, proportional electoral rules, and/or recurrent left-of-center governments are better equipped to counter globalization's displacement effects with offsetting forms of compensation (e.g., Garrett 1998). Still others call attention to how tight relationships between vertically integrated firms, industries, unions, and employer associations in coordinated market economies stave off the market-privileging forces brought on by international competition (Jensen 2011a). According to this argument, even if exposure to the world economy limits certain actions, governments can offset these by directing policy in complementary areas. By heightening demands for social protection, openness may in fact facilitate responsive policymaking – a point I confront head-on in Chapter 3.

It is no exaggeration to say that revisionist arguments have achieved conventional wisdom status, particularly if we place under this umbrella more balanced arguments that allow that globalization has reduced – though not

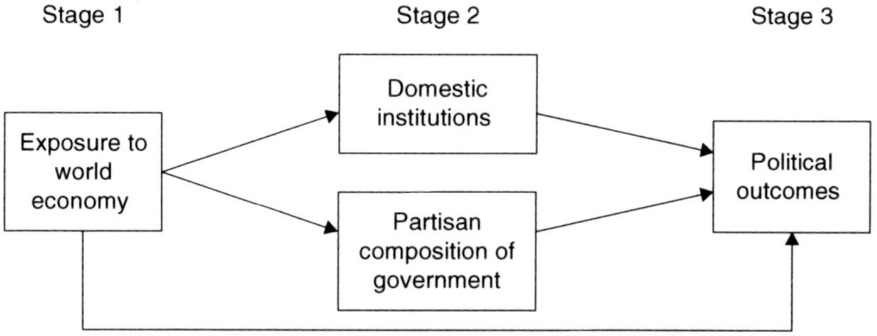

FIGURE 1.1. A standard framework linking globalization to domestic politics: markets, domestic institutions, and policy outcomes.

eliminated – the capacity of nation-state governments to pursue separate policy regimes (e.g., Hays 2009; Kittel and Winner 2005; Steinmo 2002).

These debates with respect to efficiency and compensation continue, even though efforts to reconcile the views of globalization pessimists and optimists have yielded "surprisingly little progress" (Hays 2009, 8).[4] The purpose of this book, however, is not to take sides in debates between proponents of the efficiency thesis (pessimists) and those subscribing to compensation arguments (optimists). This is not a story about policy choice under the strain of global interdependence. Rather, my objective is to emphasize what is missing from general discussions of global economics and national politics. Although the perspectives reviewed earlier arrive at different conclusions, they share a common causal framework. This general framework is summarized in stylized fashion in Figure 1.1. Economic globalization – variously gauged as exposure to international trade, the removal of restrictions on cross-border capital movements, foreign direct investment, and the like – is conceived as causally prior to and bearing on national political outcomes.[5] These political outcomes are usually conceived in terms of public spending, social transfers, and tax burdens or, in short, as policy outcomes. The general framework further posits that domestic factors, in the form of institutions and/or government partisanships, serve a

[4] Beside the central efficiency-compensation debate, a third perspective contends that relationships observed between globalization and national policy decisions are neither negative nor positive but spurious. Iversen and his collaborators, for instance, argue that factors associated with structural economic change, not globalization, account for social policy outcomes in postindustrial economies (Iversen 2005; Iversen and Cusack 2000; Iversen and Wren 1998). The implication from what we might call the *spurious effects thesis* is that globalization's effects are indirect, filtered through more fundamental structural economic changes (also see Clark 2003; Kitschelt 1994; Pontusson 1995; Rueda 2005).

[5] These measures are, strictly speaking, not exogenously determined. Figure 1.1 could also include a feedback loop reconnecting policy outcomes to globalization. However, the political science literature generally proceeds as though globalization is exogenously determined (exceptions are Mosley 2003; Adserà and Boix 2002; Bernhard and Leblang 2006; Sattler et al. 2008).

mediating role by filtering, amplifying, or otherwise shaping the domestic consequences of globalization.

But missing from Figure 1.1 is *mass politics*, defined here as the preferences and behaviors of citizens and their representatives. Most studies have little to say about political parties (apart from their roles as heads of governments) and voters. For example, a recent statement on globalization and democracy in the rich democracies is Steinmo's *The Evolution of Modern States* (2010). Steinmo argues that countries, like organisms, are different systems that adapt differently in evolving environments. This explains why "advanced capitalist states are not locked into a 'race to the bottom'" in today's globalized world (2010, 206). Although impressive in its coverage and thought-provoking in its approach, Steinmo's structural account places little import on mass politics. The relative absence of mass politics is also evident in the pages of the journal at the forefront of the study of international political economy, *International Organization*. From 2000 to 2010, the journal published twenty-three research articles on the domestic effects of economic globalization. Only one of these – Broz and Hawes' (2006) study of congressional voting – reports analyses that bear directly on the issue of political representation.

As I discuss later in this chapter, this is not to say that mass politics has gone unexamined. Existing book-length discussions, however, tend to extrapolate from macro-analyses to draw inferences for globalization and masses. For example, Swank (2002) argues that particular political institutions work to upset the "race to the bottom" in social protections that otherwise accompany financial globalization. Although concerned with macro-policy outcomes, Swank's book has a mass politics extension. Since a majority of the public supports generous social policies, and since financial market integration need not detract from delivering such policies, it follows that globalization is not damaging to healthy mass politics – at least in countries with a particular mix of political institutions. Also relevant is Hays' (2009) work on the sustainability of the embedded liberalism bargain. Hays examines aggregate policy and performance outcomes to make claims about globalization and democracy. He argues that certain electoral and labor market institutions and macro-political institutions help in our quest to understand the rise of twenty-first-century anti-globalization backlashes. Their many virtues notwithstanding, these and other studies stop short of explicitly confronting globalization's consequences for mass politics and, hence, of providing an understanding of its effects on the workings of representative democracy.[6]

[6] Another important contributor to the literature on globalization and mass politics is Kriesi et al. (2008). This work, however, does not examine the influence of economic globalization per se, but instead uses "globalization" as a summary term to characterize the new set of political issues facing democracies in Western Europe at the end of the twentieth century. I discuss this work in Chapter 6.

1.2. The Contribution of This Book

This book is set apart from previous studies in three respects. First, it reorients the study of international economics and domestic politics away from macro-outcomes and onto the actors who lie at the heart of the democratic process: individual voters and their representatives. Second, it advances an encompassing theoretical framework that joins together the many settings in which voters and elected policymakers interact. And third, it tests this argument empirically across an entire causal chain linking the components of mass politics.

This is not the first study of globalization from the perspective of parties and voters. A growing literature examines globalization with respect to mass politics. Much of this work examines public preferences over policy, and over trade policy in particular. Scheve and Slaughter's (2001) study of public opinion finds that Americans' preferences for free trade are interpretable in terms of the Stolper-Samuelson model: Owners of scarce factors of production are less likely to support free trade than owners of relatively abundant factors. Mayda and Rodrik (2005) conduct a similar individual-level analysis across a larger sample of developed and developing countries and arrive at similar conclusions (see also Baker 2005; Kaltenthaler et al. 2004; Mansfield and Mutz 2009, among others). Work on policy preferences for liberalization is growing in volume and interest among political scientists. More relevant to the current study, however, is a separate, less voluminous, literature on the individual-level implications of the compensation thesis. Compensation arguments assert that economic globalization leads to welfare state expansion by way of pressures from below. Since they have largely been performed at the country-level of analysis, tests of the globalization-welfare link have been criticized for leaving the mechanism governing this linkage unexplored. As a way to address this shortcoming, some suggest the linkage results from a game pitting elite groups vying for power against each other (Adserà and Boix 2002). Others provide tests of the linkages at the mass level. Scheve and Slaughter (2004) provide an important link between micro-analyses and the macro-based literature on policy outcomes by demonstrating that exposure to foreign direct investment increases feelings of economic insecurity among workers. Although not tested by Scheve and Slaughter, the implication is that insecurity leads to increased demands for compensation and, in turn, policies that lead to welfare state expansion. This more complete causal chain is tested by Walter (2010) using survey data from Switzerland. Walter shows that individual effects of globalization – conceived in terms of an individual's exposure to competition via her occupation – lead to greater feelings of job insecurity, greater demands for state involvement, and ultimately increased support for those political parties most likely to deliver social protections. Also notable is Margalit's (2011) work on joblessness and vote outcomes in the United States. He finds that regions of the country that experienced a greater share of jobs lost to foreign competition were more likely to vote against the incumbent president than those areas less sensitive to this offshoring threat. Margalit further shows that the anti-incumbent effect of trade-related job losses was smaller in areas where the government certified more of the harmed workers to receive special job training and income assistance.

These and other micro-level tests of the compensation hypothesis are notable both for their creativity and, as a collection, for their consistency in producing evidence in support of received wisdoms – proffered by Ruggie (1982), Katzenstein (1985), Rodrik (1998), and others about how globalization gives rise to policies to compensate those most affected. And like these studies, this book is centered on the individual voter. But it is a voter of a different sort. The individual voter commonly featured in studies of the microfoundations of the compensation argument is motivated narrowly by material interests. The voter appearing in this book evaluates globalization's effects more broadly. Taking into account her position in the national labor market, this voter assesses what globalization implies for her income and employment security and act accordingly. As with previous studies, this voter evaluates globalization in terms of its likely impact on her material well-being. But this voter also considers the broader consequences of a globalized economy. As we shall see in the following chapters, these broader consequences include the connections between globalization and non-material, or noneconomic, aspects of life.[7] They also include a consideration of what globalization means for the capacity of elected officials. Existing studies of globalization and citizen politics are by and large "bottom-up"; globalization first alters one's security or income, which, once aggregated, produces a chain of linkages leading to elite response (e.g., Walter 2010). Missing from this story, however, is an explicit consideration of the capacity of policymakers to deliver. This study, in contrast, is both bottom-up and "top-down." It recognizes that rising exposure to world markets alters citizens' belief in policy control (Alcañiz and Hellwig 2011; Fernández-Albertos et al. 2013; Hellwig et al. 2008).

This more comprehensive approach to studying the mass politics of globalization motivates my theoretical argument and ensuing empirical tests. To preview the argument, I claim that globalization reshapes the incentives of self-interested citizens and of vote-seeking politicians, and that it does so via two channels. The first is the role of issue positions, and the second is the capacity of governments to shape outcomes. These two conduits have

[7] In this book I argue that, although globalization may lead the voter to assign less weight to economic considerations, she will grant greater weight to performance considerations in areas she believes to be unrelated or only weakly affected by the economy. This latter group is composed of issues predominantly framed in terms other than their relation to the economy. These noneconomic areas could include quality of life issues, healthcare, crime, public corruption, or the environment. In this way, noneconomic is used to summarize expectations pertaining to the effects of issues and performance indicators that lie outside the area of economy, or what Jensen (2012) refers to as "life-cycle" issues.

provided the bases of communication between citizens and their representatives in western democracies. Take political issues. In democracies, position taking on the issues provides the parameters according to which elites and masses relate to one another. But engagement in world markets creates uncertainty, in terms of both who's responsible and what's to come. This uncertainty is played out among elites as political parties attempt to craft vote-maximizing strategies in a more complicated, more multifaceted, issue space. This uncertainty is also evident in the minds of voters. Regardless of their preferences for more or less globalization, all voters face the challenge of how much globalization matters in political life and, in particular, how much it matters vis-à-vis other issue positions, cleavages, and factors driving their behavior in politics.

Globalization also bears on mass politics through the channel of policymaker capacity. Politics in western industrial democracies rests on the belief that elected agents can use policy tools to maximize social welfare. Control over policy outcomes rates as an essential prerequisite to the elite-mass bargain struck in these democracies during the twentieth century. This prerequisite is undermined by globalization. Understanding how the world economy affects notions of policy control is therefore an important part of understanding connections between world markets and national politics. Indeed, this is a point emphasized by much of the IPE/CPE literature. However, this book is not a study of how globalization influences what governments can or cannot achieve – at least not directly. Rather, it is concerned with how mass politics actors – voters and their elected representatives – perceive and reason about the room to maneuver and why it matters.

References to globalization and policy capacity are reminiscent of arguments advanced by columnist Thomas Friedman in *The Lexus and the Olive Tree*. According to Friedman, globalization puts national policymakers in a bind he called the "Golden Straitjacket." Once in the Golden Straitjacket, a nation's economics grows and its politics shrinks.

> [It] narrows the political and economic policy choices of those in power to relatively tight parameters. That is why it is increasingly difficult these days to find any real differences between ruling and opposition parties in those countries that have put on the Golden Straitjacket, its political choices get reduced to Pepsi or Coke – to slight nuances of tastes, slight nuances of policy, slight alternations in design to account for local traditions, some loosening here or there, but never any major deviation from the core golden rules. (Friedman 1999, 87)

Friedman's popular account of globalization and democracy was put forth more than a decade ago. Economists and political scientists have subsequently engaged in these themes in more sophisticated ways. Rodrik (2011) argues that the contemporary world economy affects representative democracy in a negative fashion. Borrowing both from Friedman's Golden Straightjacket and the Mundell-Fleming "trilemma" from open economy economics (Cohen

1993),[8] Rodrik asserts the existence of a political trilemma in which only two of three outcomes are possible: 1) the nation-state, 2) mass politics, and 3) integrated national economies. If we have numbers 1 and 2, we must exclude number 3. Such was the logic of the Bretton Woods compromise following World War II. Choose 1 and 3 and we must, as Friedman notes, excluded mass politics. The third outcome then is the exclusion of the nation-state in favor of some form of global federalism in which a global economy is somehow responsive to mass politics.

While Friedman and Rodrik are largely speculative in their pronouncements, other researchers weigh the evidence regarding just what governments *can* do under globalization in more systematic fashion. In her study of investor behavior, Mosley (2003) argues that capital market participants consider but a few government policies when weighing investment decisions; namely those affecting national price levels' current account balances. The implication is that governments remain in control of their policy destiny in most areas, particularly those pertaining to the supply side of the economy. Boix (1998, 2000) arrives at a similar conclusion with respect to the supply-side options remaining at the government's disposal. In an analysis of the British macro-political economy, Sattler et al. (2008) report mixed evidence with respect to the room-to-maneuver thesis. They find governments to be responsive, in policy terms, to changes in popular political evaluations. However, this accountability mechanism has no impact on the real economy. Whereas the first point supports a responsive government claim, the second questions whether real room to maneuver (still) exists. And more recent studies of tax policy emphasize the extent to which globalization constrains fiscal policy action and does more to discern under just what conditions political, institutional, and economic factors create openings for distinct economic policies even in an era of globalization (see, e.g., Busemeyer 2009; Plümper et al. 2009).

Current scholarship, in short, produces a picture much more nuanced with respect to the political implications of globalization. Where does this leave current work on notions of policy compensation and constraint, of embedded liberalism and government room to maneuver? While not claiming to have all the answers, evidence presented in this book suggests that we can come a good way toward addressing this question through a more serious consideration of politics as *mass politics*. It is one thing to identify the effects of globalization on policy; understanding connections between globalization and mass politics – the relationship between citizens and their representatives – is something else. As will be evident, my argument is informed by existing research on how politics still matters, even in a world of seemingly porous borders. However, I also take to heart more nuanced views on the limitations of the compensation/

[8] The "trilemma" refers to an implication of the Mundell-Fleming model from open economy macroeconomics; that is, policymakers may choose from two of the following three: fixed exchange rates, monetary policy autonomy, and liberal capital markets.

embedded liberalism arguments by assuming that perceptions of globalization are as important for politics as objective reality.

Like Friedman and Rodrik, I am concerned with what globalization means for policy choices and, in turn, what it means for democracy. But this book ranges beyond Friedman's conception of a narrow room to maneuver in two ways. For one, I delve deeper into the consequences of limited policy latitude for representative democracy. Representative democracy operates on two levels: as an *ideal* standard, a means for distinguishing democratic and non-democratic regimes, but also as an *evaluative* standard. Two political systems may appear equally democratic in their institutions and protections but may attain very different democratic standards. As regards this second standard, representation works when citizen-principals are able to select among a range of potential politician-agents, some of whom possess policy preferences similar to their own. This is less likely to occur, however, if the room to maneuver shrinks. In the limit, the absence of policy options means only one position is credible. So where Friedman sees the discipline of the Golden Straitjacket as a defense against profligate policies for political gain, my mass politics perspective suggests less optimistic conclusions for democracy. In terms of democracy, the straitjacket is not necessarily golden.[9]

This book breaks the narrow straitjacket metaphor by incorporating a much wider range of political issues. Not all policy outcomes are similarly limited by the dictates of market liberalization. Where uncertainty over policy control may have a large influence on matters of economic policy, it may have little direct effect on policy room to maneuver in areas like, say, healthcare, education, or the environment. The theory advanced in Chapter 2 applies to the effects of globalization's constraints not just for managing the economy but for policy options more broadly. I reason that exposure to the world economy shifts the voter's calculus away from economic determinants of party choice and onto other considerations. These other considerations fall under a broad noneconomic rubric.[10] In shifting voter considerations, the global economic context creates incentives for competing politicians to minimize economic differences. Although there is much to suggest that globalization narrows the

[9] In this respect, I share Rodrik's (2011) assertion of a political trilemma in which global economic regimes cannot simultaneously have integrated national economies, independent nation-states, and mass politics. Rather, if we assume globalization, we are left with a choice between a Golden Straitjacket, in which mass preferences matter not for national politics, or a system of global federalism, in which mass politics exists but without independent nation-states directing policy.

[10] It is true that when it comes to public policy, all but a few regulatory matters can truly be designated noneconomic in the sense of being budget neutral. However, as we shall see in Chapters 3, 5, and elsewhere, mass publics associate certain issues as more intimately related to economic policy, broadly construed. Others are more weakly associated with strict economic frames. These include the social and moral issues, the environment, freedom of expression, healthcare, and so on.

range of what is politically possible, it need not mean the end of democracy. Elite-mass ties may remain strong; increasingly, however, these ties pertain to areas perceived to be unrelated to market integration.

In emphasizing the multi-issue nature of mass politics in advanced capitalist democracies, this book parts ways with extant political economy discussions of globalization and the room to maneuver (e.g., Clark 2000; Garrett 1998; Hays 2009; Swank 2002; Steinmo 2010, among other book-length discussions). Yet, while the IPE/CPE literature has paid scant attention to differences across policy issues, such dimensionality has been prominently featured in comparative politics. The focus on multidimensionality means this book shares something with a separate body of work in comparative politics on the rise of non-material lifestyle, or expressive, issues in western democracies. Inglehart (1977; 1990; 2008) has delved deeper than anyone in cataloging these broad-based changes in mass opinion. Drawing on survey data from the 1970s onward, Inglehart shows that through a process of cohort replacement mass publics have increasingly come to value "post-materialist" considerations, such as freedom and self-expression, over materialist ones, such as economic and national security. To Inglehart, the causal force behind value change is the result of differences in socialization and a process of intergenerational change.

To Inglehart, the source of policy opinion change stems from the public's shifting values, away from material sentiment toward post-materialist values. Others observe wide-scale shifts in policy sentiment but identify forces other than cultural factors as responsible. For these scholars, changes in the organization of domestic economies have reshaped political attitudes and, in turn, political party success. Some argue that economic change weakens traditional class-based attachments. Others highlight the role of citizens' market and organizational experiences in the production sector of the economy. Included among such arguments is Kitschelt's (1994) account of the shift in popular attitudes away from a socialist-capitalist cleavage dominated by market and redistributive concerns to a left-libertarian–right-authoritarian divide that encompasses both economic and noneconomic considerations. Kitschelt (1994, 30–31) describes the forces underlying these shifts in mass politics:

> In the transformation of capitalism since World War II, the rise of the Keynesian welfare state, together with the transformation of the economic structure that expanded the portion of labor market participants who are highly educated, work with clients, and are female, has shifted the main axis of voter distribution from a simple alternative between socialist (left) and capitalist (right) politics to a more complex configuration opposing left-libertarian and right-authoritarian alternatives.

Kitschelt's argument has been especially influential in studies of European politics in that it produces implications both for voter preferences and for the strategies of office-seeking elites, particularly those on the center-left (see, e.g., Kriesi et al. 2008).

In examining the democratic consequences of economic globalization, this book shares Kitschelt's emphasis on how economic change leads to change in policy opinions and, in turn, in voting behavior and party strategies.[11] But while Kitschelt extrapolates to politics from changes in national production schemes and from changes in the social organization of economic life, this study starts with something more straightforward: the political economy's exposure to the world beyond national borders. For Inglehart, policy opinion stems from the public's shifting values produced by generational replacement. For Kitschelt, the source for such change rests in the structure of the economy in postindustrial societies. In this book, the source rests in exposure to the international economy. And unlike Inglehart, or even Kitschelt, my story emphasizes the importance of policymaker competency.

1.3. Approach to Inquiry

My approach to inquiry – and the organization of this book – is from the bottom up; from mass to elite. I begin with the individual citizen in her role as evaluator of government performance, proceed to consider communication flows between masses and elites, and finally examine the strategies of competing political elites. This approach means that this book trades the usual lens used to study the consequences of a global economy – that of policy outcomes – for one informed by the contemporary literature on voting behavior and party politics.

However, while outcome variables are pitched at the micro level, the explanatory factor is realized at the macro level of analysis. Globalization is a structural phenomenon that affects whole economies and, by extension, whole societies. Like most studies of globalization and domestic politics referenced herein, I begin with the simplifying assumption that globalization shapes, rather than is shaped by, domestic politics.[12] Of course, "economic globalization" potentially refers to a great number of things. And my conception is indeed broad. By economic globalization I mean the long distance flows of goods, capital, services, and labor, as well as information and perceptions that accompany market exchanges (Keohane and Nye 2000; Dreher 2006). Three features of this definition deserve attention. First, this conceptualization associates economic globalization with a range of phenomena, including international trade, foreign direct and portfolio investment, private market capital flows, and trans-border migration. Second, although broad, this conceptualization excludes direct consideration of other forms of globalization, such as environmental, social, cultural, or military, and emphasizes only those components that bear on the economy. Lastly, the reference to "information and perceptions" means that

[11] See, respectively, Chapter 3 on policy opinions, Chapters 5 and 6 on voter choice, and Chapters 7 and 8 on elite strategies.

[12] It might be argued that this approach wrongly assumes causality runs in one direction but ignores the possibility that economic openness is also a product of domestic politics. The likelihood of such reverse causality is less evident, however, when we consider domestic politics as mass politics. That said, where possible, I examine the possibility of "endogenous" globalization in the empirical analyses in Chapters 3–8.

this definition carries with it both *objective* and *subjective* meanings. We know that voter behavior is often more closely associated with subjective assessments than with objective reality. Thus, where possible, I examine objective as well as subjective forms of globalization.

In situating this research within the context of voters and political parties, my claims are tested mainly through statistical analyses of public opinion, vote choice, and party positions, supplemented with interview evidence. The analytical leverage comes from employing globalization as a force reshaping already-developed ties between voters and their elites in established democracies with at least a modicum of responsiveness. The cases employed in this study thus are taken from the set of advanced industrial democracies in Europe, North America, Japan, and the Antipodes.[13] In order to leverage temporal sources of variation, many analyses pool data across time. Analyses combine "large N" cross-national investigations with single country case studies – in France (Chapter 3), Denmark (Chapter 7), and Sweden (Chapter 8). Although data come from a variety of sources, a key source of evidence stems from two original datasets built by the author: one pertaining to public opinion, the other to elites (Hellwig 2011; Vowles et al. 2009).

1.4. Organization of the Book

Understanding how globalization shapes mass politics requires going beyond the standard framework as shown in Figure 1.1. Accordingly, a revised theoretical framework is developed in Chapter 2. It offers a deeper motivation for the earlier-mentioned assertion that globalization affects mass politics through the structure of issue politics and through the capacity for political control over outcomes. The second half of the chapter grounds these two points in a pair of models, one describing the "demand" side of representative democracy's bargain – the preferences of voters, and the other, party representatives, providing the "supply" side. Incorporating claims about the effects of globalization into rational-actor models produces a novel set of expectations about how globalization matters for domestic politics.

These expectations are tested empirically in the chapters that follow. This study is the first to offer up a comprehensive treatment of how country ties to the world economy have impinged on a whole range of settings that, together, form the bases of mass politics. These settings include

- public demands for government action,
- sanctioning politicians,
- selecting representatives,
- channels of influence between masses and elites, and
- behavior of vote-seeking political parties.

[13] One of the analyses in Chapters 5 includes a slightly wider set of cases.

I begin in Chapter 3 with a consideration of citizen policy preferences. Does globalization matter for policy attitudes? If so, how? The theory of "balancing demands" advanced in Chapter 2 asserts that exposure to the world economy affects government expectations. The extent to which signals from the world economy affects preferences, however, depends less on individual self-interest than on issue domain. Voters respond to signals from the world economy by demanding less in areas where constrained governments can no longer deliver but more where they still can. I show that although globalization has no consistent influence on general support for government action, it does matter for the *composition* of policy preferences. This expectation is tested three ways: an examination of individual policy preferences, a pooled analysis of globalization and aggregate preferences, and a study of French issue priorities. In contrast with the compensation thesis' expectations, these analyses show that globalization affects public preferences by shifting citizen demands away from policy provisions in economic areas. Globalization carries the opposite effect, however, in social or noneconomic policy areas, increasing popular demands for government response.

I next examine how changing preferences and issue priorities associated with globalization affect mass behavior. I look at behavior both in terms of public *sanctioning* of politicians and in terms of individuals *selecting* among alternatives for the future. Chapters 4 and 5 address political accountability. In an economy with porous political boundaries, who's responsible? How do citizens residing in open economies assign responsibility for observed outcomes, and does it matter? In Chapter 4, I present findings from an original data set of publics in ten democracies. I show that signals from the world economy reduce voter tendencies to credit or blame their governments for the economy – a finding which raises questions about the applicability of economic voting in globalized settings. I further show that globalization makes it more likely that voters attribute responsibility for the economic conditions at home to fluctuations in the international economy. Chapter 5 takes up the consequences of this shift. I show that attributing responsibility to the world economy weakens the bonds between evaluations of the economy and support for political incumbents. Lastly, I test the macro-implications by modeling incumbent support as a function of country exposure to the world economy and citizen performance evaluations. Consistent with a "balancing demands" argument, I find that globalization increases the importance of noneconomic forms of performance voting.

Where Chapters 4 and 5 are retrospective in orientation, Chapter 6 is prospective. Does a world of integrated markets influence whether and how voters select representatives based on policies for the future? Original data of voter and party positions in ten countries provides estimates of the influence of policy-based appeals on voter choice, not only in terms of more general issues pertaining to the scope of government, but also in terms of the globalization issue. I show that the language of politics in terms of "left" and "right" still resonates with voters in western democracies. To this point, I show that the structure of issue politics is not one- but two-dimensional, and issues related to globalization contribute greatly to this second dimension. The axis of party competition with respect to globalization-related issues cuts across traditional policy divides, thereby complicating the policy bases of electoral competition.

Chapters 7 and 8 turn the tables from voters – the demand side – to parties – the supply side. Conventional wisdom has it that, in democracies, it is in parties' interest to align their own issue preferences with those of the voters, but what effect might globalization have on these incentives? Chapter 7 evaluates the impact of globalization on political representation. I draw on the balancing demands argument to develop a set of expectations for how elite and mass preferences are communicated across different issues. The argument predicts that for those issues associated with economic policy and redistribution – issues on which most party representatives have staked out relatively stable identities – communication flows should run from the elites to the masses. However, on noneconomic issues, messages run from the masses to the elites. I find that while elite-mass communications are reciprocal, communication flows in an elite-to-mass direction are relatively stronger for "economic" issues, like taxes and spending. Mass-to-elite signals, on the other hand, appear comparatively stronger for issues associated with globalization. These findings receive corroborating support through a Danish case study. Implications of these directional distinctions for the performance of representative democracy are discussed.

Chapter 8 investigates how globalization shapes the tendencies of political parties to respond to voter preferences. Reasoning from its influence on issue politics and policy capacity, I argue that globalization should weaken party responsiveness to public opinion insomuch as it constrains the policy space in which parties can maneuver. However, per balancing demands arguments, this conclusion should apply only for party and voter positions on economic matters. For noneconomic considerations, strategic political parties should be no less or more attentive to the wishes of the public under a context of greater market integration. If anything, a policy context of globalization may induce parties to become more responsive as they seek out issues on which to credibly demonstrate their attentiveness to public sentiment. This reasoning is assessed in two ways: through a cross-national study of party and voter position shifts in eighteen democracies and in a case study of party behavior in Sweden.

Chapter 9 revisits study findings with respect to the theoretical argument. I discuss the study's implications for public opinion, voting behavior, party strategies, and political representation in the advanced capitalist democracies for the twenty-first century. In the wake of the financial crisis and economic stagnation, understanding how the world beyond national borders shapes national politics is more critical than ever.

2

Theoretical Framework

Political Demand and Supply in Globalized Economies

Globalization is a defining characteristic of our time. No longer limited to the behavior of activists and G8 meetings, it has been cited as cause for the rise of extremist political parties, declining participation in political life, and growing electoral volatility. Tendencies to view economic globalization adversely appear on the rise. In 2000, a majority of Americans viewed foreign trade as an opportunity, against only one third who viewed it as a threat. Just five years later, views had changed such that perceptions of threat from trade outstripped beliefs in its opportunities (Scheve and Slaughter 2007). Similar trends are found in Europe. According to Eurobarometer public opinion data, in 2003, publics in the fifteen member states of the European Union were considerably more likely to view globalization overall as an opportunity (56 percent) than as a threat (39 percent). But by 2008 things had changed, with more viewing globalization as a threat (45 percent) than as an opportunity (42 percent) (European Commission 2009).

Government responses have done little to quell anti-globalization sentiment. Unpopular neoliberal reforms – deemed essential by governments of the right and left alike – are often cited as culprits in accounts of the recent meltdown in world financial markets. The economic crisis that came to a head in late 2008 has only underlined the depth of country dependence on world markets. For example, in Ireland, the implosion of an asset bubble has meant that political elites have out of necessity become attentive to bond ratings – and arguably have done so against the wishes of the median voter. The series of EU-engineered austerity packages imposed on Greece has led to a rolling back of social protections and entitlements popular with most of the electorate. And the tumultuous nature of Italian politics is tightly linked with the world economy. In December 2010, the government was put to and passed a vote of confidence. The government's success was not because Prime Minister Silvio Berlusconi's policies were popular with Italian voters but because investors feared speculation by globally minded financial market actors. And Berlusconi's eventual ouster took place in the face of external concerns that the government could not fulfill its promises to reform in the face of default pressures.

The political implications of market dependence have not gone unnoticed, not even by political scientists. Yet researchers on the political economy of advanced industrial democracies remain focused on a surprisingly narrow set of globalization's effects. In particular, most accounts are concerned first and foremost with outcomes as *policy* outcomes. We must consider just how globalization shapes domestic politics where "politics" is defined in broad terms. These concerns must be expanded to consider globalization's consequences more broadly. This book is an attempt to do so in the direction of mass politics. How does globalization matter for the essential components of representative democracy: individual citizens and their representatives? This chapter advances an argument for how globalization has altered the bases of mass politics in advanced industrial societies and provides a framework to guide the empirical inquiries to follow in Chapters 3–8.

In this chapter, I present a pair of models of political behavior, one pertaining to voter utility and the other to political parties. The voters represent the demand side of democracy's bargain; party elites provide the supply. For each side of this mass-elite game, I develop a set of claims for how economic globalization reshapes the incentives of these actors. Incorporating signals from the world economy into models of actor utility produces a novel set of expectations about how globalization matters for domestic politics. But before doing so, it is necessary to elaborate on two channels through which masses and elites relate to one another: *preferences over issues* and *control over policy*. Together, these channels provide the boundaries for mass politics.

2.1. Globalization and Mass Politics: Two Channels of Influence

2.1.1. Issue Politics

The integration of national economies is not new. As growth strategies, states have relied on trade relationships and overseas investment for decades or more. According to certain indicators, the world was more "globalized" in times past than it is at present (Berman 2009).[1] But what has changed is how globalization has played out in *issue politics*, in the sense of how the international economy has reshaped the boundaries of political debate. In the United States, debates began in earnest with trade politics, brought to the fore in the North American Free Trade Act and the 1992 presidential election (Destler 2005; Yergin and Stanislaw 1998). Economic relations with China provide a more recent example. American policymakers have argued that the trade imbalance

[1] A globalized political economy is distinguishable from an "open" one. Globalized refers to the actual degree of integration. An open economy refers instead to the absence of restrictions on the movement of goods, services, people, and capital across borders.

between the two nations is propped up by an undervalued renminbi, making Chinese exports competitive and more factory workers employed. U.S. Treasury officials have been pressing China for years to lift controls on the currency. Yet American voters and lawmakers have only recently seized on exchange rates as a political issue. And spurred on by a world financial crisis, the "Great Recession" of 2007–2009 also brought renewed focus on the costs and benefits of market deregulation and other liberalizing reforms. This has led voters in some countries to question anew their government's commitment to globalization (Hays 2009; Rodrik 2011; Scheve and Slaughter 2007).

While globalization is increasingly salient to national electorates, the broader implications of living in a globalized economy remain uncertain. For example, a 2000 *Washington Post* poll found that 43 percent of Americans admitted they did not understand the meaning of "globalization of the world economy." Americans are not alone when it comes to uncertainty about the international economy. A 2001 survey of Europeans found that more than one third of respondents had not heard of the World Trade Organization, while another 26 percent confessed to "only know[ing] the name" of the WTO but not what it does (Christensen 2001). And a 2006 Dutch survey found that more than one third of respondents were unable to say whether they thought globalization was good, bad, or neither for their country (Gallup 2006) – and this from residents of a country whose reliance on the world economy runs as deep and has persisted for as long a time as anywhere else on the planet. Such uncertainty matters for the role issues play in democracies.[2]

If the existing structure of issue opinions accommodated or subsumed globalization *as an issue*, then uncertainty with respect to its effects would be of little consequence for mass and elite political behavior. While voters in the main tend to be ignorant on matters of policy (Converse 1964; Zaller 1992), they can still function effectively as voters by leaning on partisan heuristics or complementarities among issue positions with varying degrees of salience. Such facilitators, however, are unlikely to be available when it comes to globalization. Political issues tend to rise to salience well before politicians accommodate them within their policy platforms. An issue may rise from relative obscurity to serve as catalyst for eventual party system realignment. An issue new to the political stage can bring about feelings on the part of the electorate that cut across, rather than reinforce, existing cleavage lines.

The environment offers an example. During the late 1970s and 1980s in Europe, pressure groups concerning energy, acid rain, and conservation of

[2] Contributing to this uncertainty is an apparent "aggregation bias": when pitched in terms of personal costs and benefits, individuals are more likely to view globalization in adverse terms than when it is associated with their country's national welfare. For example, a 2004 Eurobarometer survey found that in all countries surveyed, a greater share of respondents agreed that "globalization is a good thing for our country" than agreed that "globalization is a good thing for me" (Eurobarometer 61.0).

resources gained strength. Such issues, however, were not championed by parties on the mainstream "left" or "right."[3] These tensions were met in some countries by the formation of new parties. In other places, environmental movements have been accommodated by existing party systems (Dalton 2009). Other issues on which public positions have crystallized, evolved, and served to realign party systems are race, in the United States (Carmines and Stimson 1989), and political integration, in Europe (Evans 1998).

Whereas the American party system has realigned in response to the civil rights movement, and whereas many European party systems have had to adjust to issues of the environment and energy, party positions on issues related to globalization remain in tension with dominant cleavage divisions. Globalization defies placement into existing social divisions that structure vote choice (Dalton 2002, 194). Debates about globalization's negative effects neither align neatly with older, class-based divisions nor can they be reduced to some sort of alternative cleavage divide. Rather, globalization raises the incentives to form cross-cutting alliances between class-based divisions. Workers and their employers often are of the same mind when it comes to, say, the benefits of industry protection from international trade. Thus, rather than being subsumed under existing divisions over the role of government in society, spending on public services, and the distribution of wealth, party positions on globalization generally "cut across" and compete with long-dominant domestic political alignments.

2.1.2. Policy Control

Questions of popular control lie at the heart of debates on democracy and markets (Freeman 1989). Since the postwar consensus, observers have assumed that politics can control, direct, tame, and otherwise influence social and economic outcomes. Insomuch as elected policymakers could take action to maximize the general welfare, this was a good thing. Keynesian models of economic management developed in the post–World War II era gave the state broad responsibility to steer the economy. Voters came to expect such actions from their politicians. Economic valence issues, such as employment, growth, and stable prices, have long ranked highly among the public's concerns (Hibbs 1977; Anderson 1995).

However, the expansion of world markets into more and more aspects of the economy has led voters to question whether their governments can, in fact, fine tune or otherwise control the economy. To borrow from Keohane and Nye's

[3] Dalton (2009, 163) elaborates: "Parties on both the left and right typically had difficulties reconciling their traditional economic programs and these new environmental policies. Leftist parties experienced a tension between their support for economic growth as a means of improving the life conditions of the working class and the new demands for environmental protection that might challenge economic development projects and pro-growth policies.... Conservative parties also struggled with these tensions.... Anti-nuclear groups frequently found themselves facing an alliance of labor and business ... who favored the development of nuclear power. Similar cross-cutting alliances often occurred on other economic development projects."

(2000) definition, voter "perceptions that accompany market exchanges" are such that greater openness means less control by governments. Polling evidence finds that many voters question their governments' capacity to manage globalization. For example, A 2001 survey of publics in fifteen European countries found more than twice as many agreed that "globalization cannot be controlled by governments" as disagreed (Christensen 2001). A 2003 poll of publics in the same set of democracies found that more than half felt that their country lacks sufficient influence to shape the process of globalization (Christensen 2003). And a poll done a year later asked publics to identify which, among a variety of actors, they trusted to "get the effects of globalization under control" (Papacostas 2010). Less than one in four Europeans said they trusted their national government to control globalization, a share eclipsed in number by "the European Union" and by "citizens themselves."

It is one thing to believe individual governments are unable to steer the world economy writ large, it is something else entirely to believe globalization renders individual governments incapable of controlling their *own* economies. This question of policy capacity, or what I call the room to maneuver, is central to mass politics in liberal democracies embedded in a world of independent nation-states. If citizens believe in the room to maneuver, then their support or opposition for certain policies should be based on an understanding that the policy outcomes they observe – economic or otherwise – are in part a function of what their governments do. If, on the other hand, voters perceive national governments as incapable of autonomous action, then preferences over policy ought to be of little consequence for evaluating politicians.

Yet polling data shows a decline in the ranks of these room-to-maneuver believers. Take, for example, the views of the French public in 1997, just in the wake of paralyzing public sector strikes famously billed as the world's "first revolt against globalization."[4] In a poll taken during the legislative election – in which the center-right government was badly beaten – 44 percent of the public reported that the French government either maintained "a great deal" or "quite a lot" of room to maneuver in the economy against 56 percent saying instead "not much" or "hardly any" (CEVIPOF et al., 2001). Since then, *la mondialisation* has penetrated public debate. Thus, when a similar question was put before the French public in 2008, slightly more than a quarter of respondents perceived the presence of (a great deal or quite a lot) of room to maneuver, while nearly three in four said globalization meant little to no room for autonomous political action (Hellwig 2011).

Similar trends are found elsewhere. In Britain, the share of believers in the room to maneuver declined from 55 percent in 2001 to 31 percent in 2008 (Heath et al. 2002). This trend is evident even in the United States, with its large domestic economy and privileged position in world markets. A 2005 poll found that nine in ten Americans were of the belief that the government had at

[4] Erik Israelewicz, "La première révolte contre la mondialisation," *Le Monde*, 7 Dec. 1995.

least "quite a lot" of influence on the U.S. economy (Hellwig et al. 2008). By 2008, the size of this group registered only 31 percent of the U.S. public – the same share as in Britain. Additional evidence in support of this trend comes from surveys about the government's power to shape the economy. In the fall of 2008, Americans (55 percent) maintained that their government "still has the power to fix the economy." The implication being that the economy would likely matter in that year's election outcome. Two years later, however, the percent of Americans who felt similarly slid into the minority (40 percent), with 55 percent believing instead that "the federal government cannot fix the economy so easily these days because the U.S. is part of a global economy" (CCES 2010). Indeed, large shares of the public in many countries believe that openness in fact does reduce the capacity of politicians to control policy (Hellwig 2011).[5] Figures 2.1 and 2.2 summarize these trends.

In sum, I argue that globalization penetrates mass politics through two channels: issue politics and political control over policy outcomes. For the former, globalization inhibits a congruence of issue positions across voters and political parties. For the latter, globalization weakens the link connecting policy outcomes and policymaker survival. These two claims serve as guides for the analyses reported in this book. The remainder of this chapter explicates these claims through utility models of mass and elite behavior. I first offer a model for how globalization reshapes the "demand side" of electoral politics. I then do the same for party behavior on the "supply side."

2.2. The Demand Side

I begin on the demand side with a model of voter utility. I first present the model in the context of a closed political economy and then in a globalized context. For simplicity, I do so with reference to two ideal types: closed and globalized political economies. In reality, the differences are not dichotomous but continuous. And, in particular, no economy is closed in reality. I refer to these contexts simply as closed political economies for ease of presentation.

2.2.1. Voter Utility in Closed Economies: Position and Performance Considerations

The foundation for the model is the standard spatial representation in which voters evaluate parties according to their proximity along a policy interval (Downs 1957; Enelow and Hinich 1984). The utility of voter i for party j is expressed in terms of a quadratic proximity function as the negative squared distance between the voter's preferred position x_i and the party's location at location s_j:

$$U_{ij} = -\left(x_i - s_j\right)^2. \qquad (2.1)$$

[5] Chapter 4 describes the surveys in greater detail.

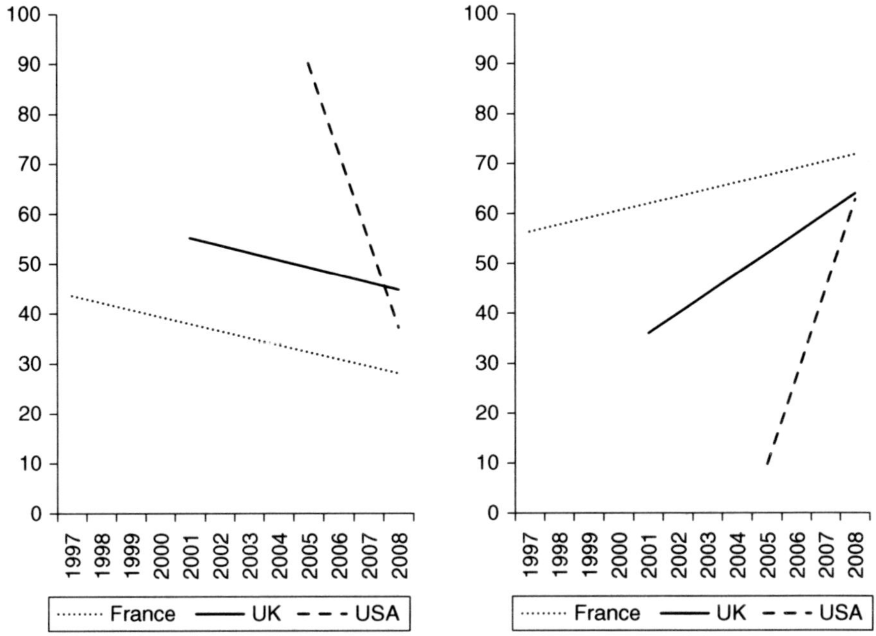

FIGURE 2.1. Trends in perceptions of the policy room to maneuver, select countries.
Notes: The graph on the left displays the percent of respondents classified as "believers in the room to maneuver," and the graph on the right does the same for "non-believers in the room to maneuver." Classifications are defined here. "Don't know" and "no answer" responses omitted.

- France 1997: "In your opinion, does globalization still leave the French government with a great deal, quite a lot, not very much, or hardly any room to maneuver in the economy?" (CEVIPOF 2001). Believers = great deal + quite a lot, Non-Believers = not very much + hardly any
- UK 2001/United States 2005: "In today's worldwide economy, how much influence do you think the British/American government have on Britain's/America's economy?" Believers = a great deal + quite a lot, Non-Believers = not very much + hardly any
- All 2008: "In your opinion, does globalization leave [country's] government with a great deal, quite a lot, not very much, or hardly any ability to choose its own economic policies?" Believers = a great deal + quite a lot, Non-Believers = not very much + hardly any

To this basic specification I add a performance component:

$$U_{ij} = -a\left(x_i - s_j\right)^2 + \beta y_j, \tag{2.2}$$

where y_j is some measure of the observed performance outcome attributable to party j. The parameters α and β describe the relative importance (weight) that

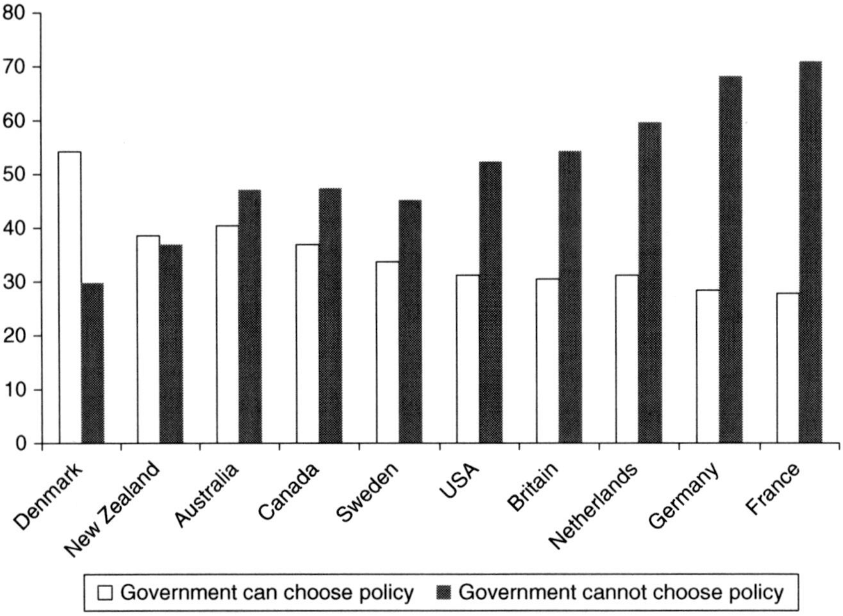

FIGURE 2.2. Globalization and room to maneuver perceptions in ten countries, 2008.
Note: Frequencies based on responses to the following: "In your opinion, does globalization leave [country's] government with a great deal, quite a lot, not very much, or hardly any ability to choose its own economic policies?" White bars equal the percent in each country responding "a great deal" or "quite a lot." The grey bars represent the percent responding "not very much" or "hardly any." "Don't know" and non-responses are not shown.
Source: Hellwig 2011.

the voter *i* assigns to each component. These two components, issue proximity and policy performance, match up with the two channels described earlier through which globalization influences mass politics.[6]

The proximity component, $-(x_i - s_j)^2$, is straightforward and requires no further elaboration.[7] Two clarifying points are in order, however, with respect to the performance component. "Non-proximity" components of this sort are often taken to represent the totality of non-policy attributes shaping *i*'s preference for *j*. These "valence" issues might pertain to a whole host of factors, including the party leader's reputation with respect to performance competence,

[6] By linking policy performance to voter utility, the model assumes that voters believe elected officials possess some degree of policy control over observed policy outcomes, the degree of which is captured by β.

[7] Later, I relax the assumption conveyed in equation 2.2 that the issues may be deduced into a single dimension.

integrity, charisma, and other valued characteristics (Stokes 1963). However, here I limit this component to performance (or competency) considerations such that y_j represents some observable performance outcome and β expresses the relative influence voter *i* accords to party *j* as a function of *j*'s competence as a policy manager. Second, as epitomized by a large literature on economic voting, empirical tests of performance-based voting generally conceive of *y* in terms of *economic* performance. But performance evaluations need not focus exclusively on the economy. Indeed, we will see that extending this closed economy utility model to a globalized setting will require us to disaggregate this observable performance outcome *y* into different performance domains, some pertaining to the economy and others not.

2.2.2. Voter Utility in Globalized Economies: Discounting and Multiple Policies

I now incorporate the reality of a global economic context into the model of voter utility. I suggested at the beginning of the chapter that globalization can affect the demand side of mass politics both by complicating the political issue space and by weakening connections between observed outcomes and policymaker actions. This means globalization affects both components of the utility function, the issue space, $\alpha - (x_i - s_j)^2$, and performance outcomes, βy_j. Here I describe how these mechanisms are incorporated into the standard model by using a policy discounting model.

According to utility models with policy discounting, voters anticipate the extent to which parties are able move outcomes from the status quo position to implement their preferred policy. Parties, however, cannot be assured of implementing their preferred policies even in those very rare instances in which they have full control over the policy levers. Rather, party policy capacity is conditioned by "situational constraints" (Grofman 1985). This means that preferred policies are implemented with some probability less than one. Further, we assume voters have knowledge of this and update their decision calculus accordingly (ibid.; Kedar 2009; Merrill and Grofman 1999; Adams et al. 2005). As Downs (1957, 39) observes, the voter "cannot merely compare platforms; instead he must estimate in his own mind what the parties would actually do were they in power."

The "situational constraints" bearing on party *j*'s policy capacity may be represented by a discount factor d_j such that $0 \le d_j \le 1$. If $d_j = 0$, there is no discounting and party *j* is expected to fully implement its preferred policies. If $d_j = 1$ there is complete discounting of policy capacity, meaning the party has no ability to execute – or, put differently, *j* has no policy room to maneuver. In this situation, rational voters should make no consideration of party positions. These are the extreme cases, of course. Practically, *d* is between 0 and 1. For example, if $d_j = .25$, then voters discount *j*'s capacity to influence policy by 25 percent.

With the discount factor, I rewrite the model as

$$U_{ij} = -\left(1-d_j\right)\alpha\left(x_i - s_j\right)^2 + \left(1-d_j\right)\beta y_j. \tag{2.3}$$

As earlier, the first term on the right-hand side is the proximity component. But because voters know that parties face constraints in their ability to enact their preferred policies, the impact of $\left(x_i - s_j\right)^2$ is now modified by some discounting parameter. This modifier, $1-d_j$, indicates that the salience of issue proximity is greater when the voter believes the party, if elected, will successfully enact its preferred policies – that is, when d_j is low. The second term, describing performance-based retrospections, is also modified to allow for discounting. In equation 2.3, the voter updates her utility calculus for *j* based on *j*'s management competency, or capacity to control policy outcomes. Attached to βy_j, the discount parameter is equivalent to *j*'s *performance weight*, which is affected by the party's own competence but also by room-to-maneuver constraints – like globalization – that "can be expected to prevent implementation of its policies" (Grofman 1985, 233). Thus, the discount factor recasts the simple utility model in two ways: policy direction, which is related to the structure of issue politics, and policy performance, which bears on the capacity to control outcomes.

A discounting framework provides an attractive way of thinking about globalization's impact on voter behavior. But how, exactly, does economic openness affect the discounting parameter? Confronting this question, researchers have posited a relationship between discounting effects and institutional features such as the organization of the party system (Kedar 2005) or the vertical and horizontal separation of powers (Alesina and Rosenthal 1995). Kedar (2005) argues that voters adjust a party's policy appeals in light of the latter's presumed contribution to policy after the election. For example, the policy positions of parties forced to govern in coalition should be discounted because the voters realize that parties will need to moderate their positions as a member of a multiparty government. Rather than constraints arising from domestic political structures, I emphasize international economic ones. I argue that the policy discount increases with country exposure to the world economy. In terms of equation 2.3, it follows that $0 \le d_{cj} \le d_{gj} \le 1$, with *c* subscripting the discount parameter attached to party *j* in closed economies and *g* doing the same for globalized economies.

With respect to the demand side, we are nearly there. But equation 2.3 may still be unduly parsimonious. Even though it incorporates proximity as well as performance components, politics in this representation remains one-dimensional. We remain tied to a single dimension of policy distance (proximity) and a single basis for judging party performance. The size of the bias introduced by modeling the issue space along a single continuum depends on how much party competition on salient issues aligns on a single structuring dimension. Granted, empirical tests of voting models often rely on single indicators for issue positions (e.g., left-right scales) and performance evaluations (e.g., the economy). However, in postindustrial, globalized political economies it would be unwise to assume unidimensionality (see, e.g., Andrews and Money 2009; Kitschelt 1994; Kriesi et al. 2008; Hellwig 2008).

To allow for multiple issues and multiple performance indices, equation 2.3 may be re-expressed so that the salience attached to party positions (α) and performance evaluations (β) to vary according to m (m = 1, …, M) issue areas:

$$U_{ij} = -\sum_m \left(1-d_j^m\right)\alpha^m\left(x_i^m - s_j^m\right)^2 + \sum_m \left(1-d_j^m\right)\beta^m y_j^m. \tag{2.4}$$

In (2.4), x_i^m is the position of voter i on issue m, s_j^m is j's position on m, and y_j^m is the observable performance level (or status) attributable to party j for issue m. The parameters α^m and β^m are the corresponding issue-specific salience weights. Note that the discount factors also vary according to policy area. This is necessary for consistency with the argument that policies in all areas are not equally constrained, be these constraints due to the nature of political competition, to how domestic institutions aggregate preferences, or to exogenous shocks.

The complexity of the utility function in (2.4) can be simplified if we are willing to assume that parties make policy-based appeals in not M but two dimensions, m and n. This allows us to write

$$\begin{aligned} U_{ij} = &-\left(1-d_j^m\right)\alpha^m\left(x_i^m - s_j^m\right)^2 - \left(1-d_j^n\right)\alpha^n\left(x_i^n - s_j^n\right)^2 \\ &+\left(1-d_j^m\right)\beta^m y_j^m + \left(1-d_j^n\right)\beta^n y_j^n. \end{aligned} \tag{2.5}$$

More compactly, we have

$$U_{ij} = -\left(1-d_j^m\right)\left(-\alpha^m\left(x_i^m - s_j^m\right)^2 + \beta^m y_j^m\right) + \left(1-d_j^n\right)\left(-\alpha^n\left(x_i^n - s_j^n\right)^2 + \beta^n y_j^n\right). \tag{2.6}$$

In this model, there exist two kinds of issue areas governing the voter's decision, m and n. The voter assesses her party options over these two policy domains both on performance (y_j^m and y_j^n) and position-taking ($s_j^m$and s_j^n) grounds. Discount weights are attached to these issue areas to describe the relative effects of economic globalization. The first compound term on the right-hand side assigns a discounting parameter, d^m, to j's relative *position* on issue m and to j's relative *competence* on issue m. The second term does the same but with reference to issue n.

Different weights allow for different expectations for how globalization affects voter choice. Take performance evaluations. For most of the postwar era, Keynesian macroeconomic models and their monetarist alternatives implied that policymaker actions could, for better or worse, directly influence the national economy. But for some time now, the trend has been one of governments controlling less and non-elected forces doing more. External demand pressures, price levels from abroad, and shocks from commodity and financial markets have influenced larger segments of state activity. These global economic developments should lead voters to question the credibility of government control over macroeconomic policy levers. Realizing that her government's opportunities for policy manipulation have become few and far between, the rational voter might downgrade, or *discount*, the importance of how the system performs on economic considerations.

It is important to make clear the distinction between issues with economic frames and those with noneconomic frames. In this book I argue that, while globalization may lead the voter to assign less weight to economic considerations, she will grant greater weight to performance considerations in areas she believes to be unrelated or only weakly affected by the economy. This latter group is composed of issues predominantly framed in terms other than their relation to the economy. These noneconomic areas could include quality of life issues, healthcare, crime, level of public corruption, or the environment. Noneconomic is used to summarize expectations pertaining to the effects of issues and performance indicators that lie outside the area of economy, or what Jensen (2012) refers to as "life-cycle" issues. So if issue area m pertains to some economic area and issue area n is noneconomic, then in open economies $1 \geq d_j^m > d_j^n \geq 0$.

Discount weights also provide expectations for the issue voting component in the model. If ties to the world economy weaken the electoral salience of national economic conditions, then the salience of political issues may increase as voters shift their bases of evaluation from those factors over which policymakers have little control – the national economy – toward those on which they continue to have an impact – the issues. There is, however, considerable variation across issue types. As we will see, citizen positions on the relevant issues tend to cluster on two dimensions in the advanced capitalist democracies. The first concerns the proper role for the state in the market. The second relates to positions on "new politics," concerns such as attitudes toward authority, the environment, gender and minority rights, and cultural diversity. Globalization should affect the salience of these two issue dimensions differently. If market integration reduces the credibility of domestic policy levers, then elite positions on economic issues may have little impact on the voter's decision. The world economy should be less of a constraint on policymaker capacity over noneconomic issues. Rather, the noneconomic dimension should play a compensating role, increasing in salience as the rational voter searches for a basis for judging elites. In terms of the magnitude of the parameters, the expectation again is $1 \geq d_j^m > d_j^n \geq 0$.

2.3. The Supply Side

I now examine the "supply side" of the mass politics story, the behavior of political elites conceived in terms of political parties. As "an instrument, or an agency, for *representing* people by *expressing* their demands," political parties rank as the primary means through which people are represented in democracies (Sartori 1976: 27; italics in the original).[8]

2.3.1. Party Incentives in Closed Economies: Responding to the Median Voter

This book adopts the assumption that parties are first and foremost strategic actors with vote-maximizing goals. Elites may trade principle – if such appeals are limited in their constituency – for actions to appeal to a broader spectrum of the electorate. But this is not to mean that parties seek votes as an end all to itself. Votes are not valuable in themselves; they are a means by which other objectives, such as office or policy, may be realized (Riker 1962; Strøm 1990). Even if not the end goal, vote maximization remains an efficient strategy for office- and policy-seeking parties alike. In the former case, increasing vote share ceteris paribus enhances the party's position for post-election coalition negotiations. In the latter case, it may be assumed that as a policy-seeking party's electoral strength increases, it gains leverage to pull the governing coalition's policy in its preferred direction.[9] So regardless of whether we take them to be motivated chiefly by votes, the spoils of office, or policy influence, parties are driven by incentives to respond to voter preferences.

The responsiveness of elected elites to mass preferences, however, partly depends on the broader issue environment. The issue environment matters in two respects. The first pertains to the distribution of electoral preferences. The ability of elites to respond to voters is facilitated by the electorate sending a clear and unambiguous signal about its preferred outcome on any given issue. Put differently, party representatives should be more likely adopt strategies to appeal to the median voter when the public's view on the issue is "single-peaked." If instead the electorate's preferences are multi-modal, then parties face the difficult decisions of which sets of voters, if any, to direct their policy appeals toward. Second, the environment shapes parties' capacity to be responsive actors in terms of issue salience. The greater the number of issues

[8] This is not to say that the behaviors of politicians as individuals are not important, but in most advanced industrial democracies, politicians achieve their goals acting through parties. Parties uniquely aggregate public preferences by channeling them into national policy debates. And parties – not individuals or, for that matter, governments – are essential for structuring the alternatives that are offered to citizens in elections, particularly in the parliamentary systems prevalent among the set of established democracies (Budge 1996).

[9] Adams and Merrill (2009), for example, show that parties in multiparty systems are motivated to adjust their policies in response to their beliefs about the median voter's position, rather than in response to the diversity of voter ideologies.

viewed as salient to the voters, the more difficult it is for party actions to be guided by public opinion. When a single issue – for example, taxes – frames the contours of political debate, and when the distribution of preferences on that issue is known, then party responsiveness is relatively straightforward. But when there are multiple issues of equal importance, all requiring position-taking – for example, taxes, the environment, immigration, international trade – then the vote-seeking party faces a position-taking dilemma: if it appeals to the greatest number of voters on one issue, it may risk slighting the majority of voters on some other issue of (near) equal salience (see Chapter 6).

These two factors – the variation of preferences across voters and the range of salient issues – jointly influence party strategies. As a vote-maximizing strategy, responding to public opinion works best when the variation of citizen demands and the range of salient issues are both *low*. Such a scenario approximates the issue environment in most western democracies during the "closed economy" years of the postwar era.[10] The years from the end of the Second World War to the energy-induced downturns of the 1970s were characterized by a broad consensus among parties and citizens alike with respect to the government's role in society. Consensus politics gave priority to the government's capacity to tame markets (e.g., via Keynesian demand management) and to advance the public welfare (via fiscal expansion). Parties in office were viewed as having responsibility not only for peace but also prosperity. And in order to meet the goals, political elites could employ fiscal instruments to serve the goals of full employment and steady, non-inflationary growth. These economic objectives, along with the concomitant social protections of healthcare, pensions, and unemployment insurance, made up a narrow range of salient issues on which elite performance was judged. A tight range of voter preferences on the key issues and a clear sense of which issues were most important facilitated a course of action for parties: Adopt broad-based strategies aimed at providing public goods, generally in the form of welfare benefits, to society at large. This prescription is consistent with arguments that began in the 1950s and 1960s, that successful parties were those that crafted policy positions to appeal to a wide array of constituencies (Kirchheimer 1966; Katz and Mair 1995).

When the number of salient issues is low and when voters broadly agree on the correct course of action, then parties have incentives to respond in kind to public opinion, to prioritize policies to improve or sustain the public's material welfare, and to display their ability to deliver on these grounds. But each of these incentives is undermined when we relax the assumption of a closed political-economic context.

[10] Of course, the economies were not closed in absolute terms. A more appropriate term may be Ruggie's (1982) notion of embedded liberal economies.

2.3.2. *Party Incentives in Globalized Economies: Many Actors, Constrained Capacities, and Reduced Expectations*

I have argued that globalization influences mass politics through two paths: the nature of issue politics and the capacity of government policy to affect outcomes. I now describe how a shift from a closed to a globalized political economy reshapes these paths with respect to the incentives of party elites.[11]

In closed economy settings, it is permissible to assume that party actors have strong incentives to align their position-taking behavior to that of the median voter on the most salient issues of the day. But even in the hypothetical closed economy environments, party actors may find such a prescription too simplistic. Parties, of course, are never without constraints on their action. Rather, choices between policy, office, and votes are trade-offs, the boundaries for which are conscribed by the wider environment. As regards the political environment, previous work on party behavior emphasizes the influence of political institutions in constraining parties (Müller and Strøm 2000; see also Laver and Schofield 1990; Huber 1996; Samuels and Shugart 2010).[12] By reducing their ability to achieve certain objectives, institutional arrangements can direct parties to pursue alternative strategies.

Just as the organization of domestic political institutions erects constraints on party behavior, so too can the organization of world markets redirect the strategies parties pursue. Consider how the wider political-economic environment is altered by heightened integration of markets across national boundaries. Beginning in the mid-1980s, increases in trade openness across Europe, the United States, and elsewhere meant export markets became increasingly important for propping up national income. Increased capital mobility meant foreign investment became all the more important as a source of growth. Governments were pressured to make credible signals to investors abroad, to attract investment capital, and to prevent capital flight at home. Under such circumstances, the effectiveness of fiscal policy instruments to finance goods provision declined. This basic story by now is quite familiar to scholars of international and comparative political economy (IPE/CPE) interested in questions of whether globalization leads to cross-national convergence – or divergence – in national policy regimes (Mosley 2003; Rodrik 2011). To some, globalization of capital means a race to the bottom in tax rates. Others assert instead that factors other than tax rates drive investment and, thus, claims of a race to the bottom are overblown (e.g., Swank 2002).

[11] Again, referring to closed and globalized economies is not to impose a false binary distinction but is meant to facilitate comparison.

[12] An example of such an institutional constraint is the electoral system. In disproportional systems with high thresholds, parties are unlikely to reap the spoils of office that comes from being a junior coalition partner. In this case, "office" objectives may be stymied in favor of alternative strategies, such as striving to influence policy through committee assignments.

Less familiar than the openness-government policy connection is how changing political-economic environments alter the strategies of political parties vying for power. With respect to these party strategies, globalization matters in three ways. First, in globalized economies, the number of players shaping policy outcomes increases. These actors are diverse, ranging from overseas consumers and domestic and foreign-based private sector investors to financial markets and sovereign credit rating agencies. Leaving aside the issue of whether Western governments in the postwar era ever "controlled" their economies, this certainly is not the case today. Today, the sources of economic growth, stability, equity, and so on are increasingly likely to be driven by decisions made by non-elected, non-accountable decision makers. These "non-electorally dependent decision makers," as Duch and Stevenson (2008, 139–140) describe them, include "individuals, firms, interest groups, non-electorally dependent (entrenched) bureaucrats, foreign leaders, the WTO, and many more." With an expanded number of actors, the government's job has changed. Since it is no longer the government's purview to respond to conditions directly, it has become all the more critical for politicians to provide an environment attractive to international market actors. Herein lies the new "consensus politics" (Kavanagh and Morris 1994) for the age of globalization. The postwar consensus has shifted. Less prevalent is the once-widely held belief that governments are providers, as in providing basic material benefits. More prevalent is the notion that governments must be facilitators, as in facilitating transparent, market-oriented policies for private-sector actors.[13] This has implications for mass-elite ties. While voters may update preferences in response to changing conditions, in a globally connected context, these preferences may not inform the actions of party representatives, at least not to the degree they would in closed market economies. By expanding markets' scope and complicating the interactions between markets and elected and non-elected decision-makers, globalization renders less clear the correct policy response.

A second way globalization reshapes party strategies is by weakening links between policy outputs and policy outcomes. In a world of closed economies, vote-maximizing parties carve out positions on the issues of the day to appeal to the greatest number of voters. Analyses of party responsiveness in a variety of democracies have shown this to be the case. Empirical research on party behavior, however, generally fails to acknowledge that this "median voter" strategy is credible only if the policies preferred by the median voter are attainable. But execution of popular policies, which often include such initiatives as the distribution of cheap credit, short-term growth, and the delivery of public services through fiscal expansion, becomes less attainable when policy

[13] The European (German) response to the financial market crisis of late 2008 reflects this consensus – rather than pushing for an injection of funds to address solvency issues, European policymakers put their support behind efforts to deepen and increase the transparency of financial market regulation.

latitude is restricted. Such is the case with globalization. Economic integration increases the popular demands for public goods and for insurance against market risk, but at the same time it undermines the ability of policymakers to finance policy obligations. This "globalization dilemma," as Rodrik (1997, 2011) calls it, pulls parties in different directions. The party's reputation as a competent manager of globalization might be enhanced by taking more pro-market, anti-expansionary, right-of-center positions, as an efficiency argument might predict. Alternatively, parties may find success in countering liberalizing trends by adopting more expansive policy positions, a position consistent with compensation arguments from IPE/CPE. Or the most credible response may in fact be no response at all. Since any action could well be met by an offsetting action, parties may decide that the best action is to stay the course, even in the face of changing voter preferences.

This raises a third way in which globalization affects elite behavior – by lowering the electorate's expectations. The use of fiscal tools to deliver public goods preferred by the electorate at large was effective in a closed economy. This "catch-all" strategy is likely to succeed as long as fiscal expansion is deemed possible. But it becomes less credible in globalized political-economic environments. Instead of making welfare-enhancing promises on which they cannot deliver, successful parties adapt by downsizing constituent expectations. The modal party strategy is to compete over less (Blyth and Katz 2005). Rather than make welfare-enhancing promises on which they cannot deliver, parties change strategies – away from delivering policy promises and toward one of downsizing constituent expectations. In this way, globalization matters for party behavior because it acts as a constraint on the realm of what's possible.

In sum, in closed economies, political parties have incentives to respond to the median voter, to propose policies to enhance the public's welfare, and to demonstrate their managerial competence. Yet each of these is compromised when the national economy becomes subjected to international economic conditions. First, globalization weakens party incentives to respond to the preferences of the electorate. Second, globalization means that the performance of the national economy is influenced by an expanded set of national and international actors. Lastly, under globalization, efforts to convey policy competence should be relatively less credible. Rather than being managers of policy, parties become managers of voter expectations.

If these claims are correct, then the implication is that political elites – and particularly elites with experience in office – should have an interest in communicating globalization's effects to the electorate in a way that serves their own interests. It was argued earlier that globalization affects voter behavior via its effect on individual perceptions of policymaker capacity such that belief in a constrained room to maneuver weakens ties between observable performance outcomes and the vote decision. Yet notions of a limited room to maneuver may also be fomented by politicians' own self-serving behavior. Given the need to face the voters at recurrent intervals, politicians have an interest in claiming

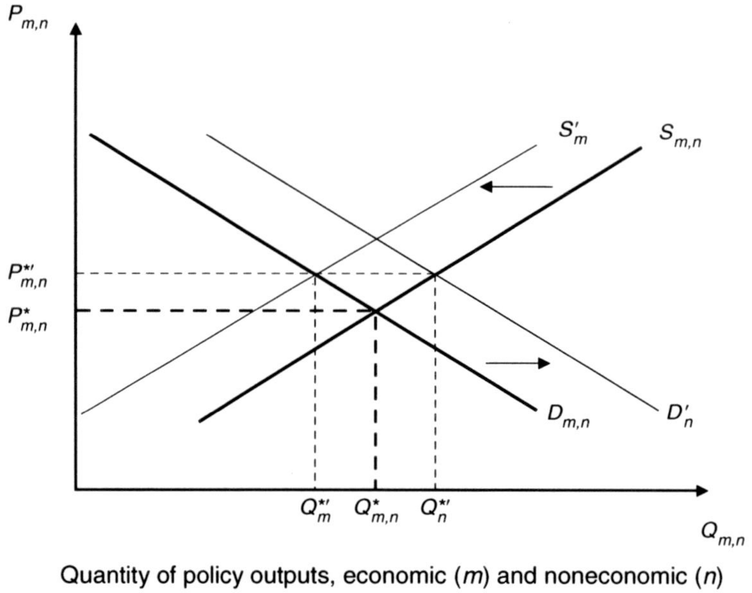

FIGURE 2.3. The supply and demand for policy in closed and exposed economies.
Note: Arrows indicate shift from a closed to an open economy. See text for additional information.

credit and deflecting blame. In closed economies, it is difficult for politicians to escape blame for poor economic performance. In contrast, highly open economies provide politicians a convenient vehicle for blame avoidance (Pierson 1994). Much in the way that elected officials can deflect blame through a discourse which highlights domestic political constraints, such as power-sharing arrangements produced by multiparty or divided governments, globalization offers politicians a tool for shifting responsibility for adverse conditions to forces beyond their control.

2.4. The Demand and Supply for Policy in Closed and Globalized Economies

This chapter has laid out a framework for understanding how globalization affects mass politics in established democracies. Having provided a set of expectations separately for the demand (masses) and supply (elites) sides, I now bring the two sides together to better illustrate globalization's joint influence on party and citizen behavior. This is shown in Figure 2.3. The figure graphs the demand and supply for policy in a simplified political economy in which the policy output is either economic, represented by subscript *m*, or noneconomic, represented by *n*. Governments have a choice of supplying *m* or

n, which, for present purposes, are assumed to be substitutes. The initial closed economy equilibrium quantity of policy supplied for both domains is located at $Q^{*}_{m,n}$ at a cost to current or future taxpayers of $P^{*}_{m,n}$. The supply curve $S_{m,n}$ applies solely to the closed economy case.[14] With the opening up of national economies comes a new set of circumstances. Under these new circumstances, the expectation is that there will be less of policy m, the "economic" policy, supplied at all levels of popular demand. The supply curve for economic policy thus shifts from $S_{m,n}$ to S'_{m}. The result is that the quantity of m supplied decreases (to $Q^{*'}_{m}$) and prices rise (to $P^{*'}_{m,n}$).

Were we to stop there, the story would be one in which globalization means voters pay more for what they desire but get less in return. This assumes that all policies citizens demand are influenced by economic globalization in the same direction and magnitude. But this may not be the case. Figure 2.3 instead implies that, when faced with globalization and a decline in the quantity of some economic benefit m, such as welfare provisions, citizens will compensate for this loss by *shifting demands* onto other issues. These alternative issue domains, n, remain unaffected by global economic ties. In fact, as a substitute, the relative demand for n at all levels of supply increases. This substitution effect is displayed in the figure by the outward shift in the demand curve from $D_{m,n}$ to D'_{n}. The resulting quantity supplied, $Q^{*'}_{n}$, is greater than its closed economy equilibrium level. In this way, globalization shifts what citizens demand and what parties supply.

In this chapter I have provided a lens through which to examine the consequences of globalization for the behavior of political actors – voters and their representatives. Studies of globalization and domestic politics out of the tradition of mainstream international and comparative political economy identify governments, domestic pressure groups, and international actors of various stripes among the most frequently employed actors for explaining policy decisions and outcomes. Using tools more familiar to students of voting behavior and party competition, I instead view globalization's drama through the lenses of citizens and their representatives, through the perspectives of those who make demands of the political system and those in a position to meet them. Particular emphasis is accorded to sketching out how globalization matters for issue politics and for political control of policy outcomes. I argue that by complicating the structure of issue politics and by reducing the effective political control over outcomes, signals from the world economy upset the bases of mass politics within advanced industrial democracies. This reframed argument produces a set of expectations pertaining to globalization's effects across different policy domains. The chapters that follow are devoted to examining these expectations across a range of settings on which electoral politics plays out.

[14] No assumption is made about the slope of the curves other than that demand is price elastic and that supply is upward-sloping such that as parties propose more "policy," the cost (or "price") of delivering this policy increases.

3

The World Economy and the Composition of Policy Demands

> Thirty years ago, the government had an influence on policy. Today, the room to maneuver has narrowed, evidently due to globalization.
>
> Party advisor on finance, Union pour un Mouvement Populaire[1]

Policy preferences are central to the dialogue between citizens and their representatives. This is particularly true for modern welfare states, where debates revolve around issues of taxation, redistribution, and the scope for the government in the market. The context of these debates, however, has changed with time. Economies in Europe, North America, and elsewhere have experienced broad structural change, transitioning from engines of growth tied to domestic manufacturing to a more stagnant situation resting on some combination of reliance on a services-based economy, an expanded public sector, and demand from abroad. Do these changes affect what citizens expect from their representatives? Does the shift from a world in which markets and borders are more or less coterminous to one in which markets cross borders produce a shift in voter expectations and, in turn, demands for policy responses? In short, does the integration of national markets matter for policy preferences?

These questions matter for how representative democracy works. For example, if the majority prefers more spending on public services, then a responsive government might increase spending or allocate a larger share of the budget to services (Soroka and Wlezien 2010). But what if public beliefs are affected by signals from the world economy? The median voter might view spending cutbacks as necessary in light of externally imposed constraints and, in turn, demand less in the way of policy response. Alternatively, the electorate might support a liberal world economic order only in the event that liberalizing reforms are coupled with reinforced social safety nets. Regardless, to the extent that global economic

[1] Personal interview, Paris March 2003.

signals alter public perceptions, a responsive government should adjust its policies, delivering "less" or "more" policy than previously. Whether such an attendant shift occurs speaks to globalization's compatibility with what Pitkin (1967) holds up as policymakers' active representation of citizens' preferences.

This chapter examines how the forces of globalization shape public policy preferences. As noted in Chapter 1, this is a subject on which work on the political economy of advanced capitalism has had relatively little to say. Those studies that do examine public opinion tend to focus on how individual self-interest directs globalization's effects (e.g., Baker 2005; Mayda and Rodrik 2005; Rehm 2011; Scheve and Slaughter 2004; Walter 2010). In this chapter, rather than focusing on individual self-interest, I argue that the effect of economic globalization on public preferences is domain specific. In some issue areas, there is broad agreement on globalization's influence, and, hence, voters are able to make cause and effect associations. But in other domains, the domestic policy implications of market integration are not so apparent. The former scenario characterizes mass demands for government action in the economy; the latter pertains to preferences for policies in domains perceived to be less affected by macroeconomic constraints.

This argument carries a novel implication: Voters balance demands for policy action. When reasoning about the connections between exogenous economic shocks and assessments of government capacity, individuals differentiate with respect to policy domain. This argument, as will be shown, contrasts in important ways with existing claims of the compensating effects of globalization, on the one hand, and of the importance of self-interest for policy preferences, on the other.

The chapter proceeds as follows. I first review existing accounts of the determinants of policy preferences. Building on the theoretical framework presented in Chapter 2, I then suggest how economic globalization might affect policy demands. Theoretical claims are tested in three sets of analyses: a cross-national analysis of individuals, a macro panel analysis, and a case study of issue concerns in France. Results from each of the investigations point to a common finding: economic globalization matters for public preferences, and how it matters depends on issue area. Consistent with the model of supply and demand for policy outcomes (Figure 2.3), results show that citizens respond to signals from the world economy by demanding less in areas where governments can no longer deliver, such as on economic areas (domain m), but more where they still can, such as cultural, post-material, or noneconomic domains (domain n). The implication is that globalization shapes the *composition* of mass preferences over policy.

3.1. The Determinants of Policy Preferences

Where do policy preferences come from? While answers to this question touch on a range of factors, approaches fall broadly into one of two camps, "economic" or "sociological." The former assumes that policy attitudes derive from individual utilities. Utility is positively affected by policy actions that increase material welfare and adversely affected by those that reduce it. In Meltzer and Richard's (1981) influential model, demand for redistribution increases as the income of the median voter declines. In the aggregate, this means more policy effort to reallocate resources under conditions of high income inequality. Extending the Meltzer-Richard set-up, Moene and Wallerstein (2001) model the effect of income inequality on preferences dependent on how benefits are targeted via the welfare state. Iversen and Soskice (2001) also begin with Meltzer-Richard but argue that human capital matters more than income levels. Other economics-based accounts of policy preferences emphasize performance rather than distribution. Analyses of aggregate opinion have shown across different contexts that public support for more government policy is pro-cyclical: It rises during times of strong economic performance and declines during slow-downs (Durr 1993; Kayser 2009; Stevenson 2001). Erikson et al. (2002) show that aggregate policy sentiment moves with the real economy, becoming more conservative as price levels rise but more liberal with increased unemployment. This result finds parallels in a recent work on aggregate opinion in specific issue areas. For instance, Soroka and Wlezien (2010) show that preferences for spending in a particular domain (e.g., defense or social policy) are negatively related to actual spending in that area.

Sociological approaches provide a contrasting account, emphasizing less mutable factors, such as institutions and group memberships. A prominent example is Brooks and Manza's (2007) "embedded preferences" account of social spending levels in OECD countries. Observing long-standing persistence in the scope of the welfare state, they maintain that "economic change or crisis, by itself, would be insufficient to fully dislodge the stakes individuals were assumed to have in existing institutions and social arrangements" (Brooks and Manza 2007, 103). A sociological approach to understanding policy attitudes would predict, for example, that citizens in encompassing welfare state regimes support higher levels of public spending than those in means-tested systems (Larsen 2008). Informed by early work on the development of social cleavages (Lipset 1981), others have found that religious traditions influence preferences for activist government policies. Likewise, factors that impinge on feelings of collective identity, such as ethnic diversity, have been shown to dampen support for policy outputs (Iida and Matsubayashi 2010).

3.2. Policy Preferences and the World Economy

How does globalization figure into this, if at all? I identify three distinct paths linking globalization to policy attitudes. One argument, commonplace in the political economy literature, is that globalization increases public preferences for protection from more volatile, less secure markets (Rodrik 1998). The reason is that globalization presents a trade-off for governments. Engaging in world markets yields efficiency gains, but in order to sustainably reap these gains and diffuse public backlash, policymakers must broker a bargain of "embedded liberalism" by increasing spending and redistributing wealth to the losers of globalization. More broadly, this perspective holds that the organization of domestic interests, as shaped by political institutions and welfare-production regimes, works to diffuse the impact of global economic forces (Hall and Soskice 2001; Iversen 2005; Swank 2002).

This compensation logic has much in common with economics-based accounts of policy preferences; performance of the national economy affects citizen welfare through changing price levels, employment (in)security, the quality of publicly funded services, and so on. Voters respond to these changes by demanding "more" or "less" policy. Thus, publics should prefer more in the way of programs to redistributive wealth and to prop up social insurance schemes as growth slows or becomes more volatile or as the distribution of incomes widens. Assuming a positively skewed income distribution, and assuming that the costs attributable to globalization borne by the losers are equal to or greater than the benefits awarded to the winners in advanced capitalist economies, then we would expect globalization to be associated with heightened public preferences for policies to compensate the losers. The more reliant the nation's economy is on world markets, the more likely citizens are to prefer policies for social protection.

Yet the micro-political basis of this positive globalization-spending connection remains underdeveloped. Research examining individual responses to globalization tends to emphasize material interests produced by globalization's asymmetrical effects on individual welfare (e.g., Hays et al. 2005; Walter 2010). Though unstated, such arguments rely on a particular pattern of associative linkages (Sniderman et al. 1986). Specifically, individuals receive signals about the scope of the world economy, update beliefs about their susceptibility to market dislocations, and adjust the level of pressure placed on governments to deliver policies to compensate against risks. But what if voters fail to respond to the particular stimuli – in this case, signals from world markets – in this way? We might expect a very different kind of voter response. Mass opinion about globalization's consequences may be filtered not by changing perceptions of market-induced risk (e.g., Rodrik 1998), but by changing beliefs about the policymaker capacity.

This alternative perspective is rooted in work on the cognitive process of causal attribution. Many researchers have demonstrated that the attribution process affects political attitudes and behavior (e.g., Lau and Sears 1981; Gomez and Wilson 2006). These studies suggest that the process of linking stimuli to observed outcomes is far from straightforward. Making causal attributions requires that individuals are first *informed* about a stimulus and then that they correctly *associate* that stimulus with its rightful sources. And the quality and source of this information affects the multi-stage attribution process in "multiple and sometimes confounding ways" (Gomez and Wilson 2006, 130).

As with the attribution process, understanding how market dependence bears on policy outcomes requires individuals to make cause and effect connections. This understanding may require some level of sophistication on the part of voters. Recent work on policy attitudes suggests, however, that all segments of society – not just sophisticates – incorporate economic information into their policy opinions (Enns and Kellstedt 2008). The capacity to make associative linkages may also be communicated by political elites. To capture the gains from competing abroad, the argument goes, businesses must have access to investment capital, export markets, and the like. Such access can raise the costs of putting up taxes, of spending on popular services, and of priming demand via expansionary policies. In the face of these constraints, political elites wishing to shirk blame for inaction have incentives to signal to the public that globalization limits their policy room to maneuver. Voters, in turn, will construct a path of associative linkages in which heightened exposure to the world economy tempers beliefs that national policymakers can influence real outcomes. Citizens may still pressure governments for policy but at levels lower than those they would in a closed-economy setting.

This argument, it should be noted, does not rest on whether a "race-to-the-bottom" is realized in terms of actual policy decisions. What matters are citizens' perceptions of policy control (see Chapter 2). On this point, there is little evidence to discredit the existence of race-to-the-bottom reasoning. Indeed, opinion surveys show that majorities in nearly all countries believe globalization limits rather than enhances the policy room to maneuver (see Chapter 1).

3.2.1. Globalization and the Composition of Preferences: Balancing Demands

While these arguments draw opposite conclusions, both assume that global economic signals affect public opinion similarly across policy areas by either increasing (compensation hypothesis) or decreasing policy demands (constraint hypothesis). A third possibility, however, is that globalization's effects are heterogeneous. The impact of signals from the world economy may vary systematically by issue domain. The public's ability to make sense of politics varies by issue area (Carmines and Stimson 1989; Converse 1964). For some issues, opinions are relatively constrained, in the sense that they are interpretable by citizens in terms of well-known cues, but for many others this is not the case. Issue domains may also vary in the extent to which voters are supportive of government involvement. For example, in his work on the dynamics of preferences for spending in different domains, Wlezien (1995) reports evidence of a guns-butter trade-off in the public's preferred levels of spending, finding that preferences for social spending decrease in response to preferences for greater defense allocations. He asserts thus that the public, "seems to have a level of spending in mind that it allocates to defense and nondefense programs based on the need for defense spending" (Wlezien 1995, 997).

The structure of issue politics plays an important role in research on mass preferences. In Wlezien's work, the international political environment shapes Americans' preferences for national defense, which in turn helps explain opinions on social spending. Similarly, the structure of issue politics guides citizens' perceptions of the international economy, particularly with respect to its influence on policy preferences and policy demands. The constraint hypothesis maintains that voters use information about the world economy to downgrade expectations regarding political control. But as work on attribution processes indicates, this should be the case only when complex and distinct pieces of political and economic information can be brought into congruence.

Not all issues are equally affected by constraints arising from the world economy. Information required for drawing connections is more accessible for some policy areas than others. The former set maps closely onto the set of issues on which policy contestation in developed welfare states has been based – for example, issues pertaining to the role of the state in the market. On these issues, parties and voters are well-conditioned to think about the consequences of government (in)action. And for these, the constraints levied by economic openness are quite apparent. For other issues, however, associative linkages are either absent or circuitous; thereby making it more difficult to bring information into congruence. As regards processing signals from the world economy, I suggest this to be the case for cultural, post-material, or otherwise noneconomic issues.[2]

This argument anticipates compensation of a different sort – not of governments compensating losers but of citizens voicing preferences in awareness of room-to-maneuver constraints. In certain policy domains, such as the national economy, ties between globalization and policy outcomes may be relatively straightforward (see Chapter 4). But in other issue areas, such as healthcare, the environment, pensions, and the like, achieving such distal consistency is difficult. As such, public demands for government action should remain high. Recognizing constraints on national policy capacity in certain issue areas (e.g., the economy), individuals may, in compensating fashion, increase pressures for policy action in other areas. Given the relative ease of bringing information about the assumed cause (exposure to the world economy) and effect (the policy room to maneuver) into congruence, voters should be able to recognize the extent to which the capacity to fine tune the economy is constrained. But in other issue areas, like healthcare, the environment, pensions, and the like,

[2] In terms of their effect on national budgets, few policy outcomes are in fact unaffected by globalization's constraints. However, because of the structure of issue opinions and variations in the development of associative linkages, the constraining effects of signals from the world economy may be perceived as less of a constraint on the government's policymaking capacity on issues less directly related to the national economy. For this reason, it is appropriate to speak of economic and noneconomic issue areas.

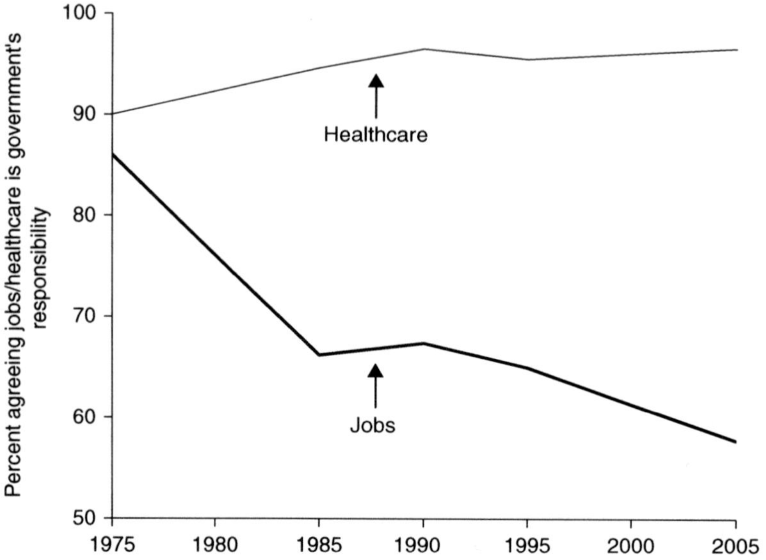

FIGURE 3.1. Public preferences for government responsibility in jobs and healthcare in eight countries.

Note: Lines report the percent of respondents who (strongly and somewhat) agree that it is the government's responsibility to provide jobs and to provide healthcare. Percentages are averages from eight countries: Australia, Britain, (West) Germany, Ireland, Italy, Norway, Sweden, and the United States. Dates are approximate, and values for 1980 and 2000 are interpolated. Not all countries included in each time period.
Sources: Barnes and Kaase (1979), various ISSP surveys.

achieving such distal consistency is difficult. In these areas demands should remain high.

Trends displayed in Figure 3.1 are consistent with these claims. It displays opinion in two areas, employment assistance and healthcare, from the 1970s to the 2000s. Government assistance in job provision provides an example of an economic policy demand and healthcare provision represents a noneconomic issue. The figure charts the percentage of individuals, averaged across eight countries, who agree that it is the government's responsibility to provide a job and to provide healthcare to everyone in need. While support for government action in an economic domain – jobs – has declined, opinion about the governments' role in the noneconomic domain – healthcare – has remained constant.[3]

[3] Evidence from factor analyses of issue preferences reported later in this chapter supports the claim – made for now only on grounds of face validity – that the structures of preferences for jobs and for healthcare are unrelated. Indeed, each loads strongly on a different dimension (see Table 3.1).

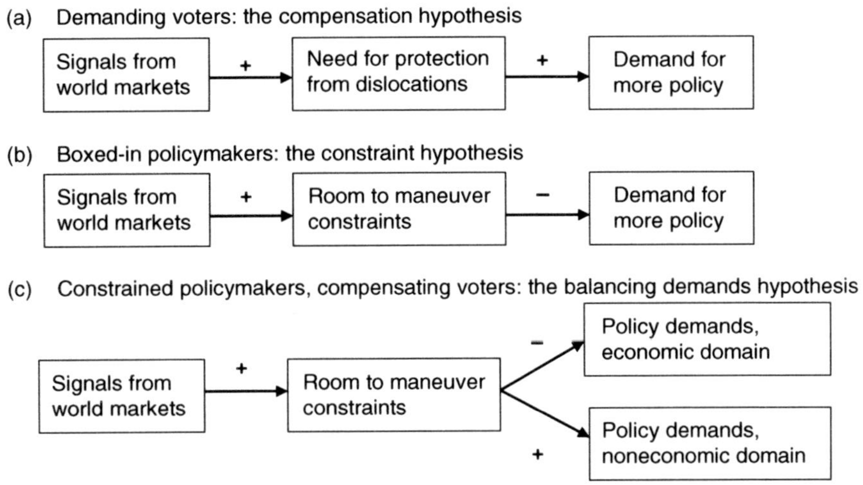

FIGURE 3.2. Economic globalization and policy demands: hypotheses.
Note: +/– denote expected direction of relationship.

Figure 3.1 does not provide definitive support for an openness-induced effect. For instance, voters may wish for governments to do less in the area of jobs simply because they have lost their trust in the state. Or it might be that a decline of postwar consensus politics and the growing push toward free markets has shifted policy preferences away from a belief that government can have a positive effect. Other explanations are possible as well.[4] Nevertheless, the differential trends characterizing jobs and healthcare push us toward a third causal claim which contrasts both with straight compensation and constraint accounts: As a result of perceptions of differences in policy capacity, economic globalization reduces public demands for government policy response in some areas but not others. While reducing preferences for action in the economic realm, signals from the world economy serve to increase preferences for policy outcomes in noneconomic policy domains. This "balancing demands" argument finds support from interviews with political elites. For example, a high-ranking Liberal Democrat MP in Britain told me, "Britain is moving to a situation where health and education and things like that are becoming more ... of a factor than the economy."[5]

By way of summary, Figure 3.2 depicts three competing claims linking globalization to policy demands. According to the *compensation hypothesis*, signals from the world economy are viewed as a source of volatility and insecurity. The public thus increases pressure on government to offset the dislocations (Figure 3.2a). The *constraint hypothesis* predicts that citizens interpret signals

[4] I thank an anonymous reviewer for making this point.
[5] Personal interview, London, February 2003.

from world markets as a constraint on the range of credible policy responses, and, thus, they demand less in terms of a policy response (Figure 3.2b). The *balancing demands hypothesis* assumes globalization limits policy action but not to the same degree across issue domains. Economic signals are assumed to alleviate pressure on governments to deliver solutions for issues related to the economy. But this is not the case for domains where the structure of issue politics and the absence of clarifying cues create barriers to making distal associations. Rather, voters balance reduced demands for government action in the economy by increasing demands for attention in other, noneconomic areas (Figure 3.2c).

3.3. Globalization and Mass Preferences: Micro Cross-Section Analysis

To test these competing expectations, I perform a pair of statistical analyses, first of individuals and then of aggregated opinion. The analyses are complementary. With the first, we can control for individual and party-level attributes, while the second enables us to consider change over time. The individual-level analysis employs public opinion data from seventeen countries using data from the 2006 International Social Survey Programme's (ISSP) Role of Government IV Survey.[6] The 2006 ISSP module asks respondents for their opinions on the proper role for government over a wide set of policy issues. Respondents were asked "On the whole, do you think it should or should not be the government's responsibility to

- provide a job for everyone who wants one?
- keep prices under control?
- provide healthcare for the sick?
- provide a decent standard of living for the old?
- provide industry with the help it needs to grow?
- provide a decent standard of living for the unemployed?
- reduce income differences between the rich and the poor?
- give financial help to university students from low-income families?
- provide decent housing for those who can't afford it?
- impose strict laws to make industry do less damage to the environment?"

Item responses are on a four-point scale from "definitely should be" to "definitely should not be" such that higher values indicate stronger support for government policy involvement. These items have been employed in previous research on policy preferences (Iversen and Soskice 2001; Rehm 2011; Wlezien and

[6] Fieldwork was carried out in participating countries between early 2005 and early 2008. The countries included are Australia, Canada, Denmark, Finland, France, Germany, Ireland, Japan, Netherlands, New Zealand, Norway, Portugal, Spain, Sweden, Switzerland, the United Kingdom, and the United States.

Soroka 2012). Wlezien and Soroka (2012) argue that these responsibility items are a proxy for the public's "preferred level of policy." As Brooks and Manza (2007) show in their longitudinal analyses, responses to these items vary over time, indicating that they do not simply measure views on the legally prescribed purposes of government. Rather, the survey items reflect changes in public views of the areas where governments should be more or less involved in delivering policy responses. In short, previous analyses of these questions indicate they are appropriate as measures of the underlying concept of policy demands.

These items are used to create three measures of policy preferences. The first combines the ten items additively, giving equal weight to each policy area. I label this broad-based measure *general preferences*. The other two policy measures are generated from factor scores. Principal components factor analysis of the ten preference items, displayed in Table 3.1, show they load on two dimensions. The first dimension captures attitudes on many policies pertaining to economic or material concerns. Issues related to jobs and unemployment, inequality, and prices all load strongly on this dimension. The second dimension pertains to more multifaceted concerns that mix economic concerns with issues often framed in more social or post-material terms, such as healthcare and the environment (see, e.g., Dalton 2009).[7] Using regression scoring techniques, I generate two factor scores (Kim and Mueller 1978). Variation on the first factor is driven chiefly by job provision, redistribution, and unemployment protection. Variation on the second dimension is attributable mainly to attitudes on healthcare, the environment, and pensions. I label the first factor *economic preferences* and the second *noneconomic preferences*.[8]

The key predictor is a measure of globalization. To account for multiple ways which the world economy influences the nation's economy, I use Dreher's (2006) index of an economy's objective level of exposure to world markets. The measure combines information on foreign trade in goods and services, foreign direct investment, portfolio investment, and income payments to foreign nationals. I also, however, perform analyses with other globalization indicators as a way to gauge the robustness of results.

Models control for other macro-level factors shown to affect policy preferences.[9] To address pro-cyclical arguments that changes policy preferences

[7] In uncovering two dimensions, one material and one post-material, this result is consistent with other research on the structure of issue attitudes (Hooghe et al. 2002; Kitschelt 1994; Kriesi et al. 2008; also Soroka and Wlezien 2010, 77; Wlezien 2004, 6). It might be added that two items, preferences for public provision of housing and financial aid for university students, load strongly on both dimensions. This makes sense on face-validity grounds as both of these (particularly financial aid) are viewed in economic and noneconomic terms.

[8] Again, I do not wish to argue that the two dimensions cleave neatly according to issues that lie in and out of the economy. Instead, these labels pertain to the general ways individuals view these two sets of issues – a claim substantiated by much research. See the previous note.

[9] All macro measures are recorded from the year before the particular country survey was in the field to allow for information processing.

TABLE 3.1. *Policy responsibility items factor loadings*

	Factor 1 Economic preferences	Factor 2 Noneconomic preferences
Provide jobs	**0.78**	0.06
Reduce income differences	**0.72**	0.18
Provide living std for unemployed	**0.67**	0.30
Keep prices under control	**0.58**	0.24
Provide industry with help	**0.47**	0.28
Provide housing	**0.59**	**0.45**
Provide aid to university students	**0.46**	**0.47**
Impose laws to protect environment	0.08	**0.61**
Provide living std to elderly	0.26	**0.75**
Provide healthcare	0.14	**0.78**
Variance explained	0.28	0.22

Note: Principal component factors, varimax rotation. Factor loadings greater than |0.4| are in bold. Cronbach's alpha = .824, N = 19552.
Source: ISSP Role of Government IV Survey.

relate positively with economic conditions (Wlezien 1995; Stevenson 2001), models include per capita GDP, both as the percent annual change and as the (natural log of) national income. To address claims that the size of the welfare state conditions public sentiment favoring government action (Brooks and Manza 2007), I include a variable for welfare effort measured in terms of social transfers as the after-tax change in the Gini coefficient. To account for longstanding cultural factors shaping public beliefs over the state's role in society, I follow Iida and Matsubayashi (2010) and include a measure of ethnic diversity and a measure of the percentages of Catholics in society. Also included is a variable for federalism, which, by vertically diffusing powers, may temper preferences for policy activism.[10]

Models include a set of individual-level covariates. Two of these are particularly relevant with respect to globalization. Compensation arguments imply that losers of globalization will prefer more levels of government activity and winners less. Accordingly, I construct a variable *globalization loser*. Based on their human capital endowments and labor market positions, individuals scoring high on this measure are more likely to see their income levels suffer on account of competition from abroad.[11] Political knowledge may also matter insomuch as it is required for individuals to receive signals from the world economy and link

[10] I also ran models with a dummy variable for European Union member countries, on the grounds that EU membership also signals a diffusion of political control. In no specification, however, was the EU indicator close to statistically significant.

[11] *Globalization loser* is constructed using information on respondents' income and occupation. See Appendix 3.1.

them to policy outputs (however, see Enns and Kellstedt 2008). I thus include a measure of the respondent's subjective political knowledge.[12] I also include measures to control for partisan dispositions. Since left-leaning partisans are more likely to prefer expansive policies, and right-learning partisans less likely, I include indicator variables for individuals identifying with a party on the left and right sides of the political spectrum. Partisanship may also matter with respect to the respondent's affinity toward the government in power. On the one hand, co-partisans may demand less from the government – for instance, they are more apt to see the status quo in a positive light than are members of other parties. Alternatively, co-partisans may be more likely to endorse active government because they share similar policy preferences to those in power. Finally, models control for formal education, gender, and age.

Since covariates are measured both at the individual- and country-level, statistical analyses are performed using hierarchical linear modeling with random intercepts. Table 3.2 presents model estimates. *General preferences* is the dependent variable in Model 1. Results show globalization losers, left-leaning partisans, non-co-partisans, the less educated, and women are more likely to prefer government involvement in all policy areas. National context also matters; individuals are more likely to demand government policy if they reside in countries with stronger growth rates, higher incomes, and policies in place to reduce inequities, in ethnically homogenous societies, and in places with greater proportions of Catholics. These results are consistent with findings from previous research. Note, however, that signals from the world economy have no discernible impact, either positively, per the compensation hypothesis, or negatively, according to the constraint hypothesis.

The next two models examine preferences for government responsibility in economic and noneconomic policy areas. Model 2 estimates show that globalization negatively influences mass preferences in economic areas. As indicated by the coefficient on *globalization flows*, individuals demand less from governments on matters such as jobs, redistribution, and unemployment protections when exposure to world markets is greater. More substantively, an index score increase akin to that of the United States (*globalization flows* = 0.41) to that of the Netherlands (0.95) reduces citizen preferences for government provision of economic policy by about 10 percent.[13] By increasing the importance of issues related to economic globalization, parties can steer policy preferences. This result is consistent with the argument that globalization, working through the preferences of the electorate, places limitations on the policy capacity of national governments.

[12] Lacking an objective knowledge item, I employ a measure of subjective knowledge: "I feel that I have a pretty good understanding of the important political issues facing our country."

[13] This result is produced by taking the difference between 0.95 and 0.41, multiplying it by the estimate on *globalization flows* from Model 2 (–0.77) and then expressing this result as a percentage of the total in-sample range (excluding individuals at the 1st and 99th percentile) on *economic preferences* (or 0.42/4.12 = 0.10).

TABLE 3.2. *Multilevel models of government policy responsibilities*

Dependent variable	General preferences (1)		Economic preferences (2)		Noneconomic preferences (3)	
	Est.	SE	Est.	SE	Est.	SE
Globalization flows	−.08	(.12)	−.77**	(.28)	.91**	(.44)
Δ Growth	.05**	(.02)	.10**	(.05)	.03	(.07)
GDP per capita	.28**	(.10)	.49**	(.22)	.31	(.35)
Welfare effort	.01**	(.003)	.04**	(.01)	−.003	(.01)
Ethnic fractionalization	−.004**	(.001)	−.0003	(.002)	−.01**	(.003)
Catholic	.45**	(.05)	.93**	(.12)	.29	(.20)
Federalism	−.10**	(.04)	−.29**	(.10)	.06	(.15)
Left partisan	.12**	(.01)	.20**	(.02)	.14**	(.02)
Right partisan	−.17**	(.01)	−.29**	(.02)	−.17**	(.02)
Co-partisan	−.06**	(.01)	−.08**	(.02)	−.09**	(.02)
Globalization loser	.05**	(.01)	.11**	(.01)	.01	(.01)
Political knowledge	.004	(.003)	−.02**	(.01)	.05**	(.01)
Education	−.04**	(.002)	−.10**	(.01)	−.004	(.01)
Female	.10**	(.01)	.19**	(.01)	.09**	(.01)
Age 35–49	−.02	(.01)	−.12**	(.02)	.10**	(.02)
Age 50–64	.002	(.01)	−.08**	(.02)	.11**	(.02)
Age 65+	.04**	(.01)	.03	(.02)	.12**	(.02)
Constant	−2.53**	(.98)	−5.39*	(2.23)	−4.07	(3.53)
Var: Country level	.003**	(.001)	.02**	(.01)	.04**	(.01)
Var: Individual level	.19**	(.002)	.76**	(.01)	.89**	(.01)
Wald chi-square	2404.24**		2223.96**		487.12**	

Note: Dependent variables are factor scores produced from the factor analyses described in the text and in Appendix 3.1. The data source for the public opinion data is ISSP Research Group (2008). Standard errors are in parentheses. * $p \leq .10$ ** $p \leq .05$; (two tailed). Number of individuals: 19,208. Number of countries: 17.

Model 3 reports results for the noneconomic issue dimension. Comparing the determinants of public demands on this second policy dimension to the first is illuminating. Although globalization losers are more likely to express support for government activity in economic areas, being adversely affected by economic openness has no bearing on one's preferences in noneconomic areas. We also see that political sophistication has differential effects. Knowledge reduces demands for economic intervention – ostensibly owing to recognition of constraints – but not in noneconomic areas. And, notably, estimates on all country-level predictors differ between Models 2 and 3, in terms of sign, precision, or both.[14]

[14] Regarding the country-level predictors, GDP per capita increases preferences for government activity with respect to the economy but not for demands in noneconomic areas. This result runs

Again, our main interest is in the effect of globalization. While globalization depresses public demands for policy directed to economic areas (Model 2), preferences for government action on less overtly economic issues, such as healthcare or assistance to the elderly, are greater when exposure to the world economy is high (Model 3). A change on the order of a move from a relatively closed economy, such as the United States, to a relatively open one, such as the Netherlands, is predicted to increase the respondent's preferences for noneconomic policy by about 11 percent. This pair of results underlines the conclusion that globalization's impact on preferences is contingent on policy domain.

Additional analyses speak to the robustness of these findings. First, I examined whether results were sensitive to alternative measures of the key predictor. I found that findings are robust across several measures of globalization, including broader-based indicators, such as Dreher's economic index combining flows with the absence of policy restrictions, as well as narrower components such as trade flows and private capital flows. Second, I considered whether messages about the impact of the world economy stem more from elite discourse than they do from these broad objective measures. I did so by including in the models a measure constructed from surveys of party experts in which respondents were asked to evaluate the importance of the world economy for the party's public issue stance (Vowles et al. 2010).[15] Results show that individuals who, by virtue of their partisan attachments, receive signals about the importance of globalization from party elites are less likely to make demands with respect to the economic dimension. The inclusion of these elite-filtered signals, however, has no bearing on the impact of actual exposure to the world economy. Third, I examined whether the globalization-attitudes connection differs for globalization winners and losers. Interactive specifications indicate that winners are more likely than losers to reduce their demands for policy activity under globalization. However, this is only the case for *economic preferences*; the winner/loser distinction has no bearing in shaping noneconomic policy attitudes. Lastly, it may be the case that the more sophisticated are more likely to process signals. Thus, I estimated interactive models to test whether the influence of globalization depends on the individual's level of political sophistication. For *economic preferences*, political sophistication has no effect: globalization reduces policy

counter to Inglehart's (1990) arguments that, as societies become more affluent, citizens should want less active governments in economic areas and more active governments in noneconomic areas. I thank an anonymous reviewer for noting this finding.

[15] Experts were asked "how important has the world economy been to the parties in their public stance?" Using the median response for each party, I constructed a series of indicators for "globalization is of great importance," "globalization is of some importance," and "globalization is of little importance." These indicators are matched with respondents in the ISSP data file based on their partisan affiliation, with respondents not "feeling close" to any particular party receiving a code of zero. Comparisons with party placements from other surveys (utilizing common items, such as left-right positions) suggest that results perform well (Vowles et al. 2010). For more on the expert survey, see the appendix to this chapter.

demands regardless of knowledge level. For *noneconomic preferences*, results show that the coefficient on *globalization flows* is not statistically significant at lower levels of knowledge, implying that sophistication assists voters to work through complicated distal associations (e.g., Gomez and Wilson 2006).[16]

Thus, while economic globalization has no effect on general preferences for government action, it has substantial effects on the *composition* of preferences. Publics in open economies adjust policy preferences based on their associative linkages. Individuals levy policy demands in different issue areas in a way consistent with the relative influence of the world economy on economic life. Globalization alleviates pressures for policymakers to deliver policies in so-called economic areas – that is, the very areas in which the state has been involved since the postwar settlement years. But it raises pressure for policymakers to tend to citizen demands in other, less directly economic areas.

3.4. Globalization and Mass Preferences: Macro Panel Analysis

Evidence reported earlier in this chapter supports a balancing demands argument. This evidence, however, is based on a single point in time. The extent and orientation of the integration of national economies has changed over time. To capture these changes, I offer a test of the balancing demands hypothesis by pooling cross sections from the International Social Survey Programme from 1986 to 2006 to perform a panel analysis of aggregate policy preferences.

Items used to construct the policy preferences measures described here are not available in all ISSP survey waves. Fortunately, two items were asked on several occasions: the item on government's responsibility to provide jobs and the item on reducing income differences. Brooks and Manza (2006; 2007) have shown that these two items "summarize well the underlying dimension of mass policy preferences that are measured by the larger set of ISSP items," such as those found in the 2006 study analyzed earlier (Brooks and Manza 2007, 41). Moreover, we saw in Table 3.1 that these two load strongly (indeed, the most strongly) on the first principal components dimension in the Role of Government IV data set. I therefore pool the ISSP surveys that include these two items, perform a factor analysis of these two items, and use country-year mean values on the resulting scores to produce a macro-level value of *economic preferences* for each observation included in the analysis.[17]

[16] Results of these analyses are available from the author's website.

[17] Country-years included are Australia (1986, 1990, 1993, 1996, 1998, 2007), Austria (1986, 1993, 1999), Canada (1996, 1999, 2006), Denmark (1998, 2008), Finland (2006), France (1997, 1998, 2006), Germany (1985, 1990, 1991, 1996, 1998, 2006), Ireland (1991, 1996, 1998, 2005), Italy (1985, 1990, 1991, 1990, 1996, 1998), Japan (1996, 1998, 2006), the Netherlands (1991, 1998, 2006), New Zealand (1991, 1996, 1998, 2006), Norway (1990, 1991, 1996, 1998, 2006), Portugal (1999, 2006), Spain (1996, 1998, 2006), Sweden (1996, 1998, 2006), Switzerland (1999, 2007), the United Kingdom (1985, 1990, 1991, 1996, 1998, 2006), and United States

TABLE 3.3. *Macro models of government policy responsibilities*

	Economic preferences (1)	Noneconomic preferences (2)
Globalization flows	−.66*	.62*
	(.36)	(.35)
ΔGrowth	.04*	.01
	(.02)	(.02)
GDP per capita	−.16	.10
	(.35)	(.30)
Welfare effort	.02	.01
	(.01)	(.01)
Ethnic fractionalization	.003	−.01**
	(.004)	(.003)
Catholic	.45**	.17
	(.18)	(.17)
Federalism	−.39**	−.39**
	(.14)	(.13)
Constant	1.65	−1.27
	(3.71)	(3.63)
N	70	43
R^2	.55	.68
Rho	.32	.62

Note: Dependent variable is factor score produced from the factor analyses of ISSP survey items on government responsibility for providing employment and for reducing income inequality (Model 1), and for government provision of healthcare and a quality standard of living for the elderly (Model 2). Cells report GLS panel random-effects estimates with standard errors in parentheses. All models allow the intercepts to vary according to year. * $p \leq .10$ ** $p \leq .05$; (two tailed).

Values range from −0.89 for the United States in 1985 to 0.94 in Portugal in 1999. This variable is regressed on the same set of macro-indicators described earlier.

Table 3.3 presents the results. To account for unobserved unit (country) heterogeneity, models are estimated with random effects via generalized least squares.[18] Since we are interested in the causal effects of globalization – a

(1985, 1990, 1991, 1996, 1998, 2006). These are taken from the ISSP's Religion I and II and Role of Government I, II, III, and IV surveys. Brooks and Manza adopt a similar approach.

[18] Another approach for addressing cross-unit heterogeneity (non-random error correlations and omitted variable bias), is via country-fixed effects. Scholars have recently argued, however, that the inclusion of country-fixed effects erects a barrier to inference, particularly for cross-sectionally dominant and unbalanced panels such as the one here (e.g., Plümper and Troeger 2007). If results of these alternative specifications yield the same qualitative results, then we can be all the more assured that globalization reduces public demands in economic policy domains.

measure which trends over time – I include a battery of dummy variables for survey-year to allow the model intercept to vary over time to control for other common trending factors. As with the cross-sectional analysis, results reported in Model 1 show that mean levels of *economic preferences* are higher in countries with stronger economic performance, higher shares of Catholics, and unitary (non-federal) designs. Again, results show that exposure to the world economy negatively affects public support for more activist policies. Compare, for example, the globalization score for Italy in 1987 (29 on the 0–100 scale) to that of Ireland in 2001 (98, just prior to the September 11-induced economic contraction). The difference between these two levels reduces *economic preferences* by .46, or 25 percent of its total in sample range. Or consider a change within a single country. In Finland, the score on the index was 42 in 1985, rising to 85 in 2001. Model estimates predict that such a move matters for collective policy preferences, reducing preferences for economic policy by 16 percent. Once again, it appears that mass publics recognize the constraints policymakers face and adjust demands accordingly.[19]

What about aggregate preferences for policies considered by many as falling outside the purely economic/material domain, such as health, the environment, and pensions? Unfortunately, for many ISSP surveys, items to construct the noneconomic preference measures are not available. It is, however, possible to analyze noneconomic preferences over a smaller sample using those surveys that measure the two policy responsibility items that load most strongly on the second factor dimension: healthcare and provision of a quality standard of living for the elderly. For this subset of surveys (forty-three country-years in all), I created a measure of country-survey mean values as described earlier. The second model in Table 3.3 reports results on this reduced set of cases. Consistent with a balancing demands argument, the coefficient on the globalization flows index is positive and statistically significant.

Results of the aggregate panel analyses thus reiterate those of the micro: When it comes to public preferences, economic globalization constrains policy demands in areas related to economic performance, stability, and equity. To compensate, voters request greater assistance in areas they believe to be relatively less susceptible to worldwide markets.[20]

Additional analyses show this to be the case. Estimating models with OLS regression with robust standard errors clustered by country also produces results consistent with those in Table 3.3.

[19] To assess model sensitivity, I re-estimated the models omitting one case at a time. For Model 1, the coefficient on *globalization flows* is statistically significant and signed in the negative direction for every case. For Model 2, the coefficient on *globalization flows* is positively signed in all cases and is statistically significant at conventional levels in all cases but one; when the Japan 2007 observation is omitted, the *p*-value falls to 0.21.

[20] The macro models also provide an opportunity to separate out the different policy preferences into their component parts. Table 3A.8 in the appendix to this chapter re-estimates Table 3.3 models but with dependent variables disaggregated into preferences for providing jobs, for reducing income differences, for providing healthcare, and for providing a quality living standard for

3.5. Globalization and Citizen Issue Demands: A French Case Study

I have shown that globalization loosens mass demands for more expansive government policies and programs to support the public welfare. Our interests in political-economic change, however, are often informed by change over time. Longitudinal analysis of a single case provides a means to complement "cross-sectional dominant" research designs. Accordingly, this section reports the results of a longitudinal case study analysis of the policy priorities of the French public. With a tradition of strong government intervention in economic and social affairs, France is a good example for examining how exogenous constraints limit the influence of governments in advanced industrial democracies. And French politicians have often made connections between globalization and the credibility of their policy-based appeals.[21] The data begin in the third quarter of 1981, just after the election of François Mitterrand to the presidency, and run to the fourth quarter of 2006, near the end of President Jacques Chirac's second term.

To examine whether this sentiment characterizes the views of the French public, I conduct a time-series analysis of macro opinion. Specifically, I model mass demands for government policy attention. These policy demands are again of two types, economic and noneconomic. These indicators of popular opinion come from polls that ask "Among the following, which do you think the government should be most concerned with at the present time?"[22] The item has four response categories: "fight unemployment," "fight violence and crime," "fight high prices," and "maintain social peace."[23] I take two of these series, "fight unemployment" and "fight violence and crime" as dependent variables in a set of time-series regression analyses. These series, *unemployment priority* and *crime priority*, are measured as the percentages responding with "fight unemployment," and "fight violence and crime," as government's greatest concern. These are selected because, for one, they are the most salient and display the most over-time variation (see Figure 3.3). More importantly, they are selected because they offer examples of issue concerns from different domains. Following the balancing demands hypothesis, the expectation is that economic flows will *reduce* public demands for jobs (an economic issue) but contribute to *greater* demands to fight violence and crime (a noneconomic, social issue).

the elderly. Results are consistent with those shown in Table 3.3: *Globalization flows* carries a negative coefficient for models of economic policy preferences (jobs and income differences) and a positive coefficient for models of noneconomic policy preferences (healthcare and a quality living standard for the elderly).

[21] Evidence from personal interviews, February/March 2003, Paris.

[22] "Parmi les choses suivantes, quelle est celle dont le gouvernement doit, selon vous, s'occuper en priorité à l'heure actuelle?" The polls are conducted by SOFRES and published monthly in *Le Figaro Magazine*. I thank Carine Marcé for assistance in collecting these data.

[23] A fifth option, "maintain purchasing power," was offered regularly beginning in 1989. Responses for this option rarely exceeded 10 percent of respondents.

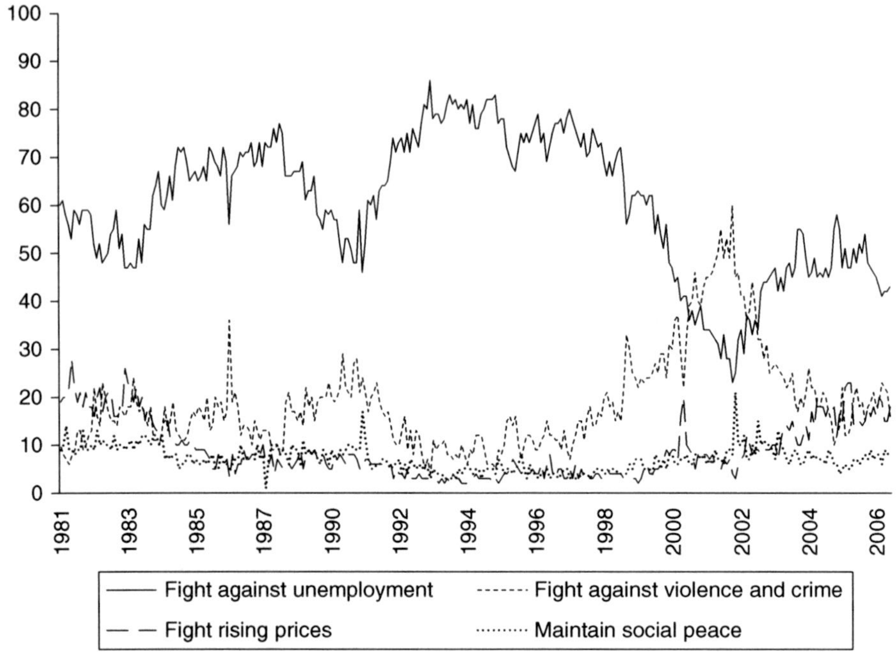

FIGURE 3.3. Issue priorities of the French public, 1981–2006.
Note: Vertical axis reports percent respondents identifying issue as the one government should be most concerned about.
Source: Sofres.

I regress these series on quarterly measures of the openness of the French economy to trade and to capital flows.[24] *Trade openness* is measured using exports plus imports. *Capital flows* is the sum of total inflows and outflows of foreign direct and portfolio investment. Both series are standardized as a percentage of GDP and come from the IMF's *International Financial Statistics*. Controls include measures for economics and politics. To control for the effect of objective performance, I include the seasonally adjusted unemployment rate and the annualized economic growth rates.[25] As the unemployment rate increases, the share of respondents who prioritize efforts to combat unemployment should rise as well. Growth may have the opposite effect, blunting

[24] While the public opinion data are collected monthly, the economic covariates are collected at quarterly intervals only. Thus, I average the macro opinion measures across the three months and estimate time-series models using quarterly data.

[25] Quarterly unemployment data are available from the Institut National de la Statistique et des Études Économiques (www.insee.fr). Quarterly growth data are calculated from constant GDP provided by the OECD. While crime statistics would also be appropriate, these data are available only at annual increments.

the urgency of dealing with joblessness and, all else equal, turning popular concerns to other issues, such as crime. Finally, models include an indicator designating periods of center-left governments. When the left is in control, public concerns regarding unemployment may be moderated since, according to issue ownership reasoning (Budge and Farlie 1983), the center-right alternative would not be seen as doing any better. According to the same logic, concerns about crime may be amplified.

Analyses are performed using single-equation error correction models (ECMs). The ECM specification – which models the left-hand side series in first differences and includes a lagged adjustment parameter – enables us to test for both the contemporaneous and long-run multiplier effects of exposure to the global economy on public confidence.[26] Also, as *unemployment priority* and *crime priority* are constructed using aggregate responses to the same closed-ended survey question, unmeasured shocks may affect both regressions (Greene 2000, 614–636; Tomz et al. 2002). To account for this possibility I estimate models with seemingly unrelated regression (SUR) to correct for correlated errors.

Table 3.4 displays the results. Models 1 and 2 examine the factors moving public concerns for unemployment, where the effects of trade and of capital flows are allocated to separate models.[27] Models 3 and 4 do the same for concerns for fighting crime and violence. Per expectations, the actual rate of unemployment has a positive and substantial influence on the net percentage of respondents who think the government should prioritize fighting unemployment. Unemployment levels have no effect on crime concerns, as we might expect. Growth, however, reduces tendencies to view joblessness as a priority for government action while increasing sentiment that policymakers address the crime issue. Government partisanship has no effect on unemployment considerations. We do find, however, that crime concerns increase under center-left governments, perhaps because of a belief that they are less competent on the issue.

Our chief interest, however, pertains to the relationship between trends in French exposure to the global economy and what citizens expect from the government. First consider the *unemployment priority* models. Coefficients the trade (Model 1) and capital flows (Model 2) series in first differences are not statistically significant, indicating no contemporaneous effect of changes in exposure on unemployment concerns. Coefficients for both series in levels, however, are negative and statistically significant; over time, economic openness reduces public

[26] There is reason to believe that the effects of economic and political shocks on public issue concerns are not (only) contemporaneous but accumulate over time. Additionally, preliminary analyses indicate that many of the series of interest are strongly autoregressive. Estimates of the fractional differencing parameter, d, indicate that the null hypothesis of a unit root cannot be rejected for the public opinion series and for capital flows. The single-equation ECM has been shown to be appropriate in this situation (De Boef 2001; De Boef and Keele 2008).

[27] The contemporaneous correlation between *trade openness* and *capital flows* is 0.78.

TABLE 3.4. *Economic globalization and French issue concerns, 1981–2006*

	Δ Unemployment priority		Δ Crime priority	
	(1)	(2)	(3)	(4)
Trade openness				
Difference$_t$	–0.06		–0.45	
	(0.40)		(0.38)	
Level$_{t-1}$	–0.54**		0.33**	
	(0.13)		(0.09)	
Capital flows				
Difference$_t$		–0.02		–0.02
		(0.06)		(0.05)
Level$_{t-1}$		–0.16**		0.10**
		(0.05)		(0.04)
Unemployment rate				
Difference$_t$	0.73	–0.22	0.81	1.76
	(2.10)	(2.19)	(2.01)	(2.06)
Level$_{t-1}$	1.46**	1.21**	0.03	–0.12
	(0.58)	(0.60)	(0.35)	(0.36)
Growth				
Difference$_t$	–0.06	–0.17	0.03	–0.12
	(0.69)	(0.68)	(0.65)	(0.65)
Level$_{t-1}$	–0.96**	–1.05**	0.64*	0.68*
	(0.39)	(0.40)	(0.36)	(0.37)
Center-left	1.01	0.09	1.36*	1.70**
government$_t$	(0.86)	(0.86)	(0.77)	(0.80)
ECM adjustment$_{t-1}$	–0.24**	–0.16**	–0.21**	–0.17**
	(0.06)	(0.05)	(0.04)	(0.04)
Constant	27.84**	3.14	–13.99**	0.69
	(6.76)	(3.59)	(5.31)	(3.77)
R^2	0.26	0.21	0.27	0.19
Ljung-Box Q	0.03	0.17	1.91	2.36
Ljung-Box Q^2	0.09	0.002	0.06	2.29

Notes: Series is quarterly, 1981Q4 to 2006Q4 (T = 101). Cells report OLS estimates with standard errors in parentheses estimated using seemingly unrelated regression. ** p < .05, * p < .10, two-tailed tests.

demands for policies aimed at ameliorating French unemployment. Specifically, the cumulative effect of a 5 percent shock to *trade openness* is an 11 percent reduction in aggregate *unemployment priority*. A shock to *capital flows* of the same magnitude reduces the mass unemployment concerns by 5 percent.[28] Greater

[28] These interpretations are based on the long-run multiplier effects of the variables. The coefficients are –2.25 (= –.54/–(–.24)) for Model 1 and –1.00 (= –.16/–(–.16)) for Model 2. Multiplying these coefficients by five produces the effects reported in the text.

economic exposure means fewer people demand that governments address and, in turn, be held responsible for jobless levels.

Yet, as I have argued – and as previous analyses have shown – globalization does not mean that public demands for government action cease. The assumed constraints arising from the interdependence of world markets mean instead that priorities shift. Public priorities move away from those issue considerations seen as closely affected by the dictates of markets and onto domains that are not. If this argument is true, then we should see globalization positively affecting the share of the public which grants priority to fighting violence and crime, since it clearly falls in the latter category.

Models 3 and 4 test this claim. In these models of *crime priority* coefficients, lagged *trade openness* and lagged *capital flows* are, indeed, positive and statistically significant. Public demands for addressing crime and violence *increase* with time as the French economy becomes more integrated into global markets. What accounts for this observed globalization-crime concerns relationship? Do individuals believe globalization in any way *causes* crime and violence? Probably not. More likely the observed relationship is a byproduct of changing perceptions of policymaker capacity. While economic concerns have dominated French politics during the postwar era (Anderson 1995, 35–36), liberalization and privatization reforms imply that governments can now do less to affect economic growth and job creation. Accordingly, globalization has meant that citizens demand relatively less from national politicians in the economy and relatively more in other issues not classified as mainly economic in nature. Taking crime as an example of a noneconomic concern and unemployment as a (or perhaps *the*) key economic concern, these results lend much support to the intuitions of a member of the French Socialist Party who told me that "the government has an important role in policies for health [and] education ... but not for managing the economy."[29]

3.6. Conclusion

This chapter has shown how the external economic environment shapes public demands for policy. The focus has been on the key intermediate step of mass preferences – a step skipped over by studies out of the international and comparative political economy traditions. Evidence from different sources and levels of analyses finds that publics in more globalized economies are not more but less likely to view their government as responsible for delivering policies to improve economic performance, equality, and stability. Objective economic globalization also shapes policy preferences by exerting greater pressures on policymakers to act in those areas where they are (still) deemed effective, such as health, pensions, and the environment. Once we re-center debates on the voter, we find that the political impact of globalization is more nuanced,

[29] Personal interview, Paris, 25 February 2003.

and not in the way anticipated in political economy studies (e.g., Garrett and Mitchell 2001). It is accurate neither to conclude that globalization produces constraining effects nor to suggest that it gives rise to offsetting compensatory actions. Rather, publics use information about integration in world markets to recalibrate their preferences, shifting demands away from economic issues and toward other domains. Globalization, in short, alters the *composition* of preferences.

Findings have implications for how we think about the consequences of market interdependence in advanced industrial democracies. The conventional wisdom is that opening up to foreign competition must be tied to some form of offsetting compensation for the globalization losers (such as those employed in import-competing sectors but lacking skills to shift into other forms of employment). Were this true, we would observe a positive association between globalization and public preferences for active labor market policy, income redistribution, and stronger safety nets. However, results of several analyses show that exposure to the world economy *reduces* demands in these areas. The explanation for this outcome rests in how signals from the world economy shape public beliefs in the policy room to maneuver. By giving reason to question the competency of national policymakers, citizens make associative linkages – reasoning from information about the world economy to beliefs about the credibility of government action in the economic, materialistic, public welfare realm.

Chapter findings also contribute to our understanding of what moves policy preferences. Here, dominant approaches emphasize the importance of individual self-interest. Income level, for example, is said to drive a wedge between those who demand more public provisions and those who do not. And, with few exceptions, studies of trade preferences tend to draw predictions based on individual factor allocations and/or sector of employment. I adopt a different approach. Rather than emphasizing how self-interest creates preference divergence, I demonstrate that support for policy action varies systematically by issue. Given heterogeneity in the public's ability to make associative linkages, I show that policy support in one domain (economic) is not governed by the same factors as support for public action in another (noneconomic).

It is clear that the consequences of economic globalization for domestic politics range beyond their effects on policy outcomes. It is equally clear that, in a democracy, the preferences of the electorate matter. However, the process by which the electorate forms beliefs about globalization is not well understood. Analyses reported here enhance our understanding of belief formation as it relates to signals from the world economy. However, more work is necessary to investigate alternative causal linkages. In particular, we know little about how globalization matters for the electoral connection. This is the topic of the next chapters, beginning in Chapter 4 with a look at the effects of the global economy on how voters evaluate politicians.

Appendix 3.1

TABLE 3.A1. *Variable definitions and sources*

Variable	Measure	Source
General preferences	Additive combination of ten public opinion items	ISSP 1985, 1990, 1991, 1996, 1998, 2006
Economic preferences	Score from first factor loading based on ten public opinion items	ISSP 1985, 1990, 1991, 1996, 1998, 2006
Noneconomic preferences	Score from second factor loading based on ten public opinion items	ISSP 1985, 1990, 1991, 1996, 1998, 2006
Globalization flows	"Economic Globalization: Actual Flows" measure from Dreher (2006)	http://globalization.kof.ethz.ch/
ΔGrowth	Percent annual change in per capita GDP	Heston et al. 2009
GDP per capita	Natural log of per capita income in constant USD	Heston et al. 2009
Welfare effort	The after-tax change in the Gini coefficient	Solt 2009
Ethnic fractionalization	1 minus the Herfindahl index of ethnic group shares in country	Alesina et al. 2003
Catholic	Percentage of those in country who identify as Catholic	La Porta et al. 1999
Federalism	1 for countries with federalism, 0 otherwise	
Left partisan	1 for supporters of parties designated by ISSP coders as "far left" or "center left," 0 otherwise	ISSP 2006
Right partisan	1 for supporters of parties designated by ISSP coders as "far right" or "center right," 0 otherwise	ISSP 2006
Co-partisan	1 for those who identify with a governing party and zero otherwise	ISSP 2006
Globalization loser	Household income quintile multiplied by a variable scored 1 for manual worker and –1 otherwise. Measure rescaled to range from +1 to –1	ISSP 2006
Political knowledge	Responses to survey item: "I feel that I have a pretty good understanding of the important political issues facing our country." Codes as follows: "strongly agree" = 2, "agree" = 1 "neither agree nor disagree" = 0, "disagree" = –1, "strongly disagree" = –2	ISSP 2006
Education	Formal education, normalized by country on a 6-point scale	ISSP 2006
Female	1 for female, 0 for male	ISSP 2006
Age 35–49, Age 50–64, Age 65+	Age brackets	ISSP 2006

TABLE 3.A2. *Convergent validity: correlations using left-right placements*

	Hellwig expert survey	**Benoit Laver expert survey**	**CSES mass perceptions**
Benoit Laver expert survey	0.957 (145)	–	
Mass perceptions	0.881 (107)	0.881(112)	–
Manifesto	0.722 (121)	0.738 (125)	0.698 (96)

Notes: (*N* in parentheses) All correlations significant at 0.001 level. Expert survey data from Benoit and Laver (2006). Mass perception data from the Comparative Study of Electoral Systems, 2001–2006 (Shapiro and Shively, 2007). Manifesto data from the Comparative Manifestos Project (Klingemann et al., 2006). All variables have been rescaled on a 1–10 basis.

TABLE 3.A3. *Correlations on social and tax-spend dimensions*

	Benoit & Laver expert survey (2006)
Social dimension	.9060 (163)
Tax/Spend dimension	.9173 (159)

Notes: (*N* in parentheses) All correlations significant at 0.001 level. Expert survey data from Benoit and Laver (2006). Variables were rescaled from 1 to 10.

Survey of Experts on Political Parties and Globalization

Analysis of Convergent Validity

Tests of measure validity were performed by comparing mean responses from the expert surveys with three other sources for generating data on party positions: a separately administered expert survey (Benoit and Laver 2006), party positions as perceived by mass survey respondents from the Comparative Study of Election Systems (www.cses.org), and a measure produced from the Comparative Manifestos Project (Klingemann et al. 2006). The expert survey data employed here correlate strongly with each of these alternative measures.[30]

[30] Specifically, using the one item each source had in common, the standard left-right scale, I find that the expert survey data correlate strongly with each of the alternative measures. The Pearson *r* correlations are 0.96 with the Benoit-Laver survey, 0.88 with the CSES data, and 0.72 with the CMP scores. Further information is provided on the author's website. I thank Dani Marinova for research assistance.

4

Globalization and the Attribution of Responsibility

Markets matter for citizen demands. Globalization reduces public demands for government activism, not across the board but more so in certain areas. These are precisely in those areas held to be of importance by majorities in most developed welfare states: growth, stability, and equality. Globalization, however, does not mean politicians are off the hook. Electorates still demand that their governments deliver, just not in the same areas. In fact, demands for governments to address issues that are not explicitly economic in nature – like healthcare, crime, and care for the elderly – increase along with ties to the world economy. All this is consistent with the balancing demands model of citizen politics in exposed economies.

But what does this imply for how elections work? As a means for linking voters to their representatives, elections serve two purposes. First, elections are the mechanism through which citizens-principals hold representatives-agents to accounts. In modern democracies, a set of political specialists is given a lease on power to carry out policies consistent with the interests of the public at large. Armed with the vote, citizens can sanction policymakers who do not perform at acceptable levels. The prospect of facing the voters at regular intervals means that incumbents, even if motivated solely by retaining office, must "anticipate performance-oriented voting in their choice of policies while in office" (Ferejohn 1986, 7). In addition to this accountability purpose, elections help select policies for the future. Elections aggregate interests and produce policies aligned with voter preferences. This is the representation purpose of elections.

However, these accountability (sanctioning) and representation (selection) purposes of elections assume a self-contained, closed political-economic system. This assumption has long been at the base of the scientific study of politics, from the "behavioral revolution" of the 1960s to the present, but, for nearly as long, the bases for this assumption have been unfounded (e.g., Cameron

1978; Alt 1985). How does politics in democracies work when we relax this assumption of a self-contained political system? A purpose of this book is to examine how the accountability and representation purposes are shaped by the dramatic opening up of political economies in advanced industrial societies. In Chapter 6, I examine the effect of the global economic context for whether and how voters select party candidates. But first, this and the next chapter take up the problem of electoral accountability. How do citizens residing in open economies assign responsibility for observed outcomes, and does it matter for how they vote, for election outcomes, and, in turn, for public policy?

This chapter advances a set of expectations for how globalization matters for political accountability – that is, for how citizens attribute policy responsibility and, in turn, sanction or reward politicians. The empirical component draws on an original ten-nation dataset on responsibility attributions to show that citizens are less likely to credit or blame governments for the economy when globalization signals are strong. I show in the next chapter that decisions to assign primary responsibility for the economy to international markets – as opposed to national governments – affect how citizens choose their representatives.

4.1. Responsibility Judgments and Democratic Accountability

Democratic accountability is premised on the concept of responsibility. If the vote is used as a tool to sanction officeholders whose performance fails to reach a certain threshold, the implicit assumption is that incumbents had some hand in – or control over – shaping outcomes. Control over outcomes may be direct, as in using fiscal and monetary instruments to stimulate a sagging economy, or indirect, such as erecting safeguards to minimize the risks stemming from financial volatility, industrial accidents, environmental catastrophes, and the like. Either way, the accountability relationship assumes voters know something about who or what is responsible for policy outcomes. While this may not be true for all issues, it is at least the case for a subset of particularly salient, easily observable ones (Key 1966; Tufte 1978; Fiorina 1981).

How do we evaluate the accountability relationship in democracies? To some, it hinges on reelection. Accountability exists "if voters can discern whether governments are acting in their best interest and sanction them appropriately, so that those incumbents who act in the best interest of citizens win reelection and those that do not lose them" (Manin et al. 1999, 40). For others, accountability is present as long as voters reward or punish political incumbents in terms of votes and not necessarily in terms of reelection/removal from office (Key 1966). Yet both these conceptions – and many others – maintain that accountability works through retrospective voting (see Samuels and Hellwig 2010). Retrospective voting requires little in the way of information processing. Voters merely strike out against the government when things go wrong. As Fiorina (1981, 5) succinctly states, "in order to ascertain whether incumbents have performed poorly or well, citizens only need to calculate the changes in their own welfare."

But many have come to question the simplicity of such models of retrospective voting. In order for retrospective voting to work for accountability, the reasoning goes, voters must first attribute credit or blame to those standing for office.

> Prior to sanctioning ... voters presumably decide the extent to which incumbents are in fact *responsible* for [the status quo]. That is, citizens must first reach the conclusion that the party is liable for "hard times" before throwing it out of office. This necessary precondition for sanctioning is ignored by adherents of Key's theory because responsible judgments are assumed to be automatic (Peffley 1984, 276, emphasis in original).

Many voters, it turns out, do not automatically render judgment on political incumbents. Public opinion research in several democracies finds that voters attach responsibility for past outcomes not only to governments but to a range of actors, including subnational and regional governing bodies, private sector actors, and impersonal market forces (Alcañiz and Hellwig 2011; Arceneaux 2006; Cutler 2008; Gomez and Wilson 2003; Hellwig et al. 2008; Hobolt and Tilley 2014; Rudolph 2003).

This chapter investigates the implications of the internationalization of domestic economies for how citizens attribute responsibility for policy outcomes. How do voters assign credit and blame in open economies? Do they judge the incumbent to be liable, or are they instead cognizant of the origin of performance signals, discerning those originating from outside the system from those which are a consequence of domestic factors? The former view would be consistent with a conventional wisdom viewing voters as myopic, ill-informed, and capable of paying attention to only the broadest performance indicators, using such minimal information to punish or reward the incumbent political party (Key 1966; Fiorina 1981; see also Achen and Bartels 2006). The latter perspective is in line with a more sophisticated perspective that citizens can recalibrate what they demand from politicians in light of changing policy constraints.

But who's responsible when it's a *global* economy? I argue that globalization leads citizens to become cognizant of the world around them and, specifically, how extra-national events bear on the national political and economic scene. This means that voters respond to signals of increased interdependence by adjusting their beliefs about politicians' ability to control the economy. As voters grow more skeptical that policymakers can control the economy, the relationship between a government's survival and its ability to create an environment for growth becomes more tenuous. And if voters believe that globalization reduces policymakers' influence over the economy, then they ought to be less apt to punish or reward them in light of economic conditions. In short, globalization means that the rational retrospective voter discounts information about economic conditions when evaluating the incumbent's performance in office.

This discounting argument may be stated more concisely in terms of the open economy model of mass politics introduced in Chapter 2. Recall the assertion that globalization shifts the political demand curve through two channels, issue politics and political control. This is captured by the voter utility function in equation 2.3, $U_{ij} = -(1-d_j)\alpha(x_i - s_j)^2 + (1-d_j)\beta y_j$, where $(x_i - s_j)^2$ is the issue politics (proximity) component, y_j is the retrospective performance component, and d_j is the discount parameter, all of which influence voter *i*'s utility for party *j*. Our focus in this chapter is on retrospections, y_j, and their effect on voter utility, β. If exposure to the world economy weakens the influence of retrospective assessments then, in terms of equation 2.3, $0 \leq d_{cj} \leq d_{gj} \leq 1$, where *c* subscripts the discount parameter attached to party *j* in closed economies and *g* does so in globalized economies.

To illustrate this relationship between globalization and the voter's calculus, consider two elections: the U.S. presidential election of November 2008 and the German federal elections of September 2009. Both of these elections occurred at a time of sharp economic decline. In the United States, the "Great Recession" was key in the defeat of the Republican Party – the party of the incumbent George W. Bush – and the return of the Democrats to the White House with Barack Obama. As hinted at in the opening chapter of this book, much of this "economic voting" effect can be traced to a belief on the part of the electorate that, for better or worse, the president bears much of the responsibility for the state of the American economy. Indeed, according to a poll taken one month before the vote, six in ten Americans were of the belief that when it comes to the economy, who is elected president matters "a great deal." Moreover, a clear majority agreed with the notion that the federal government is capable of fixing the economy.[1] This belief in the connection between government decisions and economic outcomes clearly influenced the outcome: of those who attributed responsibility for the economy to the president, 84 percent voted for the challenger Obama (Lewis-Beck and Nadeau 2009).[2]

The German federal elections occurred less than a year later. As with the United States in 2008, the German economy in the fall of 2009 was in a bad state. Growth rates shrunk for the first time in a number of years. The contraction of 5 percent of GDP was more severe than in any year since World War II. Not surprisingly, polls taken before, during, and after the campaign revealed that the economy was by far the most important issue on the voters' minds (Anderson and Hecht 2012). Given this situation, the simple reward-punishment

[1] Of those surveyed, 55 percent agreed that the government "has the power to fix the economy" (Pew Research Center for the People and the Press Early October 2008 Political and Economic Survey).

[2] This is not to argue that responsibility attributions are determined exogenously from one's political preference; it stands to reason that individuals who planned to support the Democratic ticket would be more likely to blame the Republican Party-dominated government for the sluggish economy.

expectation from economic voting predicts that voters should use news of the disastrous state of the economy to punish the Christian Democratic-led grand coalition by voting it out of office – just as American voters had punished the incumbent Republican Party. This prediction, however, did not come to pass. Rather, the election produced a solid victory for Chancellor Angela Merkel's Christian Democrats (the CDU/CSU). Even though the party experienced a slight *decline* in its share of the party vote (1.4 percent) from 2005, its historic rival on the left, the Social Democrats (SPD), suffered far more (11.2 percent). As a result, the CDU/CSU emerged from the election in a position of greater strength, able to shed its uncomfortable alliance with the SPD for a more compatible partner in the liberal Free Democrats.

What explains this unexpected result? Why didn't the voters hold Chancellor Merkel and her party accountable for the unprecedentedly poor state of affairs? The answer, as with the U.S. case of 2008, has much to do with the attribution of credit or, in this case, blame. A pre-election poll found that two-thirds of respondents classified the government's responsibility for the country's economic performance during the crisis as "nonexistent," "not particularly big," or "middling" (Anderson and Hecht 2012). And while a post-election poll found that nearly 80 percent thought the economy had worsened over the past year, only a quarter of those polled placed most of the blame on the shoulders of the federal government (Rattinger et al. 2011). Rather, most Germans realized that the financial crisis originated from the loosely regulated, internationally oriented banking sector and not from policies or neglect on the part of the government. A poll conducted a few months ahead of the vote showed that Germans were far more likely to pin responsibility for the crisis on the excessive risk-taking of national and (especially) international financial institutions than they were on the policies of their government.[3] Figure 4.1 displays polling results and compares them to Americans' responses to the same questions. As shown, Germans were much more likely than Americans to cast blame onto market actors and less apt to link the downturn to their own government's policies.

The differences between voters in the United States, most of whom attributed responsibility to the elected leadership, and those in the Germany, who mostly did not, can be traced to beliefs in their respective country's ties to the world economy. For all the talk about globalization in political discourse, the U.S. economy remains *relatively* sheltered from global competition, particularly in terms of exports. In 2008, total trade in the United States was equal to about 30 percent of GDP; in Germany it was almost 90 percent (Heston et al. 2009). The U.S. economy instead is driven in large part by domestic

[3] Twenty-seven percent of Germans said their country's economic policies contributed "a lot" to the downturn in the economy. In contrast, 78 percent said that the excessive risk-taking of national bankers contributed "a lot," and 88 percent said the behavior of international bankers contributed "a lot" to Germany's downturn.

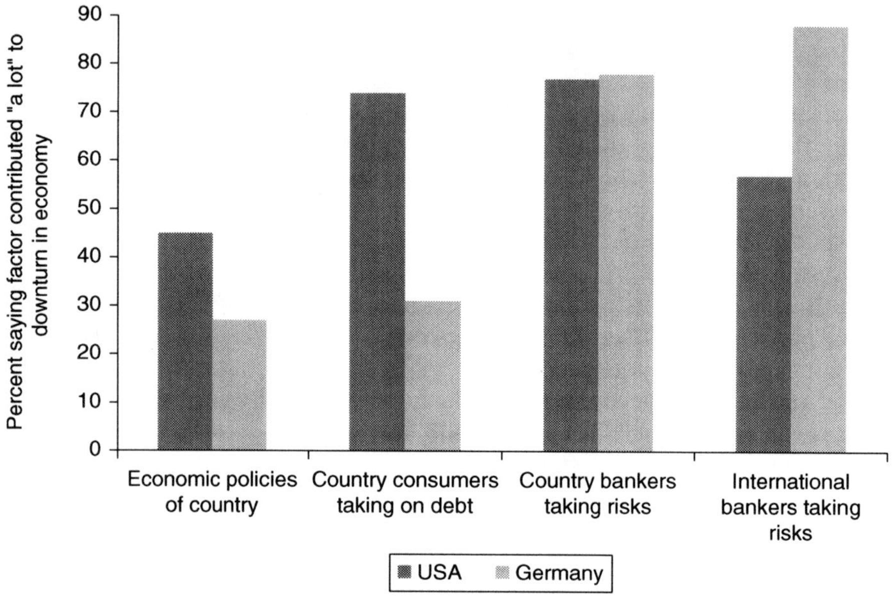

FIGURE 4.1. Public opinion on factors contributing to the economic downturn, July 2009.

Notes: Bars report percent of respondents saying that factor "has contributed a lot to the downturn."

Source: "Public Opinion on the Global Economic Crisis" poll conducted by World Public Opinion, Program on International Public Attitudes.

consumption. In contrast, much of Germany's success as the world's fourth largest economy has been led by the success of high-value added products for sale on the world market. The success of the export economy, however, has in recent times shed light on the degree to which the German economy rises and falls with *foreign* consumption. Given these differences, American voters appear relatively more likely to attribute responsibility to domestic actors and Germans relatively more apt to link assessments of economic conditions to factors other than national politicians.

Figure 4.2 illustrates this globalization-responsibility connection in general terms. In both Panel A and Panel B, the hypothesized effect of greater economic openness is to reduce popular perceptions of government policy responsibility. They differ, however, with respect to heterogeneity in performance evaluations. In panel A, the horizontal arrow linking economic performance evaluations to vote choice conveys the standard economic voting story. In this perspective, economic evaluations influence voter choice such that positive evaluations lead voters to reward incumbents and negative assessments to punish incumbents by voting against them. The display is made only slightly more complicated in granting a role for the voters' perceptions of policy responsibility. If voters

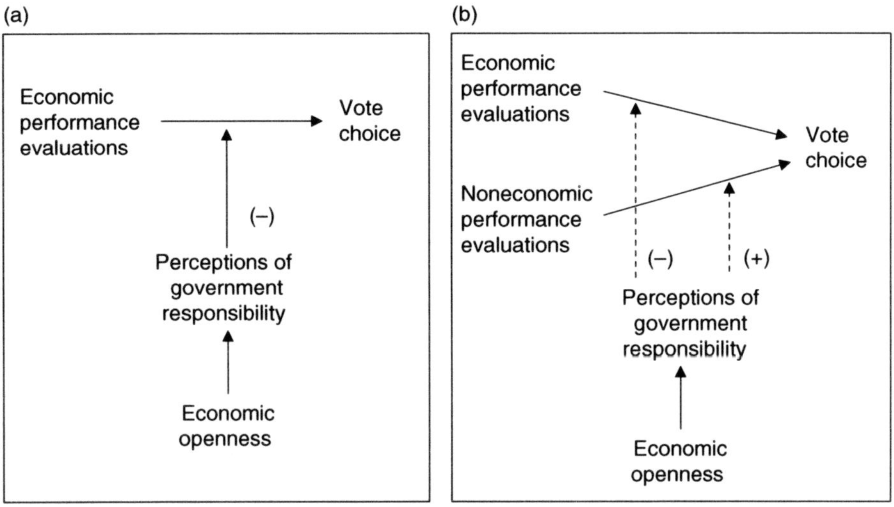

FIGURE 4.2. Globalization and accountability: causal relationships.
Note: Signs in parentheses (+/-) indicate consequences of this increase in economic openness on the *change* in the effects of perceptions of government responsibility on retrospective voting.

believe the government to be responsible for the economy they observe, then there should be a strong link between performance conditions and the vote. But if the electorate has reason to view other actors as culpable, then the performance-vote connection should become more tenuous. The world economy might reasonably be one of these actors. Insomuch as national business cycles fluctuate in unison, it is hard to avoid concluding that some factor outside the purview of national policymakers is responsible. Per the policy discounting model in equation 2.3, this is what we expect with increased frequency as a county becomes more and more exposed to the world economy.

If globalization attenuates the well-known relationship between economics and elections, does this mean that incumbents can no longer be held to accounts? Or does it mean that voters adjust how they think about performance outcomes, placing greater emphasis on policy performance in other, noneconomic domains? Normatively, the second perspective is less dire than the first. Rather than deterministically diminishing the ability of elections to serve as instruments of accountability, globalization narrows the scope of issues for which politicians are held responsible.[4] Here is where Panel B on the

[4] If true, this would be consistent with what we saw in the previous chapter: While globalization influences policy preferences, it does not affect opinions on all issues in the same way. For certain issues, such as jobs or the distribution of income, a global economic context alleviates the public's demands for policy responses. But for other issue areas, like healthcare or crime, globalization appears to be of little consequence.

right-hand side of Figure 4.2 comes in. The figure implies that globalization affects voter decisions not only by discounting the salience of national economic conditions but also by increasing the weight of other performance evaluations. If the credibility of domestic policy levers are compromised, then party positions on economic matters (e.g., taxes, spending) ought to play relatively little role in the voter's decision. The world economy, however, exerts less of a constraint on policymaker capacity over noneconomic issues. Instead, the noneconomic dimension should play a *compensating* role, increasing in salience as voters seek out rational bases for evaluating elites. This issue-specific effect is shown by the dashed lines in Figure 4.2b and by the opposite-signed hypothesized effects.

4.2. The World Economy and Responsibility Attributions: Survey Evidence

I now weigh these arguments with evidence. The first task is to establish the relationship between the world economy and responsibility attributions. The second is to demonstrate the implications of different "targets" of policy responsibility for voter choice. I rely on an original set of public opinion surveys. Conducted in 2008, respondents come from ten democracies: Australia, Canada, Denmark, France, Germany, Great Britain, the Netherlands, New Zealand, Sweden, and the United States.[5] Respondents were asked "Which do you feel is most responsible for the economic conditions in [country] in the past few years?" Specific response options varied according to country, as governed by differences in constitutional structures and membership in supranational governance structures (the European Union). However, in all countries, response options included categories for the government, businesses, workers, and, "ups and downs in the world economy." Table 4.1 reports frequency responses to this item. In nine of ten countries, most respondents do not attribute responsibility to government actors. The exception is the United States, where more than half do so: 57 percent in 2008 and nearly the same (54 percent) in 2010.[6] At the other end of the spectrum lie small open countries like the Netherlands and Sweden. This variation in holding government responsible is matched by national rates of identifying "ups and downs in the

[5] The data were collected by IFOP, YouGov, and the New Zealand Election Study. Topics addressed in these studies pertain to economic globalization, the room to maneuver, performance evaluations, preferences over policy and political issues, and participation in elections. A full description of the surveys is available at http://mypage.iu.edu/~thellwig. The data for the U.S. case in 2010 were collected as part of the November 2010 Cooperative Congressional Election Study, with information available at http://projects.iq.harvard.edu/cces/.

[6] These figures combine the percent of those responding "Congress" and "the President."

TABLE 4.1. *Responsibility attributions in ten countries, 2008*

	Public opinion: Who's responsible for economic conditions?				
	Government	World economy	Business	Workers	EU
Australia	27	53	9	6	–
Britain	29	44	10	1	8
Canada	20	60	8	6	–
Denmark	23	44	8	7	7
France	24	46	7	4	18
Germany	17	34	28	10	8
Netherlands	15	54	16	3	8
New Zealand	18	58	5	2	–
Sweden	16	54	10	5	4
United States 2008	57	14	21	3	–
United States 2010[a]	54	15	30	1	–

Notes: Public opinion figures are percentage responses to the question "Which do you feel is most responsible for the economic conditions in [country] in the past few years?" Government responsible is scored 1 in the following cases: Australia and Canada: "the federal government" and "provincial governments," the United States: "the President" and "Congress," all others: "the government." World Economy Responsible is scored 1 for "ups and downs in the world economy" in all cases except for New Zealand, in which case those saying "international trade restrictions" are included (less than 1 percent of respondents). Respondents who refused to answer, who answered "Don't know," or who volunteered other responses are not reported.

Sources: Hellwig 2011, NZES 2008, CCES 2010.

[a] The second United States entry is from the November 2010 Cooperative Congressional Election Study (CCES); all other country surveys were conducted in 2008.

world economy" as chiefly responsible, with the United States (14 percent) at the low end and New Zealand and Canada on the high end with nearly six in ten identifying the world economy as most responsible for the fate of the national economy. Figures 4.3 and 4.4 show opinions correlate with levels of economic openness.

To further probe the globalization-responsibility connection, consider that the mechanism here, signals about the world economy, likely originates from places other than actual conditions. In particular, as we recall from our definition of economic globalization in Chapter 1, the world economy may be packaged as more or less salient for mass publics by political elites. Elite messages have long been thought to be important in shaping or constraining mass attitudes. This is particularly the case for developing opinions about complex issues on such matters as foreign affairs, economic policy, and regional integration (Berinsky 2007; Gaines et al. 2007; Ray 2003; Zaller 1992). I incorporate elite cues by using an original set of surveys of county experts

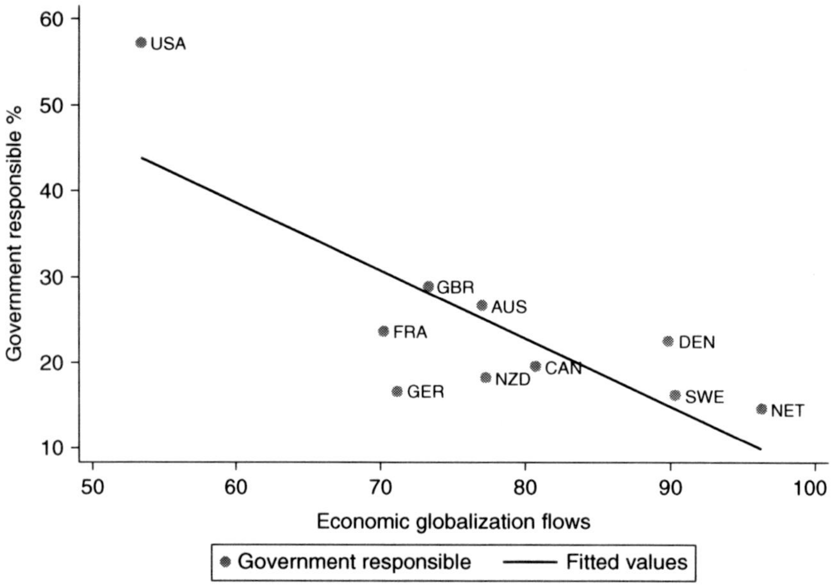

FIGURE 4.3. Objective globalization and perceptions of government responsible for economic conditions.

Note: Regression line is of percent of respondents saying "government" is responsible for national economic conditions regressed on KOF globalization – economic flows index. The bivariate correlation is $r = -0.78, p = 0.01$; the bivariate regression is *Government responsible* = 86.07 – 0.79**Globalization*, $R^2 = .62$, N = 10. With the United States omitted, the bivariate correlation is $r = -0.78$, $p = 0.16$; the bivariate regression is *Government responsible* = 42.5 – 0.27**Globalization*, $R^2 = .26$, N = 9.

Sources: Cross-National Public Opinion Surveys, Hellwig (2011); Dreher (2006), "Economic Globalization: Flows" index.

conducted at the same time as the public opinion surveys were in the field (Vowles et al. 2010).[7]

Elite messages on globalization are measured along two dimensions, party salience and party cohesion. Both salience and cohesion ought to amplify signals. Regarding the first, country experts were asked "we would like you to think about the salience of globalization to the political parties in [country]. During 2008, how important has the world economy been to the parties in their public stance?" Experts were then asked to assess the relative importance of globalization for each party's public issue stance on a four point scale

[7] Particulars about the expert surveys are available from the book's website. Also see Appendix 3.1.

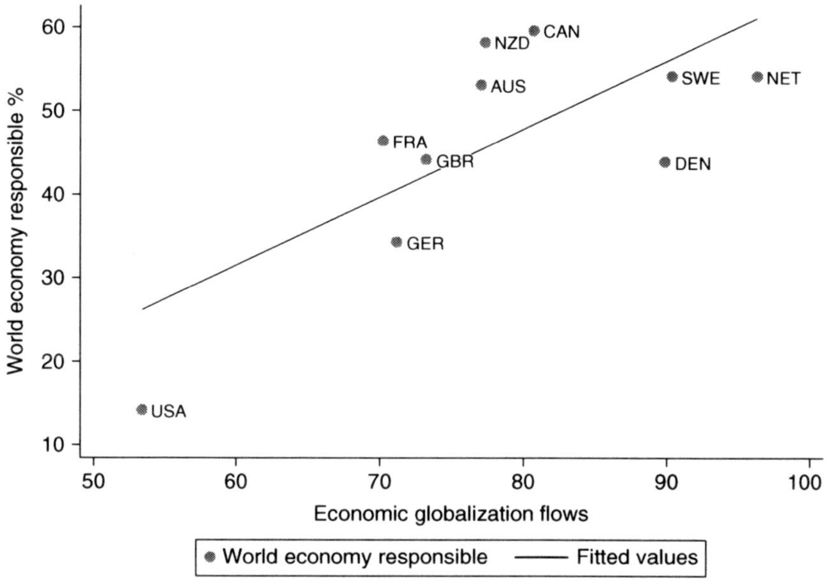

FIGURE 4.4. Objective globalization and perceptions of world economy responsible for economic conditions.

Note: Regression line is of percent of respondents saying "world economy" is responsible for national economic conditions regressed on KOF globalization – economic flows index. The bivariate correlation is r = 0.73, p = 0.02. The regression line is *World economy responsible* = –17.17 + 0.81**Globalization*, R^2 = .54, N = 10. With the United States removed, the bivariate correlation is r = 0.39, p = 0.30. The regression line is *World economy responsible* = –22.17 + 0.34**Globalization*, R^2 = .15, N = 9.

Sources: Cross-National Public Opinion Surveys, Hellwig (2011); Dreher (2006), "Economic Globalization: Flows" index.

ranging from "globalization is of no importance at all" to "globalization is of great importance." Regarding intra-party cohesion, the survey includes an item asking experts "How much internal dissent has there been in the various political parties in [country] over the national engagement with the world economy in 2008?" Experts chose from a five-point scale ranging from "complete unity" to "leadership opposed by a majority of party activists." I create country-level measures of elite messages by first averaging both items across parties and then combining them to produce an index ranging from 0 (meaning globalization is not salient and parties are internally divided) to 100 (issue highly salient and parties internally cohesive). Values on this index are reported in Appendix 4.1.

Table 4.2 reports results of two multiple regression analyses in which the dependent variables are equal to the percent of respondents identifying their

TABLE 4.2. *Modeling aggregate responsibility attributions for the government and for the world economy*

	(1) Government responsible	(2) World economy responsible
	–0.48**	0.58**
Globalization: flows	(0.15)	(0.24)
Globalization: elite	–0.79**	0.63*
messages	(0.20)	(0.33)
	24.60**	46.10**
Constant	(1.74)	(2.87)
R^2	.84	.65
N	10	10

Note: In Model 1 the dependent variable is the percent of respondents in the survey who identify the government of their country as most responsible for national economic conditions (see Table 4.1). In Model 2 it is the percent of respondents identifying the "ups and downs in the world economy" as most responsible. Cells report OLS parameter estimates with robust standard errors in parentheses. * $p \leq .10$ ** $p \leq .05$; (two tailed).

government (Model 1) or the world economy (Model 2) as mostly responsible for economic conditions. These measures are regressed on the objective globalization flows index and on the salience of elite messages on globalization described earlier. Results of estimating these models – albeit on just ten cases – find that both actual flows and elite discourse matter for responsibility attributions. When objective exposure to the world economy is less, and when the degree of political elite discourse is low, larger shares of national publics attribute credit or blame to the government. The opposite holds for perceptions that the variations in the world economy are mainly to be responsible for domestic economic conditions. These two variables account for a great deal of the variation in aggregate opinions of who's (or what's) responsible: 84 percent in Model 1 and 65 percent in Model 2.

In short, signals about the world economy – gauged both in terms of actual flows and by elite political discourse – shape how citizens attribute responsibility for national economic conditions. In *more* open economies, citizens are *less* likely to attribute responsibility for the economy to the government. The next chapter continues with this line of inquiry by examining the electoral consequences of globalization and retrospective performance evaluations.

Appendix 4.1. Sources of Globalization Signals

TABLE 4.A1. *Globalization signals*

	Flows	Elite messages
Australia	77.0	80.9
Britain	73.2	72.7
Canada	80.7	72.8
Denmark	89.9	80.6
France	70.2	77.3
Germany	71.3	81.3
Netherlands	96.2	76.0
New Zealand	77.3	86.9
Sweden	90.4	74.1
United States 2008	53.4	53.9
United States 2010	60.7	–

Notes: The trade and capital flows index is the "Economic Globalization: Actual Flows" measure from Dreher (2006); elite messages is an index which combines measures of party salience and party unity as provided by information from a survey of party experts (Vowles et al. 2009). Bivariate correlation: $r = 0.53$, $p = 0.11$.

5

Globalization and the Shifting Bases of Retrospective Voting

We saw in Chapter 4 that notions of policy capacity influence public opinion, particularly public beliefs about who's responsible. But demonstrating that a given phenomenon affects attitudes is not the same as showing that it affects behavior. We must examine political behavior directly. Accordingly, this chapter and the next take up globalization's consequences for voting behavior. In this chapter I examine retrospective, performance-based voting. Chapter 6 considers the prospective, issue-oriented side of the coin.[1]

Does globalization matter for retrospective voting? More to the point, do the tendencies to blame or credit fluctuations in the world economy for economic outcomes, as we observed in Chapter 4, matter for electoral accountability? I approach this question in two stages. First, I examine the impact of voter perceptions of responsibility for the economy on support for political incumbents. Doing so tests the expectation that economic conditions influence voter decisions, but they do so conditionally on the economy's exposure to world markets. As displayed on the left-hand side of Figure 4.2a, this argument implies that globalization has an adverse, reductive effect on political accountability. Individual-level analyses of survey data from ten countries support an argument that attributing responsibility to the world economy weakens the bonds between economic evaluations and support for political incumbents.

The second stage of analysis parses out performance evaluations. Analyses of retrospective voting generally take the form of economic voting. The argument of this book, however, is that it is insufficient to equate economics-based policy assessments with performance assessments in general. Globalization may help transform citizens from simple "Keysian" economic voters to voters who render judgment on government performance through consideration of a wide

[1] We also could study globalization's effect on political behavior beyond vote choice to consider outcomes like voter participation (e.g., Steiner and Martin 2012) and protest activity (Duckett and Miller 2006). These outcomes lie outside the scope of this study.

range of criteria (Key 1966). A second set of analyses thus examines retrospective voting in noneconomic performance areas – healthcare and immigration – and investigates whether the role of performance evaluations are conditioned on economic globalization, as portrayed in Figure 4.2b. Consistent with the balancing demands argument, I find that, while globalization weakens ties between the economy and elections, it renders noneconomic forms of performance voting more salient. As I discuss in the conclusion, these findings have normative implications, both good and bad alike.

5.1. Globalization and Economic Voting

I first explore ties between the world economy and electoral accountability using the ten-country survey data. In this case, political accountability is gauged in terms of voter perceptions of national economic conditions. The dependent variable is reported vote choice. In three country surveys – Canada, New Zealand, and the United States – vote choice is measured as the self-reported vote in a recent national-level election. In the other seven countries, respondents were asked a standard vote intentions item of the form "If a general election were held next Sunday, which party would you vote for?"[2] With responses to these items, I create an unordered categorical variable *vote choice*. The number of outcome categories varies from two to seven across the country cases, as per the number of major party competitors. By estimating a set of unordered discrete choice models, the analysis allows for a consideration of how retrospective evaluations and perceptions of responsibility are (or are not) reflected in the voter's choice among party alternatives.

Models posit that vote choice is a function of economic evaluations, but this effect is conditioned on whether the voter perceives economic conditions to be chiefly attributable to government action or mainly the result of forces outside of their elected representatives' control. The principal predictors thus are economic perceptions and responsibility attributions. Economic perceptions are measured using a standard subjective sociotropic measure for economic evaluations: "How do you think the economic situation in [country] has changed over the last twelve months?" Per sanctioning models, we would expect individuals who believe that country's economy deteriorated over the past year to be less likely to support the party of the sitting head of government. Responsibility attributions are measured with a pair of indicator variables corresponding to the aggregate data displayed in Figures 4.2 and 4.3. *Government responsible* is scored 1 if the respondent identifies the government as the actor "mostly responsible for national economic conditions" and

[2] The choice between recalled vote and vote intentions is a function of the timing when the survey was conducted relative to the election calendar. Duch and Stevenson (2008) show that using vote intentions or vote recall is of little or no consequence for vote choice models based on survey data.

0 otherwise.[3] *World economy responsible* equals 1 for those saying that "ups and downs in the world economy" are mainly responsible and 0 otherwise. To assess whether responsibility considerations condition economic voting, models include an interaction between the attribution items and economic perceptions.[4]

Models are estimated using multinomial logit. Since substantive effects in nonlinear models with interaction terms cannot be read from results tables (Ai and Norton 2003), I present results in terms of the survey respondent's expected probability of selecting a party given certain conditions.[5] Specifically, I use estimates from the multinomial logit models to calculate the probability that a typical voter selects a particular party – the party of the chief executive – given different combinations of responsibility attributions and evaluations of economic conditions.[6] Using particular combinations of these factors allows me to isolate the effects of the respondent's perceptions of who's (or what's) responsible.

Table 5.1 displays results. The box in the upper left-hand corner fixes ideas. It conveys expected outcomes with respect to the effect economic evaluations (listed in columns as "better" or "worse") and target of attribution (in rows as the government or the world economy) have on the probability of voting for the incumbent political party. The probability of selecting the incumbent is highest (at, say, 0.4) if the voter perceives the economy as having improved over the past year and, further, if she perceives the government as mainly responsible. This probability is the lowest when the respondent perceives a worsening economy provided, again, the government is viewed as responsible (hypothetically 0.1). A similar but moderated pair of outcomes is anticipated in the case where the respondent perceives "ups and downs in the world economy" as most responsible. The "economic voting effect" – measured by taking the difference in incumbent vote probabilities produced by different perceptions of economic conditions – is therefore weaker. Finally, a comparison of these effects across the two targets of policy responsibility produces our central

[3] For the Australian and Canadian cases, this variable is coded 1 if the respondent identifies "the federal government" as responsible and 0 otherwise. For the United States survey, the variable is coded 1 for those holding "the President" as mainly responsible for the economy. Respondents identifying "Congress," "businesses," "workers," or "ups and downs in the world economy" are coded 0.

[4] I also control for respondent ideology, age, gender, education, household income, and occupation. Ideology is measured using self-placement on the left-right scale. The question wording is "In politics people sometimes talk of Left and Right. Where would you place yourself on a scale from 0 to 10, where 0 means Left and 10 means Right?" I also ran models with partisanship, variously measured, on the right-hand side. Results of interest are no different from those reported here. These models are not reported here on the grounds that partisanship may be akin to (indistinguishable from) the actual vote intention in some countries.

[5] Full model estimates are available from the author's website.

[6] This "typical" voter possesses values on all other covariates equal to sample mean or modal values.

TABLE 5.1. *Expected probability of voting for incumbent chief executive: evidence from survey data in ten countries*

Economic voting effect in italics[a], ***Responsibility attributions effect*** in bold[b]

Hypothetical:	**Better**	**Worse**	**Diff.**	**Britain: LAB**	**Better**	**Worse**	**Diff.**
Government	0.40	0.10	*+0.30*	National government	0.84	0.14	*+0.70*
World economy	0.30	0.20	*+0.10*	World economy	0.84	0.58	*+0.26*
Difference			**+0.20**	Difference			**+0.45**
Australia: ALP	**Better**	**Worse**	**Diff.**	**Netherlands: CDA**	**Better**	**Worse**	**Diff.**
Federal government	0.60	0.54	*+0.06*	National government	0.18	0.15	*+0.03*
World economy	0.72	0.55	*+0.17*	World economy	0.16	0.16	*–0.01*
Difference			**–0.11**	Difference			**+0.04**
Canada: CON	Better	Worse	Diff.	**New Zealand: LP**	Better	Worse	Diff.
Federal government	0.45	0.15	*+0.30*	National government	0.68	0.16	*+0.52*
World economy	0.29	0.23	*+0.06*	World economy	0.72	0.25	*+0.47*
Difference			**+0.24**	Difference			**+0.05**
Denmark: V	Better	Worse	Diff.	**Sweden: M**	Better	Worse	Diff.
National government	0.40	0.09	*+0.31*	National government	0.20	0.22	*–0.02*
World economy	0.28	0.14	*+0.14*	World economy	0.55	0.20	*+0.36*
Difference			**+0.17**	Difference			**–0.37**
France: UMP	Better	Worse	Diff.	**United States: R**	Better	Worse	Diff.
National government	0.61	0.09	*+0.52*	President	0.20	0.05	*+0.16*
World economy	0.53	0.26	*+0.27*	World economy	0.50	0.32	*+0.18*
Difference			**+0.25**	Difference			**–0.02**
Germany: CDU	Better	Worse	Diff.	**United States: D**	Better	Worse	Diff.
Federal government	0.24	0.23	*+0.02*	Congress	0.34	0.33	*+0.02*
World economy	0.37	0.32	*+0.05*	World economy	0.15	0.51	*–0.36*
Difference			**–0.03**	Difference			**+0.37**

Notes: Cells report the expected probability of voting for the party of the incumbent chief executive, as labeled in the upper right hand corner of the boxes. Expected probabilities are calculated from estimates from multinomial logit models by manipulating variables of interest, holding all other model covariates at mean or modal values. Multinomial model logit estimates are available from the author's website.

[a] *Economic voting effect* = (pr. voting for party if economy "gotten better") – (pr. voting for party if economy "gotten worse")

[b] *Responsibility attributions effect* = (economic voting effect if government "most responsible") – (economic voting effect if world economy "most responsible")

interest: the "responsibility attributions effect," or a probability difference of 0.2 in this hypothetical case.

The remaining blocks in the table present predicted probabilities using actual estimates from multinomial logit analyses of the public opinion surveys. Vote choice probabilities are reported for the party of the incumbent chief executive.[7] Horizontal differences within the cell blocks display the effects of retrospective performance voting. Here, we see that in nearly all cases we observe an economic voting effect, shown in the table in italics. The probability of voting for the incumbent is greater when the individual perceives economic conditions as having "gotten a lot better" in the past year, and smaller for the case of negative economic perceptions.

The effect of responsibility attributions is ascertained by comparing probabilities vertically within the cell blocks. Per expectations, in many countries this effect is larger if voters attribute responsibility to the government and smaller if they assign credit or blame to the world economy. In Canada, for example, economic perceptions helped determine the voter's choice in the 2008 federal election. If a respondent thought the Canadian economy had "gotten better" over the past year, she was more likely to vote for the incumbent Conservative Party than if she thought instead that the economy had "gotten worse." This was only the case, however, for those who assigned *responsibility* for the economy to the federal government, as shown by the +0.30 difference in predicted probabilities. For the 60 percent who thought the world economy was most responsible, the analysis indicates economic evaluations had no effect. The table shows that similar results characterize the cases of voting for national legislatures in Denmark, France, Britain, and the United States. This responsibility attribution effect does not appear everywhere; analyses of voting for the incumbent parties in the Netherlands and New Zealand provide only suggestive (weak) support, and the models of support for Australian Labour and the Swedish Moderates run counter to expectations.

These results show that the voter is more likely to support the incumbent if she perceives that economic conditions have improved and less likely if she thinks the economy has worsened. This is true in all but one of our cases (the Netherlands). Evidence in support of this standard economic voting effect should not be surprising to students of voting and elections in western democracies, where the weight of the evidence is that retrospective performance-based voting exists.[8] More novel is to show that retrospective economic voting often

[7] The only exception to this is the United States case, for which I report results both in terms of the party of the sitting president at the time, Republican George W. Bush, and the party in control of the legislative branch, the Democrats.

[8] That is, a measure of retrospective voting prevails even if we take seriously the charge that perceptions of the economy may be partially endogenous to political disposition (Evans and Andersen 2006; Evans and Pickup 2010; Wlezien et al. 1997). Other researchers have argued the causal arrow runs chiefly from economic perceptions to political support (e.g., Lewis-Beck et al. 2008) and that the theoretical basis for the economic vote is at the level of individual perceptions (e.g., Stevenson and Duch 2013).

depends, at least in part, on whether voters attribute responsibility for economic outcomes to national governments or to the world economy. Economic retrospections generally have a strong effect if the voter deems the government responsible and a weaker impact if she accords credit or blame to ups and downs in the world economy.[9]

5.2. Globalization and Performance Voting in Different Issue Domains

We have seen that the relationship between the economy and the vote is contingent on responsibility attributions (see Figure 4.2a). In showing that the economic vote is strongest when the individual saddles the government as chiefly responsible, Table 5.1 results echo findings from previous single country studies on responsibility attributions on retrospective voting. Moreover, explicit consideration of international business cycles, or "ups and downs in the world economy," helps us understand this contingent relationship – something not shown in previous single country studies (cf. Hellwig et al. 2008). With globalization, voters are less apt to hold governments to accounts. Recalling the stylistic utility function in equation 2.3, this implies that responsibility attributions help determine how important retrospective assessments of economic performance are for voter utility. In terms of the discount parameter, d_j, the implication is that $0 \leq \boldsymbol{d}_{gov,j} < \boldsymbol{d}_{world,j} \leq 1$, where "gov" subscripts the discount parameter for those deeming the government mainly responsible for economic conditions; "world" does the same for those who believe the world economy is mainly responsible.[10]

But if globalization weakens the economic vote, does this also signal the eventual end of elections' "accountability purpose"? Perhaps. However, just because globalization weakens the link between economic evaluations and the vote, it need not follow that globalization similarly weakens connections between other types of retrospective performance evaluations and incumbent support. As we saw in Chapter 3, mass politics is multidimensional. Globalization may not reduce retrospective performance-based voting insomuch as it *shifts* the bases of accountability away from issue domains, such as the economy, in which the room to maneuver has narrowed, and onto domains in which government policies retain a good deal of influence. In terms of voter utility, we must assess whether the discount parameter attached to performance evaluations differs across economic and noneconomic issue areas (recall equations 2.4–2.6). This conditioning influence is illustrated in Figure 4.2b.

[9] Such was the case in the fall of 2008, when the ten country survey was administered. Indeed, at the time, the share of the publics in these countries that thought the economy had gotten (somewhat/a lot) worse over the course of the year averaged over 75 percent.

[10] Hellwig and Samuels (2007) show that this economic voting result holds for the aggregate level of analysis as well when the real economy is used in the place of perceptions of economic conditions.

Examinations of the influence of retrospective performance evaluations across different issue areas are few and far between. One reason, to be sure, is the lack of appropriate data on what voters think about government performance in areas other than the economy. But there also exists a well-worn belief that, as an indicator of government performance, the economy is the quintessential measure for holding governments to account. This claim might be justified if we assume that the economy is (nearly) always the most important issue to the voters. However, research by Singer (2011; 2013) shows that this assumption about the economy's electoral salience is not always the case. The importance of the economy varies across individuals and electoral contexts, and it does so in predictable ways.

To show this, Singer examines how people respond when asked to identify "the most important issue facing the country" since the sitting government has been in office. He reports that while many respondents identify an economic concern as most important, a majority of respondents across the thirty-nine country surveys identify something other than the economy as most important.[11] It is likely that national publics differ in their propensity to rate the economy as "most important" for a host of reasons. However, the theoretical argument advanced in Chapter 2 and empirical investigations in Chapter 3 point to an influence from economic globalization. Given perceptions of heightened policy constraint, citizens in more globalized economies may discount the importance of economics-based issues. At the same time, they may compensate for this discounting by placing greater importance on noneconomic issues.

Scatterplots shown in Figure 5.1 lend support to this claim. The figure employs the "most important issue" item from forty-one elections between 2000 and 2010 in twenty advanced industrial democracies to create two macro measures. *Economic issues* is the percent of survey respondents in a given election who identify an economic consideration as most important. *Noneconomic issues* is produced similarly but pertains instead to the share of respondents who identify a noneconomic concern as most important.[12] Graphs plot these measures on the vertical axes against the KOF globalization flows indicator on the horizontal axis. For the case of economic concerns, the relationship is negative: The more globalized the economy, the fewer identify an economic issue as important. But for noneconomic concerns, the relationship is positive. *Ceteris paribus*, citizens are more likely to identify some issue other than the economy as most important if they reside in more globalized contexts.

[11] The surveys are from Module 2 of the Comparative Study of Electoral Systems project (www.cses.org).

[12] The measures aggregate responses to the open-ended item as described by Singer (2011). *Economic issues* combines Singer's "economic performance and management" and "taxes" classifications. *Noneconomic issues* combines his classifications for social policy, foreign policy, immigration, the environment, and social values. I thank Matt Singer for sharing these data.

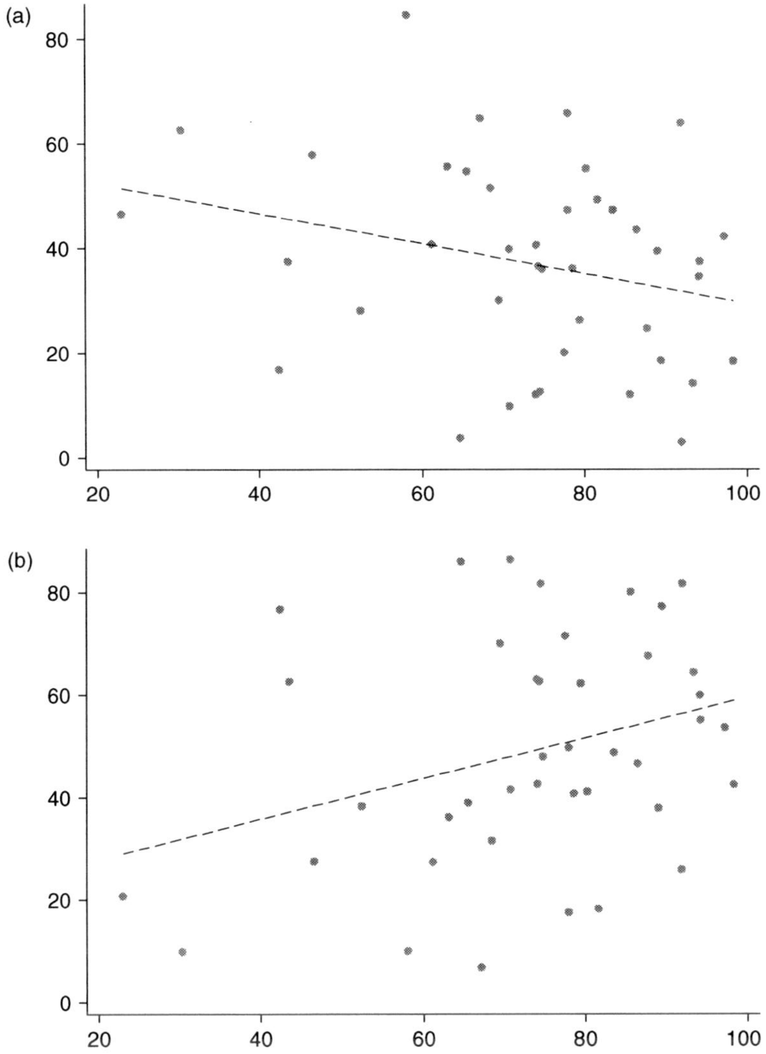

FIGURE 5.1. Economic globalization and issue priorities in forty-one elections, 2000–2010.

Notes: Vertical axes report the percent of respondents in each country year saying the issue is the "most important." Horizontal axes report country value on *globalization flows*. Elections included are Australia (2004, 2007), Belgium (2003, 2007), Canada (2004, 2008), Denmark (2001), Finland (2003, 2007), France (2002, 2007), Germany (2002, 2009), Greece (2009), Iceland (2003, 2007, 2009), Ireland (2002), Japan (2004, 2007), the Netherlands (2002, 2010), New Zealand (2002, 2008), Norway (2001, 2005), Portugal (2002, 2005, 2009), Spain (2004, 2008), Sweden (2002, 2006), Switzerland (2003, 2007), the United Kingdom (2005, 2010), and the United States (2000, 2004, 2008). The bivariate regression line shown in graph A is *economic issues* = 58.06 – .29**globalization flows*, slope *p*-value = .09. The regression line in graph B is *noneconomic issues* = 19.88 + .40**globalization flows*, slope *p*-value = .05.

Source: CSES modules 2 and 3.

These bivariate plots should not be taken as definitive. Many other factors other than exposure to international trade and finance determine voter issue concerns, not the least of which is the state of the economy itself. That said, these displays do lend support to a "balancing demands" argument; economic globalization matters, but it exerts different effects on different issue areas. Most important for our purposes is that the display points to the relevance of equation 2.4, wherein voter utility is affected by performance on more than one issue concern as described by $\sum_m (1 - d_i^m)\beta^m y_i^m$.

Until recently, data were not available to sufficiently test the effect of retrospective evaluations on the vote over different issue concerns. Fortunately, the 2009 European Election Study (EES) contains a battery of items for examining the veracity of this shifting basis of accountability.[13] With approximately 1000 respondents from all countries belonging to the then twenty-seven-member European Union, the EES provides a rich source of cross-country variation.[14] The 2009 survey is uniquely suited for present purposes in providing measures of both economic and noneconomic performance evaluations. Such items will allow us to test the claim that globalization moderates the influence of economic perceptions on vote choice but, in compensating fashion, amplifies the role of performance perceptions in other, noneconomic issue domains.

The dependent variable, *incumbent vote*, is coded 1 if the respondent expressed intentions to vote for a party in the government "if there were a general election tomorrow" and 0 otherwise.[15] Along with citizen evaluations of the economy, analyses contain perceptions of performance in two additional domains: healthcare, and immigration. At the time of the surveys, the economy, immigration, and healthcare each ranked highly in the respondents' minds. Overall, only "administrative efficiency" and the "financial crisis" ranked as high or higher in terms of the issues respondents identified as the "most important problem."[16] More importantly for present purposes, healthcare and

[13] The survey questions were designed and implemented by Sara Hobolt, James Tilley, and Susan Banducci as part of the PIREDEU design study (www.piredeu.eu/public/EES2009.asp).

[14] These countries are Austria, Belgium, Bulgaria, Cyprus, Czech Republic, Denmark, Estonia, Finland, France, Germany, Greece, Hungary, Ireland, Italy, Latvia, Lithuania, Luxembourg, Malta, the Netherlands, Poland, Portugal, Romania, Slovakia, Slovenia, Spain, Sweden, and the United Kingdom. While the EES sample is limited to European countries, this has the practical effect of yielding a more conservative test of my arguments, as the Europe-only sample limits the variation on the contextual measures.

[15] Those respondents who did not answer the question about vote intentions in the next general elections, or who said they would not vote, are excluded from the analysis.

[16] The EES also asks respondents to assess their country's recent performance in two less-salient areas: interest rate levels and climate change. Both of these pose problems for our analyses, however. Interest rate assessments are problematic in that government control over rates is unambiguous – in fact, in the vast majority of cases, interest rate decisions have been abdicated by governments to an independent central bank either at the national or European levels. Climate change assessments are also problematic because expectations are ambiguous; we might expect globalization's effect to be amplifying, in that the issue is noneconomic, but climate issues are by

immigration are ideal examples of noneconomic issue domains. As I showed in Chapter 3, in the public's mind the issue of healthcare is mostly unrelated to the economic concerns of redistribution and government involvement in the economy (see also Jensen 2011b). While immigration is a multifaceted issue, we know from previous work that it is viewed predominantly in terms of cultural threat and touches on national identity rather than on the economy.

Economic evaluations are measured using a standard item asking respondents to compare the general economic situation of their country with how it was twelve months before. *Healthcare evaluations* is similarly structured. The measure for immigration views follows a slightly different construction in that first respondents are asked to identify whether immigration has increased or decreased in the past year, and then they discern whether this change is for the better or worse. I combine answers to these two items to construct *immigration evaluations* (see Appendix 5.1). Also included in the basic model is a measure of the respondent's self-placement on the left-right dimension, adjusting direction based on incumbent government's partisan center of gravity (Nadeau and Lewis-Beck 2001). Left-right positions provide a means for controlling for the influence of policy preferences, as opposed to evaluations, on voting decisions.[17]

The purpose of this analysis is twofold. First, we wish to assess the influence of performance evaluations on voter choice with respect to the economy, the healthcare system, and immigration levels. Second, we seek to understand cross-national differences in the extent to which retrospective evaluations affect voter decisions to hold incumbents accountable. Retrospective evaluations are thus specified as affecting incumbent support conditional on a set of country-level factors. The first of these is globalization. Analysis of surveys from ten countries (Table 5.1) did not allow for the direct assessment of objective globalization. Data from the 2009 EES now makes it possible to do so. To assess whether exposure to worldwide trade and capital flows alters retrospective voting, models include the globalization flows measure for the twenty-seven EU member states. I also control for national institutional factors (Powell and Whitten 1993). Hobolt, Tilley, and Banducci's (2013) analysis of the EES data finds that factors relating to the composition of the government – including single or dominant party government, unified control, and ideological cohesion – affect the strength of retrospective voting. To control for these political factors, I include Hobolt et al.'s government clarity index. Finally, I control for the electoral cycle. This measure adjusts for the fact that we are modeling the respondent's intention to support the incumbent "if there were a general

nature global and, as such, are like interest rates in that few may expect national governments to actually shape climate policy on their own.

[17] The basic statistical model is $Incumbent\ Vote_{ik} = \beta_{0k} + \beta_{1k}Econ_{ik} + \beta_{2k}Health_{ik} + \beta_{3k}Immig_{ik} + \beta_{4k}Left\_Right_{ik} + \varepsilon_{ik}$ where the βs are parameters to be estimated, i indexes individuals, k indexes countries in the pooled analysis, and ε_{ik} is an error term.

election tomorrow." For some countries, this hypothetical general election is quite close to election day. Such is the case for Belgium and Luxembourg, which held their general elections on the same day as the European elections. But in many countries, this is not the case. Since differences in electoral calendars may matter for the association between retrospective assessments and incumbent support, I allow the strength of performance evaluations to vary according to the number of months since the last general election.[18]

Models are estimated using a hierarchical random effects specification with a logit link function. The conditional expectations of retrospections and contextual variables (globalization, political institutions, and the electoral cycle) are specified through cross-level interaction terms. Since these three contextual factors do not account for all heterogeneity in the effects of performance evaluations on *incumbent vote*, I specify a model with random coefficients on *economic evaluations*, *healthcare evaluations*, and *immigration evaluations*.[19]

Table 5.2 reports model estimates. Model 1 reports a baseline specification in which *incumbent vote* is modeled simply in terms of performance evaluations and left-right assessments, each conditioned by time elapsed since the last general election. Estimates show that economic, healthcare, and immigration evaluations each have their predicted positive influence on intentions to vote for a party. Likewise, individuals are more likely to support the government if they are in broad agreement with the party on matters of left-right policy positions.[20] Model 2 adds political institutions. Per previous research, the expectation here is that retrospections will be stronger under conditions of clear government responsibility. This is indeed what we find for the cases of *economic evaluations* and *healthcare evaluations* in which the cross-level interactions are negative and precisely estimated. The conditioning effect of *government clarity* on *immigration evaluations*, however, is weak.

Model 3 adds the economic globalization flows index. Recall that expectation that the effects of globalization should vary across types of performance evaluations. Globalization is expected to *weaken* the role of economic evaluations in shaping voter choice (Hellwig 2001). In compensating fashion, however, it should also give incentives to voters to ascribe *greater* salience to other, noneconomic performance indicators, such as healthcare standards and the state of inward migration. Parameter estimates on the cross-level interactions in Model 3 corroborate this general expectation; globalization weakens the

[18] Specifically, the measure is the number of months spanning the time from the previous general election in the country to June 2009. I take the log of the measure to account for likely diminishing marginal effects.

[19] All contextual variables are entered into models as deviations from their mean in order to facilitate comparison.

[20] Coefficients on the cross-level interaction terms with *time* all carry negative signs, suggesting that retrospective evaluations have a weaker effect when the previous election occurred further in the past. These effects, however, are estimated to be weak in magnitude and are not statistically significant.

TABLE 5.2. *Multilevel logistic regression model of incumbent vote*

	(1)		(2)		(3)	
Individual-level estimates						
Constant	−1.76**	(0.12)	−1.77**	(0.11)	−1.77**	(0.11)
Economic evaluations	0.30**	(0.04)	0.30**	(0.03)	0.30**	(0.03)
Healthcare evaluations	0.33**	(0.04)	0.34**	(0.04)	0.34**	(0.03)
Immigration evaluations	0.09**	(0.03)	0.10**	(0.03)	0.09**	(0.03)
Left-right self-placement	0.33**	(0.01)	0.34**	(0.01)	0.33**	(0.01)
Contextual-level estimates						
(Ln) Time last election	−0.05	(0.19)	−0.04	(0.18)	−0.14	(0.19)
Government clarity			−0.75*	(0.43)	−0.76*	(0.42)
Globalization					1.56	(1.04)
Cross-level interactions						
Economic x time	−0.04	(0.08)	−0.05	(0.05)	−0.04	(0.06)
Economic x clarity			0.61**	(0.13)	0.60**	(0.13)
Economic x glob.					−0.11	(0.32)
Healthcare x time	−0.05	(0.08)	−0.05	(0.06)	−0.09	(0.06)
Healthcare x clarity			0.59**	(0.15)	0.58**	(0.14)
Healthcare x glob.					0.58*	(0.34)
Immigration x time	−0.02	(0.05)	−0.02	(0.05)	−0.05	(0.06)
Immigration x clarity			0.04	(0.13)	0.05	(0.12)
Immigration x glob.					0.52*	(0.31)
Variance components						
Intercept	0.31	(0.09)	0.27	(0.08)	0.26	(0.07)
Economic evaluations	0.04	(0.02)	0.015	(0.007)	0.014	(0.007)
Healthcare evaluations	0.04	(0.02)	0.02	(0.01)	0.02	(0.01)
Immigration evaluations	0.014	(0.007)	0.015	(0.007)	0.013	(0.006)
Wald chisqr	2184.00		2324.31		2344.35	
N. obs at Level-1	18807		18807		18807	
N. obs at Level-2	27		27		27	

Note: Models are hierarchical nonlinear models with logit link function. Standard errors are in parentheses. * $p \leq .10$ ** $p \leq .05$; (two tailed).
Source: 2009 European Election Study.

slope on *economic evaluations* (coefficient = −0.11) but increases the slopes on *healthcare evaluations* (+0.58) and *immigration evaluations* (+0.52).

For a more substantive interpretation, I use Model 3 estimates to conduct a series of post-estimation analyses. Figure 5.2 charts the effect of economic evaluations on the probability of supporting a party in government. The black line reports the probability of selecting a government party for individuals who perceived the national economy as having "gotten a lot better" and the gray line is for those who believed it had "gotten a lot worse." The horizontal axis reports scores on the globalization flows index, ranging from low

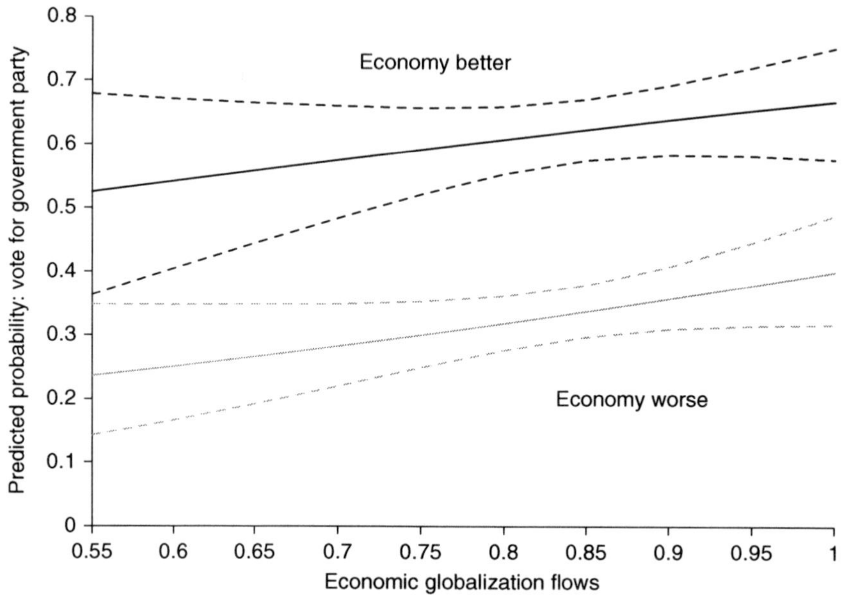

FIGURE 5.2. The effect of economic evaluations on government party vote, conditioned by globalization flows.

Notes: Figure reports the expected probability that a hypothetical individual votes for a party of the incumbent government. Expected probabilities are produced by using estimates reported in Table 5.2 model 3 and iteratively manipulating variables of interest for a hypothetical respondent with median values on all non-manipulated variables. Solid lines report mean expected probabilities from a post-estimation simulation that takes 10,000 draws from the estimated coefficients and variance-covariance matrix. Dashed lines report 90 percent confidence intervals. Black lines are for an individual who perceives the general economic situation in the country as having gotten a lot better in the past twelve months and gray lines as having gotten a lot worse.

values (close to those for Greece and Poland) to high ones (like Belgium and Ireland). If globalization reduces economic voting, then the difference in probabilities of voting for the incumbent should be smaller in more globalized economies, with incumbents both punished and rewarded less for managing the economy.

Evidence in support of this claim, however, is mixed. An individual who perceived the economy as having "gotten a lot worse" since twelve months previous was not likely to support an incumbent party. Per expectations, the probability of incumbent party support is at its lowest in the more sheltered economies and rises as we move, from right to left, to more globalized economies. Controlling for political-institutional differences, voters in more globalized economies are less likely to punish incumbents for poor economic conditions. If globalization blunts economic voting, we also should observe that citizens in more open

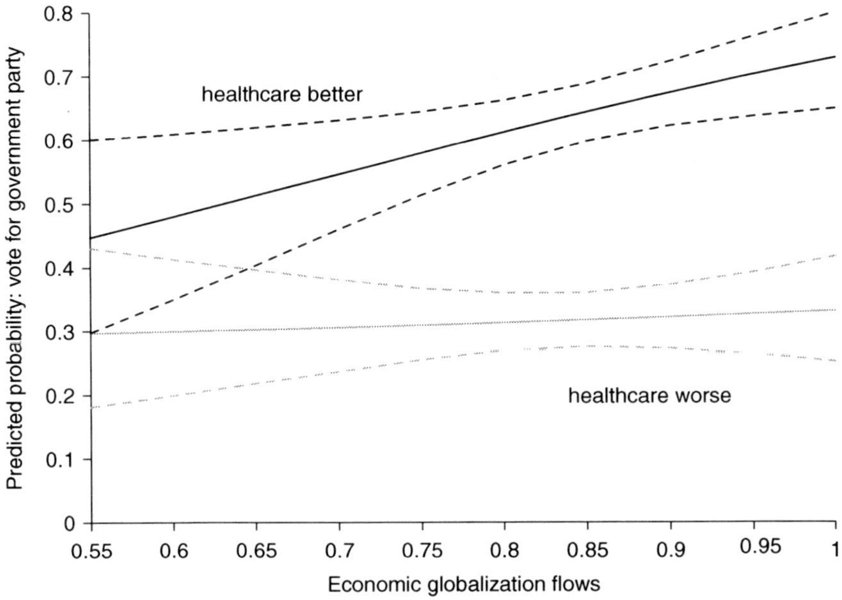

FIGURE 5.3. The effect of perceived healthcare standards on government party vote, conditioned by globalization flows.

Notes: Figure reports the expected probability that a hypothetical individual votes for a party of the incumbent government. Expected probabilities are produced by using estimates reported in Table 5.2 model 3 and iteratively manipulating variables of interest for a hypothetical respondent with median values on all non-manipulated variables. Solid lines report mean expected probabilities from a post-estimation simulation that takes 10,000 draws from the estimated coefficients and variance-covariance matrix. Dashed lines report 90 percent confidence intervals. Black lines are for an individual who perceives the standard of healthcare in the country as having gotten a lot better in the past twelve months and gray lines as having gotten a lot worse.

economies are less likely to reward politicians when times are good. However, we do not observe this expected moderating effect. I return to this point later.

Figures 5.3 and 5.4 illustrate how globalization conditions assessments of healthcare standards and immigration levels on vote intentions. We find that the electoral effect of evaluations of performance in not exclusively economic issue areas is *greater* in more exposed economies. Figure 5.3 shows that the gap in probabilities of voting for the government based on perceptions of healthcare standards is wider in more open economies. The same is true of public views on immigration; Figure 5.4 shows public assessments of changes in immigration influence voter choice such that voters are more likely to choose the incumbent when they consider the change to be for the better and less likely when they consider it to be for the worse. This result, however, is conditional on globalization. The effect of immigration perceptions on decisions to vote for

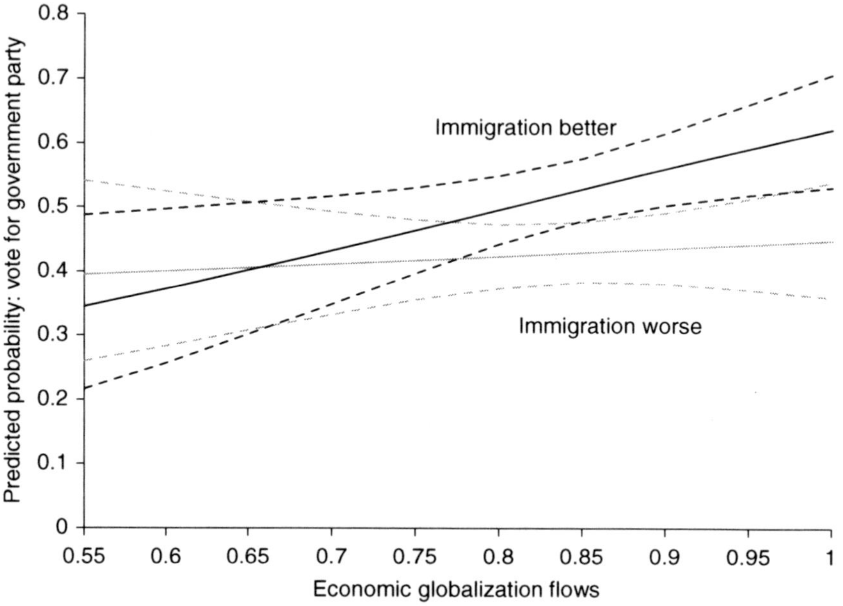

FIGURE 5.4. The effect of immigration perceptions on government party vote, conditioned by globalization flows.

Notes: Figure reports the expected probability that a hypothetical individual votes for a party of the incumbent government. Expected probabilities are produced by using estimates reported in Table 5.2 model 3 and iteratively manipulating variables of interest for a hypothetical respondent with median values on all non-manipulated variables. Solid lines report mean expected probabilities from a post-estimation simulation that takes 10,000 draws from the estimated coefficients and variance-covariance matrix. Dashed lines report 90 percent confidence intervals. Black lines are for an individual who perceives changes for the better regarding immigration in the country over the past twelve months and gray lines changes for the worse.

or against the incumbent is no longer statistically significant in economies with a value on the globalization flows index of 85 or less. Fifteen of the twenty-seven countries fall under this category.

These analyses of European Election Study data show that trans-border flows affect economic and noneconomic (healthcare and immigration) policy performance in different ways, thereby lending support to a balancing demands argument. Our statistical results, however, find the conditioning effect of global trade and capital flows on retrospective voting to be stronger for performance evaluations in noneconomic areas than in economic ones. In light of the now fairly robust finding that globalization suppresses the economic vote (Duch and Stevenson 2008; Fernández-Albertos 2006, Hellwig 2001; Hellwig and Samuels 2007; Kayser and Peress 2012; Singer and Carlin 2013), the relative weakness of the economic voting result merits some discussion.

For one, the weakness of this finding may be affected by the data sample. The EES data are from Europe only and thus do not provide a representative sample of advanced industrial democracies. Indeed, the sample may be biased toward more open economies, effectively truncating variance on the key causal variable. Timing of the surveys may also influence results. The EES surveys are ideal for testing balancing demands arguments owing to the presence of multiple performance indicators posed in multiple country samples simultaneously. However, when they were administered in June 2009, most of Europe's economies were enduring their lowest growth levels in a generation. It is difficult to leverage information from the small share of respondents who perceived – likely wrongly – that their economy had improved over the past year. Model estimates for those who believed their economies "had gotten (a lot) better" are thus informed by only a small share of respondents.

These results may also be affected by how voters receive signals about the world economy. We saw in Chapter 3 that individuals who receive signals about the importance of globalization from party elites are less likely to make policy demands with respect to the economic dimension. And we saw in Chapter 4 that perceptions of "who's responsible" for economic conditions are shaped not only by exposure to the world economy but also by perceptions of globalization's reach as communicated by party elites. Elite discourse may also affect the influence of the economy on the vote. This may be especially so given the unprecedented nature of the global recession of 2009, a time many looked to elites for help in making sense of a volatile economic environment (e.g., Hellwig and Coffey 2011). In short, it may well be that economic voting is affected by globalization but that the objective flows measure does not capture this effect.

As a way to explore this assertion, I re-estimated Model 3 using the expert-survey based measure of elite perceptions of globalization in place of the KOF flows index.[21] Figure 5.5 uses estimates from this model to graph the predicted probabilities across the in-sample values on *elite messages*, where higher values indicate greater salience and cohesion on the part of parties. The graph shows that voter assessments of national economic conditions matter for incumbent support but only in cases for which elite discourse on globalization is weak. As elite signals with respect to globalization's salience increase, the influence of economic perceptions wanes in importance until they no longer have a statistically significant difference in affecting voter support for the incumbent. This moderating effect of signals pertaining to the world economy on economic voting is just as our argument with respect to globalization and political accountability predicts.

[21] *Elite messages* combines information about the salience of globalization to political parties with information about the perceived cohesion of parties on the issue. See Chapter 4. Regression estimates are reported in Appendix 5.2.

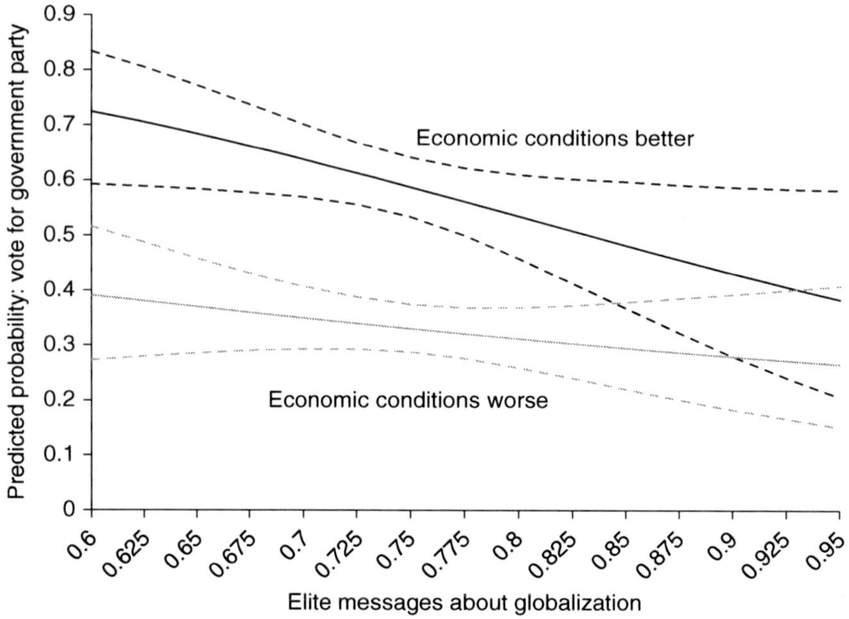

FIGURE 5.5. The effect of economic evaluations on government party vote, conditioned by elite messages on globalization.

Notes: Figure reports the expected probability that a hypothetical individual votes for a party of the incumbent government. Expected probabilities are produced by using estimates reported in Appendix 5.2 and iteratively manipulating variables of interest for a hypothetical respondent with median values on all non-manipulated variables. Solid lines report mean expected probabilities from a post-estimation simulation that takes 10,000 draws from the estimated coefficients and variance-covariance matrix. Dashed lines report 90 percent confidence intervals. Black lines are for an individual who perceives the general economic situation in the country as having gotten a lot better in the past twelve months and gray lines as having gotten a lot worse.

5.3. Discussion

Drawing on individual-level data from two sources, evidence reported in this chapter has illustrated how economic globalization alters the influence of retrospective evaluations on the standing of political incumbents. In many countries, large pluralities agree that fluctuations in markets abroad are chiefly responsible for economic conditions at home. And these perceptions are grounded – to some extent – in reality, as bivariate and multivariate analyses show. These results are consistent with previous work on the moderating effects of economic globalization on incumbent support. This chapter goes beyond previous studies to show how globalization *shifts* the bases of retrospective voting. Though weakening the "tried and true" link between economic perceptions and party choice in advanced capitalist democracies, globalization solidifies ties between the vote and assessments of performance in noneconomic areas like healthcare and immigration.

This chapter has examined the consequences of international economic integration for one of representative democracy's foundational concepts: political accountability. In today's open economies, several actors are identified by the public as responsible for the state of the economy. Further, variation in the "target" of responsibility matters for voting behavior. Economic voting exists. However, the economics-election connection is stronger in closed economies. Citizens are less likely to vote based on retrospective economic evaluations – in the sense of sanctioning policymakers for poor outcomes – if they deem the world economy (and not government policy) to be responsible. Instead, as we saw, electorally salient retrospective evaluations shift from economic performance to other kinds of policy outcomes. Globalization matters for electoral politics, at least in terms of how voters evaluate the competence of politicians in office.

These findings have implications for whether globalization binds the hands of domestic policymakers. Much previous political economy research on this point has questioned arguments that globalization reduces the room maneuver for national governments. The bases for such conclusions are generally extracted from analyses of highly aggregated public spending, macroeconomic, and economic indicators data. Yet research at the micro level lends credence to assertions that researchers interested in the domestic consequences of market integration must now "acknowledge the limitations of the kind of cross-national quantitative research that dominates the literature" (Brune and Garrett 2005, 419). I approach the room-to-maneuver question in a different way. My approach takes seriously the concerns of those who say market integration is perilous for democracy exercised through independent nation states. Unlike conventional accounts, I suggest that the concern is not so much that globalization leads to policy convergence. Rather, globalization contributes to shifts in whom (or what) citizens identify as responsible for policy outcomes.

Appendix 5.1. Variable Codes from the 2009 European Election Study

Incumbent vote (*Incumbent vote*$_{ik}$): Variable coded 1 if the respondent expressed intentions to vote for a party in the government "if there were a general election tomorrow" and 0 otherwise. Those respondents who did not answer the question about vote intentions in the next general elections or who said they would not vote are excluded from the analysis.

Economic evaluations (*Econ*$_{ik}$): Compared to twelve months ago, do you think that the general economic situation in [country] is: a lot better (coded 2), a little better (1), the same (0), a little worse (–1), a lot worse (–2).

Healthcare evaluations (*Health*$_{ik}$): And over the last twelve months, has the standard of healthcare in [country] got: a lot better (coded 2), a little better (1), stayed about the same (0), got a little worse (–1) or got a lot worse (–2)?

Immigration evaluations (*Immig*$_{ik}$): Item is calculated using responses to two survey questions. First, respondents were asked "Over the last twelve months, has immigration in [country] increased a lot, increased a little, stayed the same, decreased a little or decreased a lot?" Then they were asked whether this is a change for the better or for the worse. Taking the answer to these two items, respondent receive the following codes: 2 if increase/decrease a lot and is change for the better, 1 if increase/decrease a little and is change for the better, 0 if stayed the same, –1 if increase/decrease a little and is change for the worse, –2 if increase/decrease a lot and is change for the worse.

Left-right self-placement (*Left_right*$_{ik}$): In political matters, people talk of "the left" and "the right." What is your position? Please indicate your views using any number on a scale from 0 to 10, where 0 means "left" and 10 means "right." Which number best describes your position? Variable is coded as earlier, except 0–10 scale is reversed such that "left" is high and "right" is low in cases where the largest incumbent party is left-of-center (Austria, Bulgaria, Cyprus, Hungary, Portugal, Slovakia, Slovenia, Spain, United Kingdom).

For additional information on the 2009 European Election Study, see www.piredeu.eu.

Appendix 5.2

TABLE 5.A1. *Multilevel logistic regression model of incumbent vote, with retrospective evaluations conditioned on elite messages*

Individual-level estimates		
Constant	–1.86**	(0.12)
Economic evaluations	0.27**	(0.03)
Healthcare evaluations	0.32**	(0.04)
Immigration evaluations	0.11**	(0.03)
Left-right self-placement	0.34**	(0.01)
Contextual-level estimates		
(Ln) Time last election	–0.11	(0.21)
Government clarity	–1.02**	(0.44)
Elite messages globalization	–3.00*	(1.82)
Cross-level interactions		
Economic x time	–0.02	(0.06)
Economic x clarity	0.55**	(0.14)
Economic x elite messages	–0.65	(0.61)
Healthcare x time	–0.02	(0.07)
Healthcare x clarity	0.43**	(0.16)
Healthcare x elite messages	–0.07	(0.63)
Immigration x time	–0.02	(0.06)
Immigration x clarity	–0.13	(0.13)
Immigration x elite messages	–0.22	(0.53)
Variance components		
Intercept	0.22	(0.08)
Economic evaluations	0.013	(0.007)
Healthcare evaluations	0.02	(0.01)
Immigration evaluations	0.01	(0.006)
Wald chisqr	1836.00	
N. obs at Level-1	14743	
N. obs at Level-2	21	

Note: Source: 2009 European Election Study; Models are hierarchical nonlinear models with logit link function. Standard errors are in parentheses. * $p \leq .10$ ** $p \leq .05$; (two tailed).

6

Position Issues and Voter Choice in Open Economies

We have seen how signals from the world economy work through responsibility attributions to shape how citizens assess government performance. Stated in terms of the research on party competition, globalization affects policymakers' *valence* appeals, particularly with respect to managing economic conditions. For, as Butler and Stokes (1969: 390) noted some years ago, "issues of economic well-being are as close as any to being pure valence issues." In this chapter, we continue the examination of voter choices from Chapter 5. The orientation, however, is different. Where the lens in Chapter 5 was retrospective and concerned valence, here it is prospective and concerns issue positions. In doing so, we consider how voters select among alternative policy offerings and how globalization might affect this selection.

This book argues that signals from the world economy upset the bases of mass politics in post industrial democracies. One path through which these signals affect electoral politics is by rendering the structure of issue politics more complicated. This chapter presents an analysis of issue politics in globalized polities. Does globalization influence the voters' capacity to use the vote to shape policies in the future? How are voter attitudes over position issues shaped by a context of open markets? Are opinions on issues like immigration or globalization, which may carry noneconomic elements – in the sense of the term as used here, related to public preferences on more familiar economic issues like taxes, redistribution, and government involvement in the economy? And how salient is globalization for anchoring voters to particular political parties? Do voters choose representatives based on their positions vis-à-vis the world economy? Or do traditional cleavages continue to dominate electoral competition?

This chapter is organized in four parts. I first briefly review the model of voter choice in open economies with respect to issue voting, introduced in Chapter 2. I then examine the veracity of this model by investigating the structure of policy preferences in ten post industrial democracies using a pair of original data sets. Public opinion surveys gauge voter issue preferences, and an expert survey is used to measure the positions of political elites. Findings show that although traditional, "economic" issue cleavages remain salient, the issue space in western democracies is not one-dimensional but is consistently two-dimensional. I further show that issues associated with the broader world economy, such as trade, globalization, and, to a lesser extent, immigration, anchor a cross-cutting issue dimension that complicates rather than reinforces traditional policy bases of political competition. The last section revisits the notion of balancing demands with respect to issue voting. Consistent with the general argument, I show that economic globalization reduces the salience to parties of certain economic issues, like tax-spend, but not for other issues, like free trade and immigration, which have risen in importance alongside connections with the world economy.

6.1. Issue Voting in Western Democracies

Recall from Chapter 2 the basic model, expressed in equation 2.2, in which the utility of voter *i* for party *j* is expressed in two terms: policy position and retrospective performance. The former is described by the negative squared distance between voter *i* at location x_i and party *j* at location s_j and the latter by y_j, defined as some measure of the policy performance attributable to *j*:

$$U_{ij} = -\alpha\left(x_i - s_j\right)^2 + \beta y_j. \quad (6.1)$$

This representation of how issue positions influence the voter's calculus follows that of the spatial model of party competition (Enelow and Hinich 1984). In such models, the rational voter is predicted to choose the party (or candidate) whose position on the issues are located closest to her own. This basic prediction rests on two assumptions about citizen sophistication: first, that voters can identify the issue placements of the parties, and second, that they can separate those position issues which structure party competition from those which are less salient.

Fortunately, in many democracies the consolidation of party systems is such that these informational hurdles have been overcome. In Europe at turn of the century, parties formed in response to particular cleavages present at the time of suffrage expansion (Lipset and Rokkan 1967). With the passage of time, the issue positions adopted by these nascent organizations became part of their programmatic identity. Issue coordination between parties and electorates produced a situation of low-order line(s) of political contestation. Arising from several cross-cutting lines of social conflict, party systems eventually coalesced around dominant divisions based on one or a handful of geographic, religious, linguistic, or class divides. These dominant divisions became the basis for how voters related to parties as well as how parties distinguished themselves from one another. Changes in technology, economy, and society meant the salience of some issue divides faded with time while others became more relevant.

Policy orientations eventually conformed to a single continuum, most frequently communicated in terms of "left" and "right." By assimilating the many issues appearing before the electorate, the language of left and right provides parties and voters with a shared, limited, and manageable policy space that facilitates issue-based voting. Specific issues – like spending on public services, energy policy, women's rights, free trade, and so on – may also be important. However, as long as a single "super-dimension" captures the essence of policy debate, each issue area may be classified as more or less electorally salient on the basis of how it relates to this dimension. This helps satisfy the first assumption, that voters can identify party issue positions. In regards to the second assumption, that voters can distinguish salient issues from those which are not, the left-right continuum is an informational short-cut to help voters make sense of the issue environment. This diminishes the need to stake out positions on multiple individual issues. Rather, the bundling of issue positions onto a manageable continuum simplifies the voter's cognitive task (Jackman and Sniderman 2002; Sniderman and Bullock 2004).

The extent to which the left-right divide structures issue politics has declined with time. One reason for this is the common sentiment, heard among elites and masses alike, that the credible range of policy space on such issues has narrowed. The central component of the left-right divide is economic – "its poles contrast a more progressive and redistributive role for the state to a more conservative and market-oriented role" (De Vries and Marks 2012, 186; see also Benoit and Laver 2006; Green-Pedersen 2007; Hellwig 2008; Huber 1989; Warwick 2002). But many argue that policy distinctions on economic and material concerns, particularly among mainstream parties on the center-right and center-left, are only matters of degree rather than substance. For example, while less than one in three French citizens agreed that "ideas of right and left are obsolete" in 1981, twenty years later, 60 percent believed this to be the case (Hellwig 2008a). Others show that mass publics in Britain (Adams, Green, and Milazzo 2012) and the Netherlands (Adams, De Vries, and Leiter 2012) perceive their parties as having converged in terms of left and right.

The waning of the structuring capacity of the left-right dimension is also evident in studies of party programs. For example, Green-Pedersen (2007) finds that the extent to which parties mention left-right issues has, on average, declined in eleven of thirteen west European democracies between the 1950s and 1990s.[1] Less systematically, interviews with politicians tell a similar story. As one British Member of Parliament described it to me, "The economic

[1] Countries where parties exhibiting a decline in the share of left-right mentions are Austria, Denmark, France, Germany, Ireland, Italy, the Netherlands, Norway, Sweden, Switzerland, and the United Kingdom. The two exceptions are Belgium and Finland (Green-Pedersen 2007).

argument is dead.... Right across the center of our political spectrum it's accepted that you run an essentially market-based economy, you run it in a way that is as open as it can be to international trade and investment, that you need to have a very flexible labor market.... And I think those core principles are accepted across the parties."[2] Similarly, a French Deputée asserted that "there's not a profound difference on the economics plane between the French right and the left."[3] And, in Denmark, a spokesperson for the Social Democratic Party, speaking on economy and finance, told me that "It's very difficult to argue that the differences [between the parties] are bigger now than they used to be. On the basic economic policies, [the parties] are very close to each other."[4]

If the debates anchored by left-right considerations are perceived as less dominant, there are implications for how voters decide. As I argued in Chapter 2, it is not sufficient to model the issue proximity of voters to parties on a single dimension. In the context of the voter's utility function, this means we should relax the assumption that the salience of issue voting for voter *i* may be captured by a single parameter (α in equation 6.1). Rather, we should entertain the possibility of *multiple* issue dimensions, not all of which are equally salient. This consideration is reflected in the second component on the right-hand side of equation 2.4, restated here:

$$U_{ij} = -\sum_{m}\left(1-d_j^m\right)\alpha^m\left(x_i^m - s_j^m\right)^2 + \sum_{m}\left(1-d_j^m\right)\beta^m y_j^m, \tag{6.2}$$

where *m* indexes issue dimensions and *d* is the issue-specific discount factor (Adams et al. 2005; Grofman 1985; Kedar 2005). Indexing by *m* allows us to incorporate different issues, each with a different discount factor *d* so as to convey differences in the relative salience across issues.

6.2. The Structure of Issue Preferences in Postindustrial Democracies

6.2.1. *The Dimensionality of Issue Preferences*

This section presents a picture of the dimensionality of issue space in contemporary western democracies. I again draw on the original ten-country survey data used in the previous two chapters (Hellwig 2011). Respondents were asked for their preferences on five different issue divides: left-right ideology, taxation versus public spending, cultural issues, immigration, international trade, and globalization. On each of these, individuals were asked to identify their preferred positions along a continuum.

[2] Interview in London, April 30, 2003.
[3] Interview in Paris, March 5, 2003.
[4] Interviews in Copenhagen, March 20, 2003.

Questions are worded as follows:

Left-right: "In politics people sometimes talk of Left and Right. Where would you place yourself on a scale from 0 to 10, where 0 means the Left and 10 means the Right?"

Tax-Spend: "Some people think the government should provide fewer services even in areas such as health and education in order to cut taxes. Other people feel it is important for the government to provide more services even if it means raising taxes. Which of the following is closest to the way you feel? Would you prefer to increase services and taxes (a great deal/somewhat), that spending should stay the same as it is now, or to reduce services and taxes (somewhat/a great deal)."[5]

Cultural Issues: an index of three items, pay differences between women and men, homosexuality, and abortion.[6]

Immigration: "Do you think that the number of immigrants allowed to come to [country] to live should be reduced a lot/somewhat, stay the same as it is now, be increased somewhat/a lot."

Free Trade: "Some people are in favor of free trade with other countries as a way to increase exports and consumer choice. Other people disapprove of free trade and prefer policies to protect jobs at home. Which is closer to the way you feel? Are you (very much/somewhat) in favor of free trade, neither in favor nor opposed to free trade, or (somewhat/very much) opposed to free trade."[7]

Globalization: "Now let's talk about globalization, by which we mean the free movement of goods, people, and services across borders. What influence do you think globalization has on our society? Do you think the influence of globalization is (very/somewhat) positive, neither positive nor negative, or (somewhat/very) negative?"

[5] For *Tax-Spend*, eight surveys were given the item reported earlier, with response options on a five-point scale ranging from "increase services and taxes a great deal" to "reduce services and taxes a great deal." For the British survey, responses ranges on an eleven-point scale from "government should increase taxes a lot" to "government should cut taxes a lot." And in the New Zealand study item responses were on a seven-point scale ranging from "government should increase taxes to pay for health and education" to "government should reduce taxes and people pay more for their own health and education."

[6] Compared to the others, cultural values issues are more likely to elicit socially desirable responses and are less comparable across national contexts. These properties suggested a multi-item index construction for measuring policy positions rather than a single scale. Survey pre-testing in several national settings indicated that the three-issue battery discussed here elicits the most reliable responses across contexts. The longer British and New Zealand instruments also included items on the death penalty and nuclear power, which were combined to form the cultural issues index in those countries. Each of these responses were arrayed on a five point scale from "strongly agree" to "strongly disagree."

[7] Instead of a five-point response scale, British respondents could select from an eleven-point scale ranging from "very much in favor" to "very much disapprove" of free trade.

Country means on the issue scales indicate that Americans' left-right positions are further to the right than those in other countries (the U.S. left-right mean is 3.25 on the 1–5 scale). New Zealanders (3.19) and Canadians (3.15) also lean to the right, while the Germans (2.95) and French (2.96) are further to the left. This left-right alignment is consistent with that from other data sources (e.g., Dalton 2014, 126). U.S. public sentiment is also on the extreme, as it were, with respect to cultural issues, where the Americans tilt toward the traditional views end of the spectrum, and on trade, where they appear more protectionist than publics in other advanced capitalist economies. On other issues, Americans are closer to the ten-country mean.

I use these measures to examine associations between issues. Is an individual's location along one issue scale related to her placement on another? This matters insomuch as the likelihood of voting for a party based on its positions on the issues is greater if the voter can bundle her preferences on these many issues into a single constraining dimension. If this is possible, then the more parsimonious single-dimensional model in equation 6.1 provides a satisfactory representation of the voter's utility function. But if the voter's positions across the issues are unrelated, then bases of issue competition cannot be collapsed into a single continuum. In this scenario, the multidimensional model described in equation 6.2 is more appropriate.

To discern whether issues can be summarily communicated using a single "superdimension," I regress respondent left-right placements on their positions on tax-spend, cultural issues, immigration, trade, and globalization. Model estimates are shown in Table 6.1.[8] Results inform our inquiry into the structure of political competition in several ways. First, model R^2 statistics indicate that citizen placements on the five issue scales do only a modest job of accounting for the variations in left-right positions. Partisanship generally is a stronger predictor of left-right self-placement than ones' views on the issues of the day. This runs counter to the commonly made claims that left-right orientations encompass issue attitudes (Huber 1989; Inglehart and Klingemann 1976; see also De Vries et al. 2013). Second, the issue-based content of citizen left-right placements varies across the ten country cases. In some cases, like Denmark, Britain, and Sweden, left-right placements are informed mainly by economic considerations like preferences over taxes and spending. In other contexts,

[8] Following Huber (1989), models also include a full set of dummy variables for partisan attachments to control for the effects of parties' non-policy related appeals. The partisanship dummy variables are measured using responses to the survey item "do you usually think of yourself as close to any particular party?" The inclusion of partisanship control ensures that estimates attached to the issue positions are conservative. Rather than reporting estimates for each partisan dummy, Table 6.1 reports the result of a joint F test for the statistical significance of the partisanship information contributing to model fit. In each case, model R^2 statistics are larger with the partisan controls than without. This difference ranges from 4 percent in goodness-of-fit improvement for Denmark to 24 percent for the Swedish case. Full model results are available on request.

TABLE 6.1. *The effect of individual issue positions on left-right placements, OLS estimates*

	Australia	Canada	Denmark	France	Germany
Tax-spend	0.03	0.01	0.20*	0.08*	0.02
	(0.03)	(0.03)	(0.03)	(0.02)	(0.02)
Culture issues	0.05	0.02	0.19*	0.06*	0.09*
	(0.03)	(0.03)	(0.04)	(0.02)	(0.03)
Immigration	0.11*	0.07*	0.10*	0.08*	0.11*
	(0.03)	(0.03)	(0.03)	(0.03)	(0.02)
Trade	−0.03	0.04	−0.02	0.02	−0.01
	(0.03)	(0.03)	(0.03)	(0.02)	(0.02)
Globalization	0.06*	0.003	0.003	0.03	0.02
	(0.03)	(0.03)	(0.03)	(0.02)	(0.02)
Constant	2.32*	2.62*	2.20*	1.36*	2.24*
	(0.17)	(0.16)	(0.20)	(0.25)	(0.15)
Joint *F* test for party ID	25.39*	5.42*	3.62*	11.04*	13.68*
R^2	0.24	0.09	0.17	0.20	0.19
N	823	745	854	954	921

	Great Britain	Netherlands	New Zealand	Sweden	United States
Tax-spend	0.17*	0.08*	0.08*	0.20*	0.13*
	(0.02)	(0.02)	(0.02)	(0.03)	(0.02)
Culture issues	0.04	0.08*	0.04	0.08*	0.17*
	(0.02)	(0.03)	(0.03)	(0.03)	(0.02)
Immigration	0.15*	0.15*	0.08*	0.07*	0.06*
	(0.02)	(0.02)	(0.02)	(0.03)	(0.03)
Trade	−0.01	0.03	−0.01	0.06	0.02
	(0.01)	(0.02)	(0.02)	(0.03)	(0.02)
Globalization	0.02	−0.004	0.11*	0.04	−0.04*
	(0.01)	(0.02)	(0.02)	(0.03)	(0.03)
Constant	3.15*	2.17*	2.77*	1.90*	2.60*
	(0.14)	(0.13)	(0.17)	(0.19)	(0.18)
Joint *F* test for party ID	78.10*	11.73*	29.56*	26.55*	20.30*
R^2	0.42	0.30	0.28	0.40	0.31
N	1984	880	1614	817	839

Note: Cells report ordinary least squares coefficients with standard errors in parentheses.
* $p < .05$, two tailed test.
Source: Hellwig 2011.

cultural issues or immigration exert the strongest effects. In the United States, for instance, the content of the left-right divide is shaped to a greater degree by noneconomic cultural issues than it is in Europe.[9] Third, the effect of issues associated with exposure to the world economy, *trade* and *globalization*, are generally weak in magnitude and/or not statistically significant.

These regression estimates give us reason to be skeptical that the left-right divide serves adequately as "a sort of 'super-issue' that summarizes current political positions" (Dalton 2014, 125). Consistent with the evidence presented in earlier chapters with respect to policy preferences and responsibility attributions, Table 6.1 results suggest that voter issue preferences are multidimensional and, more to the point, differ in economic and noneconomic policy areas.

To further assess the dimensionality of the issue space, I perform principal components factor analyses on the issue scales for tax-spend, cultural issues, immigration, trade, and globalization.[10] Statistical results, displayed in Table 6.2, are notable in several respects. First, for all ten country cases we find not one but *two* dimensions of policy contestation. This is consistent with recent work on issue politics in advanced capitalist societies (Kriesi et al. 2008; Koopmans 2005). Second, the pattern of issue dimensionality is remarkably consistent across countries. On one dimension (rotated factor), most of the variation is captured by views on trade, globalization, and, to a certain degree, immigration. The other dimension is informed mainly by taxes and spending, cultural issues, and, again more weakly, immigration.[11] Across countries, the variance attributed to the two dimensions is fairly equal, implying that each dimension contributes relatively similarly to the overall structure of policy preferences.[12] However, it is notable that those issues most associated with economic openness, *trade* and *globalization*, load more strongly on the dominant, first dimension.[13] In general, the primary basis of cross-individual variation in preferences is due to issue positions on trade and globalization rather than on

[9] This finding is consistent with "culture wars" accounts of the American political landscape (Frank 2004).

[10] Kriesi et al. (2008) adopt a similar approach in their study of party systems in six European countries. But while Kriesi and his coauthors analyses rely on existing data sources, chiefly from national elections studies, I employ survey data designed and collected specifically for the purpose of incorporating aspects of globalization as a positional issue.

[11] Immigration is the only issue that loads at |0.40| or greater on both dimensions in any of the surveys, and it does so in six of ten cases. This result is consistent with research that finds that mass attitudes on immigration are driven by a multitude of factors (see Ceobanu and Escandell 2010). The signs on the factor loadings are such that positively signed-loadings indicate preferences for spending over taxes, liberal rather than traditional social policies, policies favoring the integration of immigrants rather than returning non-natives to their home countries, free trade over protectionism, and a belief that globalization's influence on society is positive rather than negative. Negatively signed loadings indicate the opposite.

[12] The first factor explains between 28 and 38 percent of the variance while the second ranges between 21 and 27 percent.

[13] The only exception is France.

TABLE 6.2. *Factor analyses of mass issue opinions in ten democracies, 2008*

	Australia		Canada		Denmark	
	Factor 1	Factor 2	Factor 1	Factor 2	Factor 1	Factor 2
Tax-spend	0.03	**0.71**	0.19	**0.75**	0.19	**0.73**
Cultural issues	0.01	**0.74**	–0.08	**0.68**	–0.08	**0.71**
Immigration	**–0.48**	**0.49**	**–0.46**	**0.54**	**–0.51**	**0.52**
Trade	**0.81**	0.07	**0.83**	0.12	**0.73**	0.12
Globalization	**0.76**	–0.02	**0.77**	–0.09	**0.80**	–0.05
Eigenvalue	1.58	1.21	1.59	1.27	1.55	1.25
Variance explained	0.30	0.26	0.31	0.27	0.29	0.27
N	852		830		879	

	France		Germany		Great Britain	
	Factor 1	Factor 2	Factor 1	Factor 2	Factor 1	Factor 2
Tax-spend	**0.75**	0.10	0.04	**0.80**	0.02	**–0.81**
Cultural issues	**0.67**	0.04	–0.03	**0.56**	0.12	**0.57**
Immigration	**0.69**	–0.27	**–0.53**	**0.42**	**–0.61**	**0.43**
Trade	–0.02	**0.79**	**0.77**	0.05	**0.76**	0.18
Globalization	0.17	**0.81**	**0.77**	0.02	**0.75**	0.09
Eigenvalue	1.60	1.32	1.53	1.08	1.53	1.21
Variance explained	0.31	0.27	0.29	0.23	0.31	0.24
N	965		931		2220	

	Netherlands		New Zealand		Sweden	
	Factor 1	Factor 2	Factor 1	Factor 2	Factor 1	Factor 2
Tax-spend	0.21	**0.68**	–0.06	**0.74**	0.21	**0.65**
Cultural issues	–0.01	**0.59**	0.02	**0.70**	–0.06	**0.71**
Immigration	–0.34	**0.68**	**–0.64**	0.14	**–0.54**	**0.47**
Trade	**0.80**	0.04	**0.80**	0.15	**0.74**	0.35
Globalization	**0.76**	–0.05	**0.76**	0.15	**0.81**	–0.01
Eigenvalue	1.44	1.22	1.72	1.04	1.58	1.24
Variance explained	0.28	0.27	0.34	0.21	0.32	0.25
N	898		1868		841	

	United States	
	Factor 1	**Factor 2**
Tax-spend	−0.06	**0.81**
Cultural issues	−0.04	**0.79**
Immigration	**−0.53**	**0.44**
Trade	**0.84**	0.13
Globalization	**0.78**	−0.18
Eigenvalue	1.91	1.21
Variance explained	0.38	0.24
N	861	

Note: Principal component factors after varimax rotation with Kaiser normalization. Two and only two factors retained in all cases based on minimum eigenvalue = 1. Factor loadings greater than |0.4| are in bold.
Source: Hellwig 2011.

issues such as taxes and spending, which have characterized political competition in developed welfare states over the postwar era.

6.2.2. *The Structure of Party Positions*

Evidence from ten country surveys shows that rather than subsumed by the left-right positions, issue opinions with respect to economic globalization are cross-cutting. In today's western democracies, *position issue* politics, to use Stokes' (1963) terminology, are multidimensional, and two-dimensional at that. But the existence of these dimensions and their relevance for mass behavior are two separate things. Whether this multidimensionality matters for voter decisions depends on the other players in the game: the political elites. Even if voters perceive both dimensions to be salient, their preferences will be of little consequence if parties are distinguishable in terms of but a single set of issues.

To better understand the consequences of the mass opinions on the issues, I examine the structure of elite preferences. Party preferences are assessed using data from the 2009 survey of party experts. The questionnaire asked country experts to place parties along issue scales in a number of policy areas. These include the left-right scale, cutting taxation versus raising spending, immigration, protectionism/free trade, and globalization.[14] I use these items to measure party positions by taking the mean response from all experts who placed it on the issue scale.

[14] Party positions based on fewer than eight experts are not used. See Chapter 6 Appendix for question wording and the appendix to Chapter 3 for a discussion of validity and reliability issues.

To examine the locations of party competitors relative to that of the electorate, I plot the locations of voters and parties on two scales. For one scale I use the left-right summary measure. As noted, it has been argued that left-right placements provide a common anchor linking voters to parties (Bélanger et al. 2006; Lewis-Beck and Lobo 2011). As such, it serves as a useful basis of comparison against other issues. For the other dimension I rely on positions on trade. Trade is selected for this illustration because this issue typically has but a weak influence on citizens' left-right positions (Table 6.1) and because it loads most strongly on the issue dimension opposite of tax spend and cultural issues (Table 6.2).[15] To summarize voter preferences in the electorate, I use respondent means on these issues, taken from the ten-country public opinion data already described. Corresponding measures for party positions are taken from the expert surveys. Means were then rescaled so that all items across both voters and parties are put on a 1–5 scale to match up with the voter positions.

The resulting two-dimensional spatial mappings are displayed in Figure 6.1. Left-right positions are charted on the horizontal axes and preferences over trade appear on the vertical axes. Party labels are described in the notes beneath each graph. Looking across the graphs, we see that mean voter positions typically bisect the left-right continuum in more or less even segments. In certain cases (e.g., the United States) the mean position lies right of center. Mean voter placement on the trade issue is also quite consistent across the ten countries. The typical voter in these democracies generally views the gains from trade outweigh the costs, being slightly more in favor of free trade than policies "to protect jobs at home."

With respect to multidimensionality, our interest is in the orthogonality of the issue positions. In a few systems, the trade issue has been assimilated into the language of left and right. For Canada, parties at the federal level are arrayed from left-protectionist to right-free trade ranging from the New Democratic Party and the Greens, to the Liberals, and finally to the Conservatives, with only the regional Bloc Québécois appearing on the "off-diagonal." This lower-left to upper-right array is approximated by party systems in the United States as well as by the main parties in Australia.[16] However, in the remaining cases there is little to suggest that the trade issue has been subsumed into a single left-right super-dimension. Instead, the spatial mappings approximate an inverted "U" pattern: Parties adopt either mildly pro-free trade positions in tandem with centrist left-right positions or a combination of protectionism with more extreme positions to the left or to the right. For example, in Denmark, each of the four largest parties is located in a separate quadrant of the two-by-two issue matrix: the Liberals in the upper-right, the Social Democrats in the upper-left,

[15] I also performed the principal components factor analyses shown in Table 6.2 with *left-right*. In no case do *trade* and *left-right* load primarily on the same dimension.

[16] Note that the Australian party system appears more "triangular" (Kriesi et al. 2008) if we consider the Liberals and Nationals (long in coalition) as two separate parties. Though the National and Liberal Parties are close in left-right terms, they part ways on the issue of international trade.

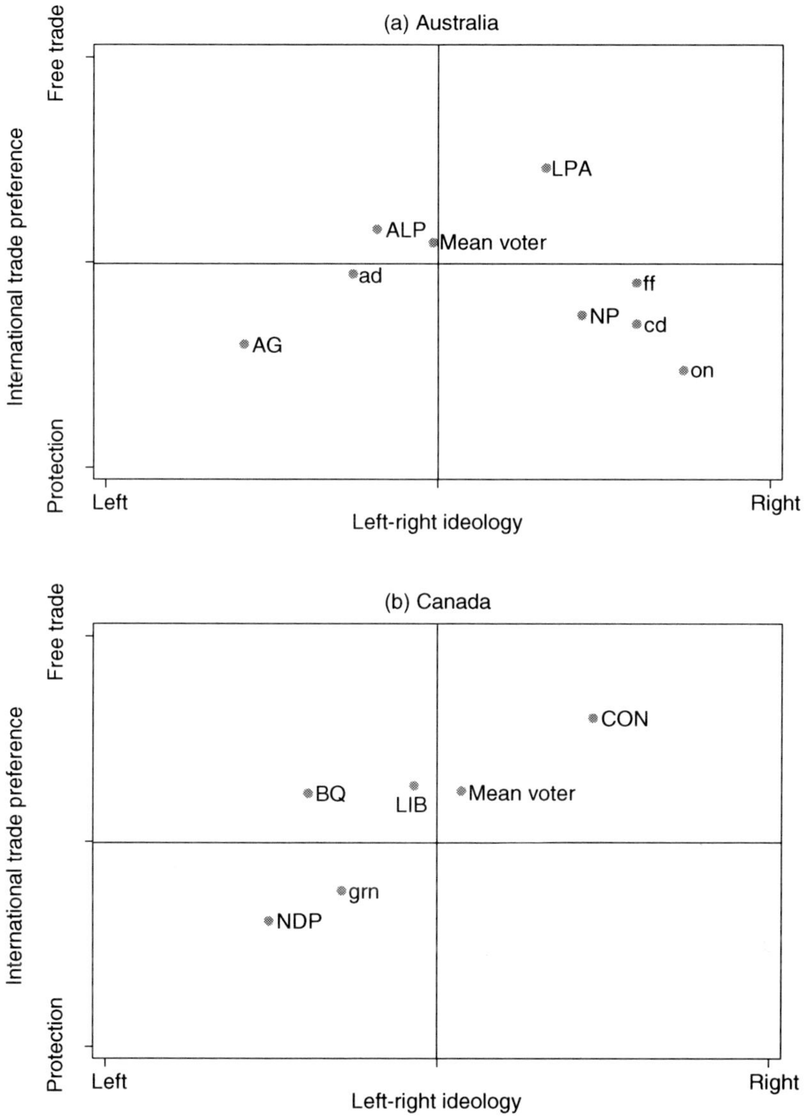

FIGURE 6.1. Location of mean voter and political parties on left-right and free trade scales in ten democracies, 2008.

(a) Party labels in capital letters designate parties with representation in the assembly. ad: Australian Democrats, AG: Australian Greens, ALP: Australian Liberal Party, cd: Christian Democrats, ff: Family First Party, LPA: Liberal Party of Australia, NP: National Party of Australia, on: One Nation Party

(b) Party labels in capital letters designate parties with representation in the assembly. BQ: Bloc Quebecois, CON: Conservative Party, grn: Green Party, LIB: Liberal Party, NDP: New Democratic Party

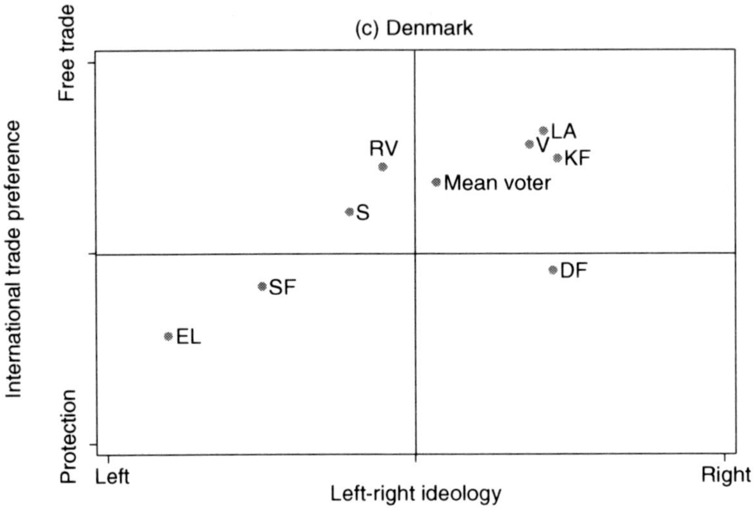

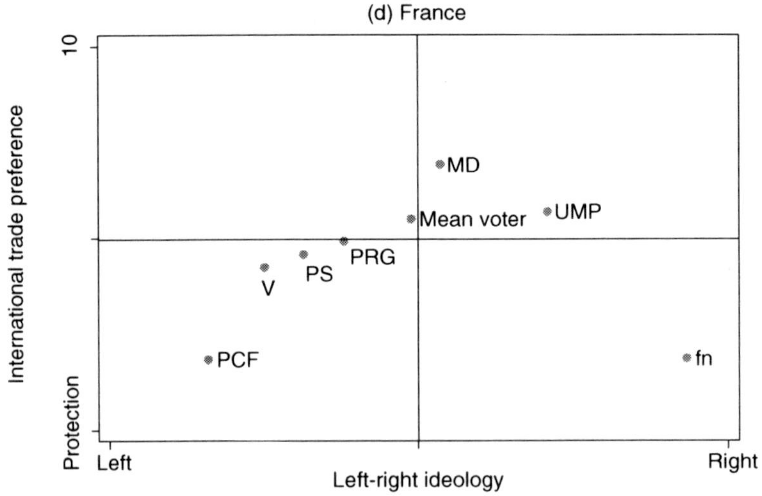

FIGURE 6.1. (*cont.*)

(c) Party labels in capital letters designate parties with representation in the assembly. DF: Dansk Folkeparti, EL: Enhedlisten, KF: Konservative Folkeparti, LA: Liberal Alliance, RV: Radikale Venstre, S: Socialdemokratieit, SF: Socialistisk Folkepartei, V: Venstre

(d) Party labels in capital letters designate parties with representation in the assembly. fn: Front National, MD: Mouvement Démocrate, PCF: Parti Communiste Française, PRG: Parti Radical de Gauche, PS: Parti Socialiste, UMP: Union pour un Mouvement Populaire

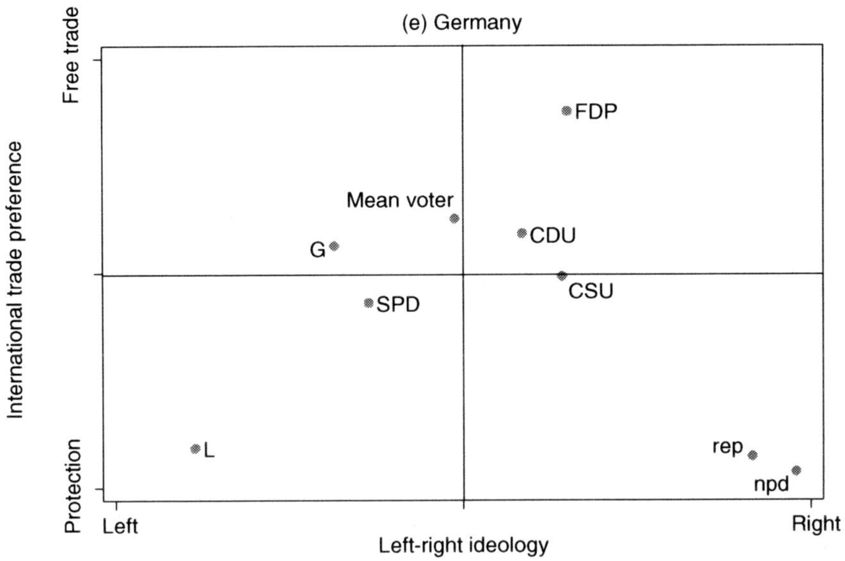

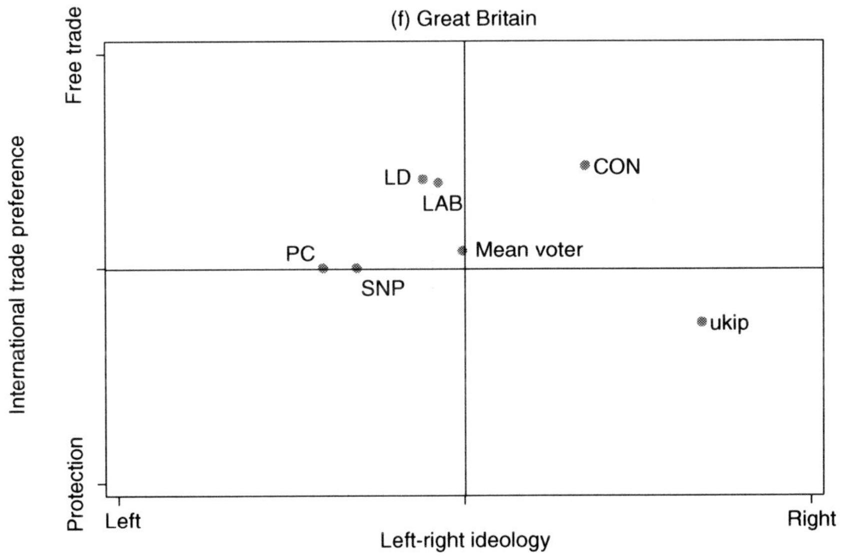

FIGURE 6.1. (*cont.*)

(e) Party labels in capital letters designate parties with representation in the assembly. CDU: Christlich Demokratische Union, CSU: Christich-Soziale Union, FDP: Freie Demokratische Partei, G: Büdnis 90/die Grünen, L: Linkespartei, npd: Nationaldemokratische Partei Deutschlands, rep: Republikaner, SPD: Sozialedemokratische Partei Deutschlands

(f) Party labels in capital letters designate parties with representation in the assembly. CON: Conservative Party, LAB: Labour Party, LD: Liberal Democrats, PC: Plaid Cymru, SNP: Scottish National Party, ukip: United Kingdom Independence Party

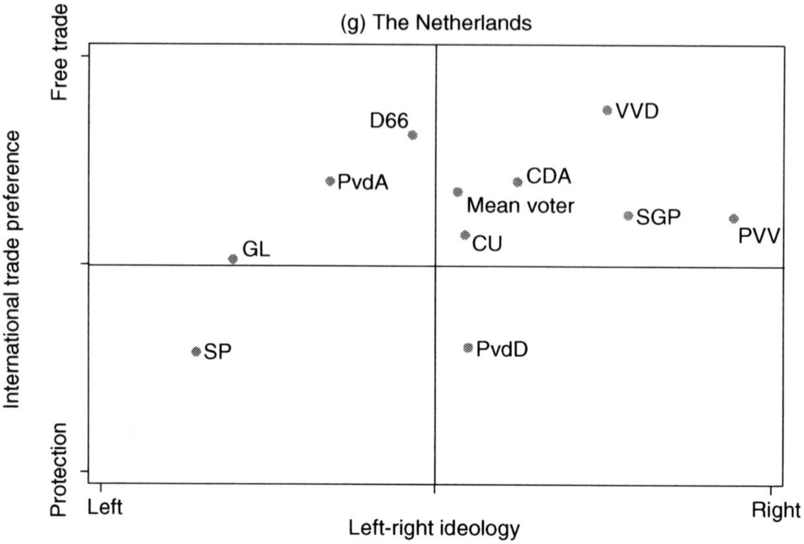

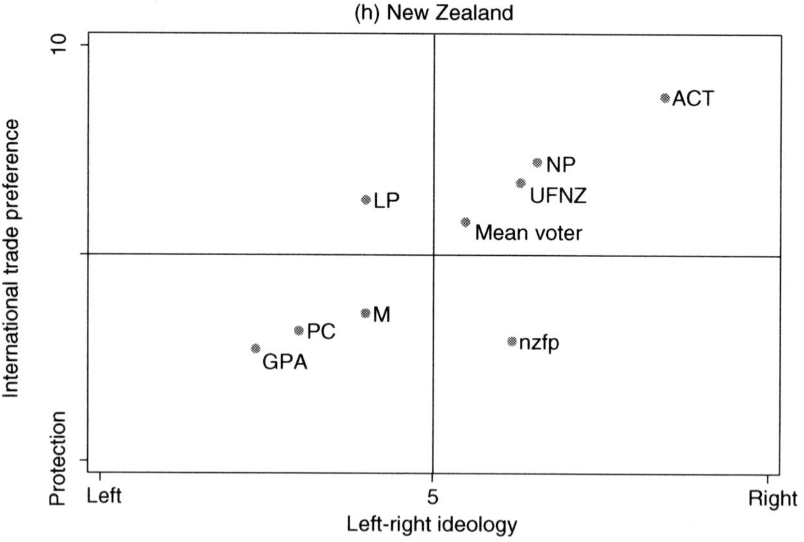

FIGURE 6.1. (*cont.*)

(g) Party labels in capital letters designate parties with representation in the assembly. CDA: Christen-Democratisch Appèl, CU: ChristenUnie, D66: Democraten 66, GL: GroenLinks, PvdA: Partij van de Arbeid, PvdD: Partij voor de Dieren, PVV: Partij voor de Vrijheid, SP: Socialistische Partij, SGP: Staatkundig Gereformeerde Partij, VVD: Volkspartij voor Vrijheid en Democratie

(h) Party labels in capital letters designate parties with representation in the assembly. ACT: ACT New Zealand, GPA: Green Party of Aotearoa, LP: Labour Party, M: Maori Party, NP: National Party, nzfp: New Zealand First Party, PC: Jim Anderton's Progressive Coalition, UFNZ: United Future New Zealand

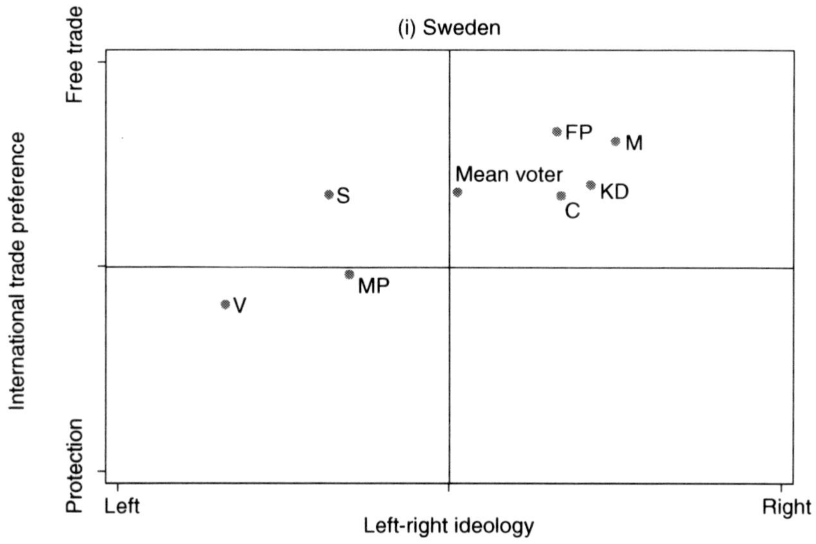

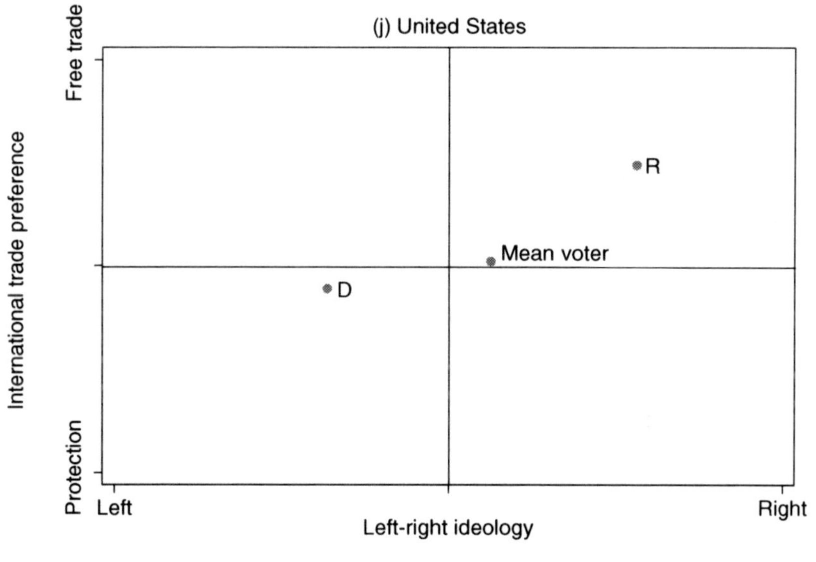

FIGURE 6.1. (*cont.*)

(i) Party labels in capital letters designate parties with representation in the assembly. C: Centerpartiet, FP: Folkparteit Liberalerna, KD: Kristdemokraterna, M: Moderata Samlingsparteit, MP: Miljöpartiet de Gröna, S: Socialdemokratiska Arbetareparti, V: Vänsterpartiet

(j) Party labels in capital letters designate parties with representation in the assembly. D: Democratic Party, R: Republican Party.

TABLE 6.3. *Mean voter and party placement on two issue scales*

	Left-right		Trade	
	Party left of mean voter	Party right of mean voter	Party more protectionist than mean voter	Party less protectionist than mean voter
Australia	ALP	LPA	Ad	APL
Canada	LIB	CON	BQ	LIB
Denmark	RV	V	S	RV
France	PRG	MV	PRG	UMP
Germany	SPD	CDU	CDU	FDP
Great Britain	LAB	CON	SNP	LAB
Netherlands	D66	CU	SGP	PVDA
New Zealand	LP	nzfp	M	LP
Sweden	MP	FP	S	KD
United States	D	R	D	R

Note: Cells identify the parties most proximate to the mean voter as indicated by the given issue scale.
Source: See Figure 6.1.

the Danish People's Party in the lower-right, and the Socialist People's Party in the lower-left. In France, the inverted U is anchored by the Communists and the National Front at the poles with the larger and more mainstream Socialists and Gaullists in the middle. The German and Dutch cases produce similar pictures. In Britain, the Labour, Conservatives, and Liberal Democratic parties are located closely together on left-right matters and are nearly indistinguishable from one another in favoring free trade. And while the New Zealand and Swedish party systems appear to be arrayed along a single "southwest-northeast" axis, in both systems this low-ordered dimensionality is upset by the pro-trade positions of the dominant party on the center-left: Labour in New Zealand and the Social Democrats in Sweden.

These two-dimensional plots highlight the complexity of issue voting for citizens in post industrial democracies. If we assume that the issue space is dominated by a single issue divide such as left-right, then the voter's task is reasonably straightforward. But in most party systems, this assumption is not tenable. Rather, the mean issue-voter is put in a spatial conundrum, located between one pair of parties on one set of issues and between another pair for another set of issues. In fact, the mean issue-voter is faced with the same pair of party alternatives, in proximity terms, for the left-right dimension and for the trade issue in only one case – the United States. Other than the exceptional two-party case of the United States, in every other system the proximally motivated mean voter faces different choice sets. Table 6.3 brings this finding to the fore by reporting the mean voter's position on the two issue scales to those of the parties most proximate to her.

6.3. The Effect of Position Issues on Voter Choice

Analyses of five issues scales across ten countries provide some of the strongest evidence to date that the issue space in post industrial democracies is two-dimensional. I now provide a more direct test of whether the multi-dimensional structure of issue preference alignment matters by modeling the voter's choice among party alternatives. Recalling the utility function in equation 6.2, we are interested in estimating the relative magnitude of each α^m for each party. To do so, I estimate a statistical model for multinomial choice where π_{ij} is the probability of individual i voting for party j. The model predicts that the probability that i selects j is a function of the voter's utility for j taking into consideration her utility for all other parties such that

$$\pi(vote_i = j) \equiv \pi_{ij} = \frac{\exp\left[-\sum_m \alpha^m \left(v_i^m - s_j^m\right)^2\right]}{\sum_{l=1}^{m} \exp\left[-\sum_m \alpha^m \left(v_i^m - s_j^m\right)^2\right]}. \tag{6.3}$$

I estimate model parameters using conditional logit.[17]

The dependent variable is individual vote choice. In seven of the ten country surveys, this is measured using the respondent's vote intentions when asked "If a general election were held next Sunday, which party would you vote for?" For Canada, New Zealand, and the United States, I used recalled vote choice because an election had just recently occurred.[18] Voter utility over party alternatives is modeled as a function of voter and party placements on the issue scales. Voter positions are derived from the survey items as previously described. Party positions are the mean values from the party expert surveys. All issues are again standardized on five-point scales. Finally, to minimize bias in the effect of issues on vote, models include a set of individual-specific controls, including education, income, occupation, age, gender, union membership, and region.[19] For each country case, I estimate two models. The first is a

[17] The conditional logit model specifies that the probability that voter i selects party j is proportional to the exponential of the deterministic component of utility and that probabilities greater than m parties sum to one. For the two-party case of the United States, I estimate instead a binary logit model in which the dependent variable equals 1 for Republican voters and 0 for those who reported voting Democratic. The model includes measures of respondent issue distances to the Republican and Democratic Party positions. For ease of presentation, estimates shown in Table 6.4 are distances to the Republican Party position only.

[18] There is no evidence that vote intentions perform any differently than recalled vote for the purposes of these analyses (Duch and Stevenson 2008, 109–112). Parties with fewer than forty voters are excluded from the analyses.

[19] To facilitate presentation, estimates on the control variables are not displayed in the table.

baseline specification in which voter and party issue preferences are captured on a single dimension in terms of left and right. The second model relaxes the unidimensionality assumption and employs each of the five issue scales (tax-spend, cultural issues, immigration, international trade, and globalization).

Model estimates are reported in Table 6.4. Consider first the single-dimensional models, appearing in the "A" columns of the table. For each of the ten country models, the coefficient on *left-right* is negatively signed and precisely estimated. The greater the distance between voter *i*'s left-right preferences and party *j*'s left-right position, the less likely *i* will select *j*. But while voter-party proximity on the left-right dimension appears salient across our cases, the multidimensional models (reported in the "B" columns) show this is not true for all issues in all countries. Voter-party proximity on taxes-versus-spending has a statistically significant influence on voter choice in Canada, Denmark, France, Britain, New Zealand, Sweden, and the United States, but not in Australia, Germany, and the Netherlands. Positions on cultural issues are salient (i.e., attain statistical significance) in all cases save Britain, the Netherlands and Sweden. Immigration is shown to affect voter choice in seven of the cases, with publics in Germany and the two North American cases being exceptional. Finally, coefficients indicate that the trade and globalization issues tend not to be relegated to afterthoughts in the minds of voters but instead help shape the bases of party competition, even within a crowded issue space. With the sole exception of the United States – the least globalized economy in the sample[20] – in all cases the coefficients on *trade*, *globalization*, or both are negatively signed and at or close to acceptable levels of statistical significance.

Table 6.4 provides information on the extent to which voter-party proximity structures electoral competition. Yet the single choice-specific parameter estimate attached to the issue distances masks differences in the influence of a given issue for a given party choice. And it would be wrong to assume that all parties' are similarly affected, in terms of vote share, by their position-taking behavior on a given issue. For example, voters may put more weight on left-right considerations when evaluating parties associated with the mainstream center-left and center-right. The fortunes of green parties, on the other hand, may not be as tightly linked to "old-politics" divides associated with the state's role in the economy. And the success of parties on the far right may be especially affected by their positions on immigration.

Thus, to compare the effects of issue positions across parties, I use model estimates from Table 6.4 to calculate the predicted probability that the voter selects each of the parties. I examine the effect of voter-party proximity on vote choice by manipulating the values on variables of interest and recording

[20] With respect to the KOF Index of Globalization (Dreher 2006) rankings, the United States easily rates as the least globalized among these cases, scoring 63 on a 0–100 scale for 2008. In comparison, the next lowest (Australia) has a rating of 72. The Netherlands' index value is 92.

TABLE 6.4. *The effect of issue proximity on voter choice: conditional logit estimates*

	Australia		Canada		Denmark		France		Germany	
	A	B	A	B	A	B	A	B	A	B
Left-right	−0.34*		−0.15*		−0.13*		−0.44*		−0.29*	
	(0.03)		(0.05)		(0.02)		(0.06)		(0.05)	
Tax-spend		−0.05		−0.17*		−0.26*		−0.11*		−0.04
		(0.04)		(0.04)		(0.05)		(0.03)		(0.03)
Culture issues		−0.20*		−0.06*		−0.14*		−0.08*		−0.18*
		(0.03)		(0.03)		(0.05)		(0.03)		(0.05)
Immigration		−0.09*		−0.04		−0.15*		−0.12*		−0.06
		(0.03)		(0.05)		(0.02)		(0.03)		(0.04)
Trade		−0.09*		−0.11*		−0.04		0.05		−0.04
		(0.03)		(0.04)		(0.03)		(0.05)		(0.03)
Globalization		−0.06		0.04		−0.11*		−0.16*		−0.001
		(0.04)		(0.04)		(0.03)		(0.04)		(0.03)
Log Lik.	−677.43	−729.90	−504.53	−490.18	−1160.70	−1119.34	−805.61	−845.27	−893.37	−923.37
Pseudo R^2	0.24	0.18	0.17	0.20	0.12	0.16	0.19	0.16	0.20	0.17
N	810	810	439	439	743	743	724	724	726	726

(*continued*)

TABLE 6.4. (*Cont.*)

	Australia		Canada		Denmark		France		Germany	
	Great Britain		Netherlands		New Zealand		Sweden		United States	
	A	B	A	B	A	B	A	B	A	B
Left-right	−0.63*		−0.10*		−0.34*		−0.57*		−0.52*	
	(0.04)		(0.02)		(0.03)		(0.07)		(0.16)	
Tax-spend		−0.36*		−0.01		−0.09*		−0.18*		−0.27*
		(0.04)		(0.02)		(0.01)		(0.04)		(0.09)
Culture issues		−0.05		−0.01		−0.06*		−0.07		−0.23*
		(0.03)		(0.04)		(0.02)		(0.08)		(0.08)
Immigration		−0.22*		−0.12*		−0.09*		−0.33*		−0.09
		(0.03)		(0.02)		(0.02)		(0.07)		(0.13)
Trade		−0.02		−0.04		−0.08*		−0.18*		−0.004
		(0.03)		(0.02)		(0.02)		(0.05)		(0.06)
Globalization		−0.12*		−0.02		0.05		−0.002		−0.10
		(0.05)		(0.02)		(0.03)		(0.04)		(0.09)
Log Lik.	−1701.80	−1844.82	−1375.75	−1371.36	−2519.26	−2620.78	−559.67	−724.42	−646.03	−592.09
Pseudo R^2	0.33	0.28	0.05	0.05	0.39	0.37	0.43	0.27	0.26	0.32
N	1856	1856	743	743	2755	2755	612	612	626	626

Note: Cells report conditional logit model coefficients with standard errors in parentheses. For the United States, cells report binary logit coefficients with standard errors in parentheses from a model in which vote for Republican = 1; vote for Democrat = 0. Models are estimated with party-specific intercepts and covariates. All models include a set of individual-specific covariates, estimates for which are available upon request. * $p < .05$, two tailed test.

TABLE 6.5. *Expected probabilities of intending to vote for the Republican Party, United States 2008*

Issue Scale	"Low"	"High"	Probability Change
Tax-spend	0.21	0.83	0.63 [0.49,0.74]
Cultural issues	0.16	0.82	0.66 [0.52,0.76]
Immigration	0.43	0.62	0.20 [−0.06,0.43]
Trade	0.38	0.65	0.27 [0.09,0.44]
Globalization	0.55	0.51	−0.04 [−0.22,0.15]

Note: Values generated by using model estimates iteratively manipulating respondent placement on the given issue scale for a hypothetical voter having mean or modal values on all non-manipulated variables in the survey. Brackets provide the 95 percent confidence interval for first differences provided by a distribution produced by taking 10,000 draws from the estimated coefficients and variance-covariance matrix from the model for the United States reported in Table 6.4. "Low" and "High" poles on the issue scales are as follows. *Tax-spend*: low=increase services and taxes a great deal, high=reduce services and taxes a great deal; *cultural issues*: low=libertarian, high=traditional; *immigration*: low=number of immigrants increased a lot, high=number of immigrants reduced a lot; *trade*: low=very much opposed to free trade; high=very much in favor of free trade; *globalization*: low=globalization very negative, high=globalization very positive.

the resulting changes to vote probabilities.[21] Recording the change in the party choice probabilities as produced by changes in the voter's preferences provides a standard measure of the relative impact of issue-based voting across issues and party alternatives alike.

By way of example, Table 6.5 illustrates this approach for the case of the Republican Party in the United States. Using estimates from Table 6.4 (United States, "B" column), I conducted a series of manipulations pertaining to each set of voter-party issue distances. For example, to measure the salience of the tax-spend issue, I first calculate the expected probability that a respondent located at the "low" end of the issue scale (i.e., corresponding to "increase services") voted Republican in the 2008 Congressional election.[22] This individual votes Republican with probability 0.21. I then examine party choice probabilities for a voter who places himself at the "high" end of the

[21] I incorporate estimation uncertainty by repeating the procedure 10,000 times for each counterfactual and construct confidence intervals using the distribution of expected probabilities (King, Tomz, and Wittenberg 2000). For non-manipulated variables, I set values at their mean or modes for the given country sample.

[22] In this rare two-party case, the probability of voting Republican is one minus the probability of voting Democrat as respondents who voted for a third party in 2008 were too few in number and are excluded from the analysis.

tax-spend scale (i.e., "cut taxes"). The voter now selects the Republican candidate with probability 0.83, for a probability change of +0.63. Comparing the probability change generated from manipulating respondent placements on *tax-spend* with those on the other issues provides us with an indicator of the relative salience of a single issue for a single party. In the case of the U.S. Republicans, Table 6.5 shows that support is driven considerably by issues of taxation and cultural matters. Party positions on trade also matter, while immigration and globalization do not produce statistically significant shifts.

Performing this exercise across all parties reveals that voter-party proximity on the economic tax-spend issue consistently yields the strongest issue-based effect. The salience of voter-party proximity on the other four issues is generally weaker. Positions on taxes and services are estimated to be salient for thirty-two of forty-six parties, or 70 percent of the cases. Voter-party proximity on the cultural set of issues registers salience in only for twenty party cases. Immigration attains statistical significance for thirty-one parties. A shift in voter preferences from "increasing the number of immigrants" to "reducing the number by a lot" appears to have an effect, in the positive direction, on vote probabilities for parties to the right and far right of center. The trade issue registers as salient for fourteen parties or about 30 percent. Lastly, results show that the globalization issue matters for voter selection over party alternatives. Of those parties examined, this counterfactual analysis indicates that nearly 40 percent would experience a change in support in the event the voter shifted her position from thinking globalization has a "very negative" influence on society to a belief that globalization's influence is "very positive." All told, the set of issues that matter in elections is considerable. This adds further evidence to the claim that the multidimensionality of issue politics complicates the voter's decision.

6.4. Balancing Demands? The Correlates of Party Issue Salience

Evidence presented in this chapter has contributed to our understanding of the effects of voter-party proximity on voter utility. Yet this evidence does not tell us the whole story. In particular, we have yet to consider *why* positions on particular issues matter more than others. Here it is instructive to recall our final expression of voter utility from Chapter 2, equation 2.6, in which the influence of issue proximity on voter utility is modeled in two dimensions, m and n. These distances $(x_i^m - s_j^m)^2$ and $(x_i^n - s_j^n)^2$ are discounted by d_j^m and d_j^n. It was further posited that the relative salience of these issue areas in part reflects the influence of economic globalization. If issue area m pertains to some economic area and issue area n is noneconomic, then in open economies, $1 \geq d_j^m > d_j^n \geq 0$. If this is the case, we expect the salience of economic issue areas will be reduced under conditions of high exposure to world markets. In contrast, the salience of noneconomic issues to the party will increase with economic globalization.

TABLE 6.6. *Party issue salience and economic globalization: bivariate correlations*

Issue scale	Globalization flows	Trade openness
Tax-spend	−0.45*	−0.32*
Cultural issues	−0.62*	−0.42*
Immigration	−0.11	−0.21
Free trade	−0.14	−0.04
Globalization	−0.08	−0.16

Note: N = 46, * $p < .05$.

As a test of this expectation, I examine the correlates of issue salience for political parties. The salience of issue dimension *m* for party *j* is measured by taking the absolute value of probability changes produced by shifts in voter positions as described earlier.[23] We can take the values on these salience measures and compare them to a set of covariates expected to affect the salience of different issue areas – tax-spend, immigration, cultural issues, trade, and globalization – for party support. I correlate the salience of these five issue sets with a pair of globalization indicators: the KOF globalization flows measure and trade openness (country exports plus imports as a share of GDP).[24]

Results are displayed in Table 6.6. The first column shows the association between party salience on the issues against *globalization flows*. The second column substitutes *trade openness* as the indicator for country exposure to the world economy. For both indicators, market exposure is inversely associated with the salience of tax-spend and cultural issues. On these issues, party positions are more salient for the voter in less globalized economies, all else equal. This is not the case, however, for the remaining issues, i.e., those related most strongly with the other "globalization" dimension. Indeed, these three – immigration, trade, and globalization – tend to load on the alternative dimension on the factor analyses displayed in Table 6.2.

Although based on simple bivariate tests of forty-six parties across ten country contexts, these findings remain consistent with a "balancing demands" perspective. Economic globalization reduces the salience to parties of certain economic issues, like tax-spend, but not for other issues that have risen in importance with the opening of national economies, such as immigration and free trade.[25]

[23] Taking the absolute value is necessary in order to gauge *salience* without regard for the *direction* of voter shifts along a given issue scale. Thus, the Republican Party scores the following values on *issue salience*: tax-spend 0.63, cultural issues 0.66, immigration 0.20, international trade 0.27, and globalization 0.04 (see Table 6.5).

[24] Given that the dependent variable, *issue salience*, is itself estimated from a statistical model (the conditional logits in Table 6.4), and given that there are only forty-six party cases from ten country cases, I eschew multivariate regression analysis and instead rely on bivariate tests.

[25] As a plausibility probe, I also correlated the party salience measures with a set of domestic, party-specific factors. These included party size, party age, and party type. We might expect

6.5. Conclusion

INTERVIEWER: What have been the main issues in Danish politics in recent years?

DANISH RADICAL PARTY MEMBER OF PARLIAMENT: The issues have been taxes, environmental issues, immigration, trade. This is the first time I've thought about it, but actually all of these issues have something to do with globalization.... You find that the old way to look at left and right has changed. A party like mine which, in economic terms, is in the center – we are liberal with a strong social program. We have always been this. But in the new areas – development assistance, immigrants, etc. – we are not center; we are very much on the extremes. So there are two dimensions now.

INTERVIEWER: A hypothesis would be that makes it more complex for the voter to process.

DANISH MP: Yes, definitely.[26]

This exchange speaks to the main thrust of this chapter: the issue space in postindustrial democracies is multidimensional, and this makes matters more complicated for the voter. The evidence presented here reveals the extent to which "position issues" (Stokes 1963) matter for voter choice. The effect of issue positions on vote probabilities varies from issue to issue and from party to party. While this may not come as a surprise, original data on voter preferences and party positions has made it possible to examine the effects of issue voting beyond the general left-right dimension. The left-right dimension remains an important component of party competition in advanced capitalist democracies, but to stop there is to ignore the entire story. Other issues also matter for structuring policy competition and do so independently of left and right. Issues related to globalization, like immigration and trade, represent a "cross-cutting" cleavage that complicates rather than reinforces traditional policy bases of political competition.

To understand the bases of party competition in post industrial democracies, this chapter has examined the *structure* of the issue environments in ten advanced capitalist societies. An original set of mass and elite surveys has made it possible to provide a more definitive test of the dimensionality of issue competition, and to do so across several national contexts. Not only do I examine the effects of issue voting in general left-right terms, as typically done in studies of issue voting, but I also assess other issue dimensions.

Analyses confirm the salience of the left-right dimension, but findings also question the commonly held view that the electorate's preferences on the relevant issues of the day can be arrayed along a single dimension. We instead see that few issues, if any, consistently inform voter positions on the left-right continuum. In places like Denmark, Sweden, Britain, and the United States,

parties that are larger, older, and embody mainstream (non- "niche") policy appeals to be more sensitive to standard issues like tax and spend and less sensitive to new issues like immigration. Bivariate correlations of these data bear out these expectations.

[26] Personal interview, Copenhagen, March 2003.

citizen left-right positions can be understood in terms of their stance on economic tax-spend priorities (Table 6.1). But in Australia, Canada, Germany, and the Netherlands, the immigration issue better informs one's left-right position than economic or, for that matter, cultural issues do. The contribution of economic and cultural issue positions to the publics' overall issue sentiment is no greater than – and perhaps weaker – than their positions on issues like free trade, globalization, and immigration (Table 6.2). And a consideration of cross-party differences reveals that while some parties' fortunes are driven by left-right-type issues (whatever they might be), this is not the case for others. Investigating mass and elite preferences on a common set of issues across multiple country studies yields a more complete understanding of the structure of issue politics in contemporary democracies.

Chapter findings also provide fresh insights into particular elections. The U.S. presidential vote in 2008 and the German federal election in 2009 once again provide helpful illustrations. Since they occurred during sharp economic declines, an observer might have predicted that elections in both countries would result in a change in government party control, and in the United States this is indeed what happened, as the Democrats retook the presidency and increased their numbers in both houses of congress. However, in the German case, the vote resulted in victory for the incumbent Christian Democrats. While American and German election dynamics differ in many ways, a consideration of issue voting offers insights. Even though the economy ranked as the most important issue among voters in both countries, analyses of the *tax-spend* dimension indicate that American voters distinguished between parties on economic grounds. German voters, however, did not do the same among their party alternatives.[27] Thus, while American voters were apt to consider how the Democrats and Republicans would differ in their economic prescriptions, the German electorate would find little basis for selecting, say, the Social Democrats over the Christian Democrats. Different structures of issue politics produce different political outcomes. In the United States, competition is arrayed largely in economic terms, with cultural issues playing a secondary role. But in Germany cultural issues play as much or more of a role than economic considerations.

The next two chapters elaborate on how globalization works through multidimensional issue spaces by further examining the interplay between voters and their representatives. Where this chapter has been static its analyses and, on balance, descriptive in its aims, the next two chapters inject a measure of dynamism to examine how globalization reshapes elite-mass communications (Chapter 7) and the responsiveness of party representatives to public opinion (Chapter 8).

[27] Results are available upon request.

Appendix 6.1

Survey of Party Experts Question Wording

In the expert survey, respondents were asked to place political parties in their country of expertise on a set of issue scales. The five items referenced in the text are:

Left-right: We would like to start this questionnaire with asking you to characterize the parties in terms of their broad ideological stances on a general left-right dimension. On the scale below, 0 indicates that a party is at the extreme left of the ideological spectrum, 10 indicates that it is at the extreme right, and 5 means that it is at the center. Names of the most important parties in [country] are listed along the top of the scale. For each party, please circle the location of each party on a general left-right dimension, taking all aspects of party policy into account.

Tax-spend: Next we would like to ask you about fiscal policy. Some political parties feel it is important for the government to provide many more services even if it means an increase in spending. Other parties think the government should provide fewer services even in areas such as health and education in order to reduce spending. Still others are located somewhere between these extremes. Using these criteria, please indicate where the parties were located at the beginning of 2008 on questions of tax and spend on the scale below, where 0 indicates strong preferences for raising taxes and increasing spending on services and 10 indicates strong preferences for cutting taxes and spending less on services.

Cultural issues: Another way parties are sometimes classified is in terms of their views on social policy. Some parties favor liberal social policies on matters such as abortion, homosexuality, and euthanasia. Other parties oppose these policies. Others are located somewhere between these extremes. Using these criteria, on the scale below please indicate where the parties are located on questions of social policy, where 0 indicates strong preferences in favor of liberal social policies on matters like abortion, homosexuality, and euthanasia, and 10 indicates strong opposition to these social policies.

Immigration: Next consider the issue of immigration. Some political parties favor policies designed to help immigrants and asylum seekers integrate into [country] society. Other parties favor instead policies designed to help immigrants and asylum seekers return to their country of origin. Still others are located somewhere between these extremes. Using these criteria, please indicate where the parties are located on questions of immigration policy, where 0 indicates strong preferences for helping immigrants and asylum seekers integrate into [country] society and 10 indicates strong preferences for helping immigrants and asylum seekers return to their country of origin.

Trade: Next consider positions on the international economy. Some parties are strong supporters of free trade as a means to increase exports and consumer choice. Other parties favor protectionist policies to protect national industry. Others lie somewhere in the middle of these views. For each party, please circle the number that corresponds to the statement that, in your mind, best describes the position toward free trade that the party's leadership has taken over the course of 2008.

Globalization: In your opinion, what is the overall orientation of each political party toward the consequences of globalization? For each party, please circle the number that corresponds to the statement that, in your mind, best describes its overall orientation toward the consequences of globalization at the beginning of 2008, where 0 indicates strongly opposed to economic globalization and 10 indicates strongly in favor of economic globalization.

7

Representational Linkages and the Room to Maneuver

A central focus of this book is how globalization contributes to a multi-dimensional, multi-faceted mass politics landscape in advanced industrial democracies. Based on the notions of the room to maneuver and of balancing constraints, I have shown that while economic openness renders certain performance criteria and policy positions less relevant, it also serves to augment the salience of other issue considerations. Traditional economic issues fall in the first category; noneconomic matters relate to the second. We have seen how globalization matters for the *demand side* of mass politics – that is, how globalization affects what citizens' demand from their representatives. And we have seen how globalization matters for policy preferences and issue-based voting. Where previous chapters have focused mainly on the attitudes and behaviors of the masses, this chapter and the next address how such room-to-maneuver considerations influence political elites. The objective of this chapter and the next is to examine globalization's consequences for how parties act – that is, for the *supply side* of the equation. Chapter 8 addresses how globalization matters for party responsiveness to public opinion, while this chapter examines the direction and magnitude of communications between representatives and their supporters in the electorate.

After a brief overview of the political science research on representational linkages, this chapter draws on the balancing demands argument to develop a set of expectations about how elite and mass preferences should be communicated across different economic and noneconomic issue types. The discussion motivates the argument that issue politics and room-to-maneuver considerations affect the *direction* of elite-mass communications. For those issues associated with economic policy and redistribution – issues on which most party representatives have staked out relatively stable identities – communication flows should run from the elites to the masses. However, on noneconomic issues, those issues on which party identities are often less established, the argument predicts communication flows from mass to elite.

Multiple methods, both quantitative and qualitative, can contribute to developing a satisfactory understanding of the phenomenon of representation (Page 1994, 26). Thus, claims are empirically assessed in two ways. The first is an analysis of the ten-country mass and elite data employed in previous chapters. The second is a study of representational linkages in Denmark during the 1990s and 2000s. The Danish case study allows us to examine the temporal interplay between public opinion and election outcomes, as well as the relationships between elite preferences and policy decisions, in a way that cross-sectional analyses of mass and elite opinion cannot. Each set of analyses reveals that the direction of representational linkages varies across issues in ways consistent with a "balancing demands" account.

7.1. Theories of Representational Linkages

The study of representation is fundamental to the study of politics, both normatively and empirically. Normatively, debates revolve around the question of what kind of representation is needed, at minimum, for democracy to function (Mansbridge 2003). Many take it as given that officeholders' actions should be guided by the wishes of their constituents. Others contend that such delegate-based models of representation, whereby elite agents take direction from the preferences of their citizen principals, are undesirable for policy outcomes, for the capacity to respond to unforeseen circumstances, and for regime stability. "Trustee" notions of representation hedge the other way, maintaining that the constituents' preferences are but one consideration among many directing officeholders actions. According to this perspective, the representative should rely chiefly on his own experiences; he "stands for" rather than "acts for" the electorate (see Pitkin 1967).

Empirical studies also grapple with what sort of representation exists, how it evolves over time, and how it varies across settings. In their path-defining study, Miller and Stokes (1963) viewed representational linkages in terms of the extent to which the roll call votes in legislatures are informed by the opinions of the constituencies they represent. Over time, research in the field has converged on two questions: what the *direction* of elite-mass ties is and how they *vary* across issue areas. With respect to direction, early studies assumed, either implicitly (Miller and Stokes 1963) or explicitly (Cnudde and McCrone 1966), that the direction of influence ran from the masses to the elites, as delegate models of representation imply. According to this view, mass preferences originate separately from the views of officeholders. A growing number of researchers, however, have questioned this exogeneity assumption. As Key (1966) suggested some years ago, the stated preferences of voters may simply reflect the limited menu of alternatives proposed by elites. Scholars have leveraged new data sources and employed new analytical techniques to show that the flow between mass and elites does not travel on a one-way street. Rather, mass opinion and policy outputs interact; often influencing each other in reciprocal fashion (Hill and Hurley 1999; Soroka and Wlezien 2010; Stimson 1999). Motivated by such findings as well as by evidence of elite-framing and control of information in general (e.g., Zaller 1992; Bartels 2002), a consensus has emerged that views public opinion as both endogenous and exogenous to policy formation.

In addition to considerations pertaining to direction, it must be acknowledged that not all issues are of the same type. Much research – including that presented in Chapter 6 – reveals that issue politics is multidimensional. Assessments of the quality of representative democracy must therefore consider elite-mass connections on not just one but multiple issue divides.[1] Not all are equally salient to the voter; not all are equally important to the politician's motivations. Research on policy representation across issue types has emphasized two sources of variation as important. The first is the issue's relationship to existing cleavage lines, as crystallized by the party system; the second is the issue's level of complexity (Bailey and Brady 1998; Carmines and Stimson 1989; Hill and Hurley 1999; Hurley and Hill 2003; Miller and Stokes 1963; Wlezien 2004; Soroka and Wlezien 2010).

Specifically, extant scholarship yields a general set of expectations about the relative strength and direction of the flow of elite-mass communications. Issue types that are simple and cleavage-reinforcing provide opportunities for two-way communication flows between masses and elites. Complex issues – those that are multifaceted and/or technical in nature and not aligned with the dominant lines of policy-based competition – are instead characterized by weak or nonexistent communication flows. In addition to these two ideal types, issues may also be simple in technical terms yet cross-cutting; on these issues, we expect linkages to flow from masses to elites. Finally, if an issue is complex but at the same time cleavage-reinforcing, mass publics should defer to party leaders, producing elite-to-mass communication flows.

7.2. Representational Linkages, Room-to-Maneuver Constraints, and Balancing Demands in Open Economies

Although it provides a foundation for theorizing about the direction and magnitude of elite-mass communications across issues, the existing scholarly work is silent on whether and how a context of globalized political economies might shape, redirect, or otherwise affect these connections. The primary contribution of this chapter is to propose and test a set of expectations for how globalization matters. I rely on two familiar concepts: the policy room to maneuver

[1] Most empirical assessments of representation in comparative perspective ignore issue dimensionality and limit their analyses to a single set of issues, usually expressed in left-right terms (e.g., Ezrow 2010; Huber and Powell 1994; McDonald and Budge 2005; Powell 2000).

and balancing demands. As argued in Chapters 1 and 2, globalization reshapes the incentives of self-interested citizens and their representatives. One path through which this occurs is via changing perceptions of the capacity of governments to shape outcomes. Further, a constrained room to maneuver – be it grounded in objective reality or not – aids the purposes of office-seeking politicians, particularly those politicians charged with delivering (welfare-enhancing) policies. Pinning blame on forces outside their direct control, like the global economy, gives politicians a means to skirt responsibility. In doing so, globalization can improve politicians' ability to stay in office, even when the system performs poorly during their watch (see Chapter 5, also Alcañiz and Hellwig 2011; Hellwig 2001).

The establishment of a discourse of constrained policy options bears on how representational linkages work. According to delegate notions of representation, the positions of policymaker-agents are strongly guided by the (revealed) preferences of the citizen-principals. However, this mass-to-elite connection is fortified by an assumption that the elected can credibly act on the preferences of their constituents and see them through to effective policy. Notions of a narrow policy room to maneuver undermine the credibility of this assumption. If political elites believe the range of options to be limited by the logic of global capitalism, then they should be less likely to bring their positions into alignment with the views of their supporters. They instead will be inclined to adopt whatever position is deemed necessary to comport with the dictates of global markets. Thus, while the standard view is that in democracies the policy positions of the representatives ought to reflect the preferences of their supporters, this elite-to-mass linkage should be weaker under perceptions of a constrained room to maneuver. Yet, per balancing demand reasoning, this weakening of elite-to-mass linkages should apply only to those economics–related issue areas in which globalization exerts a constraining effect. If the issue at hand is not economic, or at least is not attached to an economic discourse, then we should expect elite positions to (remain) informed to some extent by the views of their supporters.

This discussion leads to a pair of testable expectations pertaining to the influence of mass opinion on policymaker positions in globalized economies. For those economic issues that are limited in choice by the exigencies of a narrow policy room to maneuver, the influence of citizen preferences on elite positions is weak to nonexistent. Hence, in terms of communication flows, we would expect relatively little movement by parties in response to mass preferences. However, for those noneconomic issues not visibly bound by constrained policy options, citizen views should have an impact on the position-taking statements of the political elites.

The room to maneuver should also bear on communication flows running from elite to mass. Researchers argue that for certain issues, those which are party-defining or sufficiently complex in nature, mass opinion plays little role in influencing the position-taking behavior of party elites. On these issues, elites develop issue preferences independently from the public whose interests they are said to represent. I argue that room-to-maneuver constraints, where they exist, work similarly. When it comes to pressures arising from globalization, the public may defer to the views of trusted elites rather than develop views independently. Citizens should be more willing to compromise their existing policy opinions to align them with the preferences of party elites when the options pertaining to that issue area are limited by a narrow room to maneuver.[2]

It follows that on economic issues there is an opening for elites' opinions to shape the views of their supporters. Indeed, on the traditional bread-and-butter issues of taxes and redistribution, we expect the primary direction of communication flow to be elite-to-mass. This is not the case, however, for noneconomic issues. Relatively unaffected by globalization, I expect the mass public to develop views on these issues independently from party elites. Rather, as described earlier, for noneconomic issues we would anticipate the preponderance of communication flows to run from the masses to their elected representatives. This comports with the classic assumption that mass preferences, or constituency opinion, is the independent variable influencing elite action (Miller and Stokes 1963; Cnudde and McCrone 1966).

7.3. The Direction of Elite-Mass Communication Flows across Issue Areas: Evidence from a Ten-Country Study

Evidence to test expectations regarding issue type and direction of representational linkages comes from two distinct sources. The first analysis is an examination of the strength and direction of elite-mass communication flows using the ten-country mass and elite data introduced in previous chapters. These data provide measures of mass and elite preferences in five areas: the general left-right dimension and issue positions on tax-spend, immigration, trade protectionism, and globalization.[3] In was shown in Chapter 6 that across the ten country cases the left-right divide and tax-spend issue consistently align with economic concerns pertaining to the role of the state in society, the distribution of wealth, and the like. Mass preferences on immigration, trade, and globalization, on the other hand, tend to be but weakly related to these economic considerations and tend to contribute more to the alternative factor dimension (see Tables 6.1 and 6.2).

In order to test the nature of elite-mass communications, I pair party issue positions with mass opinion by measuring the preferences of party supporters.

[2] For instance, an individual who firmly believed in increasing spending on public welfare may nonetheless entertain cuts provided his party representatives communicate such a choice as necessary under globalization. While not relating their findings to room-to-maneuver constraints, Adams, De Vries, and Leiter (2012) report evidence consistent with elite-to-mass linkages on an economic issue, income distribution, in the Netherlands from 1986–1998.

[3] Cultural issues are not included in the analysis because the public opinion and expert survey indicators do not match as closely with one another. See Chapter 6 Appendix.

Supporters are defined as those who self-identify with the party.[4] By taking the mean score of all those who identify with the party provides a measure of supporter opinion. Parties for which I have fewer than twenty-five respondents are excluded from consideration, yielding a list of thirty-five political parties across the ten democracies.[5] Figure 7.1 plots party supporter positions against leader positions across the six issue areas. The graphs show that elite positions, displayed on vertical axes, align with those taken by their supporters in the electorate, shown along the horizontal axes. While the strength of the positional congruence varies across issues, the association is positive and statistically significant in each case.[6] In terms of elite-mass congruence, the strength of dyadic correspondence shown in the graphs is encouraging.

Demonstrating dyadic correspondence, however, is not the same as demonstrating dyadic representation. What drives this congruence? Are elite positions approximate to those of their supporters because the latter influences party representatives' policy views? Or is observed congruence attributed to partisans in the electorate who take cues from leadership, basing their issue preferences on messages received from the party elites?

Addressing these questions requires engaging in causal inference. Specifically, testing for mass to elite linkages implies modeling the influence of public opinion on party positions as

$$elite\_position_{jt} = \alpha_0 + \alpha_1 supporter\_preference_j + u_j, \quad (7.1)$$

where j indexes political parties, α_0 and α_1 are parameters to be estimated, and u_j is a disturbance. If the parameter α_1 is estimated with data to be positively signed and statistically significant, it would suggest that party elite positions are shaped by the preferences of their supporters. Likewise, to test for whether linkages run from elite to mass, we wish to estimate a model of the form

[4] Specifically, I link citizens to parties using respondents' partisan attachment. The survey item asks "do you usually think of yourself as close to any particular party?" If the respondent replies in the affirmative, she is asked "which party is that?" Other researchers link masses to elites using party voters, rather than partisans (e.g., Dalton 1985). Results of the analyses reported here using voters instead of supporters produce virtually identical results.

[5] Parties include the following. Australia: Greens, Labour, Liberal; Canada: Bloc Quebecois, Conservative, Liberal, New Democratic Party; Denmark: Conservatives, Social Democrats, Socialist People's Party, Liberals; France: Communist, Socialist, Union for a Popular Movement; Germany: Greens, Christian Democrats, Social Democrats; Netherlands: Christian Democrats, Greens, Socialist, Freedom Party; New Zealand: Greens, Labour, National Party, New Zealand First Party; Sweden: Freedom Party, Greens, Moderates, Social Democrats; United Kingdom: Conservatives, Labour, Liberal Democrats, UK Independence Party; United States: Democrats, Republicans.

[6] Mass-elite correlation on the positions are highest for left-right ($r = .89$) and tax-spend ($r = .76$) and weakest for the trade ($r = .61$) and globalization ($r = .46$) scales.

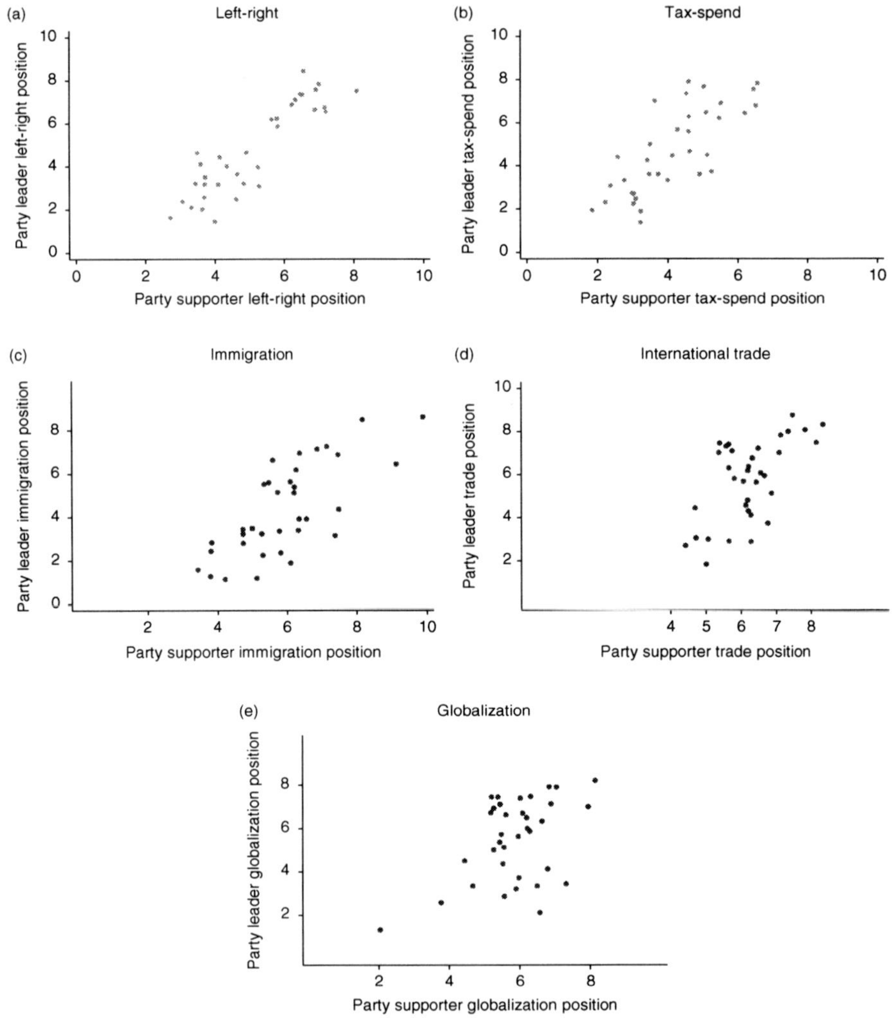

FIGURE 7.1. Dyadic correspondence between party supporter and party leader positions across issue areas.

Note: Graphs plot the mean positions of party supporters on the issue, as produced from survey data, against the positions of party leaders, measured using expert surveys.
Sources: Hellwig 2011; Vowles et al. 2010.

$$supporter\_preference_j = \beta_0 + \beta_1 elite\_position_j + v_j, \tag{7.2}$$

where the βs are parameters to be estimated, v_j is a disturbance, and the rest is as previously defined. Receptivity to elite cues, if it exists, is given by the size and precision of β_1.

7.3.1. Instrumental Variables Analysis

Estimating (7.1) and (7.2) with data must be done with consideration of the causal processes at work. Commonly used statistical analyses are unlikely to produce the sort of unbiased and consistent parameter estimates required of causal inference. This is because mass preferences and elite positions may be endogenously determined, both shaped to some extent by the other.[7] One way to address the issue of endogeneity is through longitudinal analyses, as is done in the Danish case study in the second half of the chapter. The elite and mass data used here, however, are from a single point in time. I address endogeneity concerns arising from a single cross-section by using instrumental variables. The intent of instruments is to "exogenize" the effects of elite positions on supporter opinions and vice-versa. Measures employed to create the instruments must satisfy two conditions: They must be caused by forces outside the system of equations, and they must not be correlated with the model error terms (Wooldridge 2009, chapter 15).

I first exogenize party supporter positions. Following Carrubba (2001), I estimate a model to exogenize the issue preferences of supporters of party j by regressing supporter mean positions on aggregated measures for age, income, gender, political knowledge, and three occupational indicators: employment in professional occupations, in services, and in manual labor occupations.[8] Measures for age and income are the mean values taken from the public opinion surveys in group i; the measure for gender is the percentage of respondents in group i who are female, and indicators for professional, service, and manual are the percentages who identify with these occupational groups.[9] I then estimate the model using OLS to obtain exogenous measures for $supporter\_preference_j$, repeating the process for each of the five issue areas. I conduct a similar process to instrument for elite positions. This time, I draw on research by Gabel and Scheve (2007). The authors construct party-specific instruments from three factors: the age of the party, the party's share

7 The direction of the bias depends on whether the source stems from the endogeneity consideration (in which case, OLS estimates will overestimate the effects of, say, mass preferences on elite positions in equation 7.1). If random measurement error is the main culprit, then OLS estimates will underestimate the impact of public opinion.

8 Carrubba (2001) creates instruments for mass preferences using indices based on the demographic characteristics of party supporters. His instruments for the preferences of a group on the issue of European integration are produced using information on the group's average age, education, income, and household size. He also includes as instruments the proportion of group members who are women and who belong to one of eight occupational categories.

9 The variable *age* is measured in years. Since the income measures vary across the ten public opinion surveys, I create a standardized measure income scaled from 0 for lowest income group to 1 for highest income group. The measure of political knowledge is similar in motivation to Gabel and Scheve's (2007) use of political awareness as an instrument. The measure is the (country-centered) average level of political knowledge for the party's supporters as based on responses to three factual items in the surveys.

TABLE 7.1. *Assessing mass-to-elite communication flows, 2SLS estimates*

	Left-right	Tax-spend	Immigration	Trade	Globalization
Estimated supporter Preference ($\hat{\alpha}_1$)	1.27*** (0.18)	1.95*** (0.27)	2.16*** (0.36)	2.41*** (0.37)	2.50*** (0.46)
Constant ($\hat{\alpha}_0$)	–1.59 (1.28)	–0.95 (1.01)	–6.98*** (1.87)	–7.82*** (2.30)	–9.43*** (2.95)
R-squared	0.62	0.58	0.64	0.62	0.57
N	35	35	35	35	35

Notes: Cells report two-stage least squares estimates with Huber-White robust standard errors in parentheses. All models include country fixed effects. *** $p < .01$, ** $p < .05$, * $p < .10$, two-tailed test. First stage regressions reported in Table 7.A1 in Appendix 7.1.

of votes in recent elections, and an indicator for the family in which the party belongs.[10]

Estimates from the instrumental variables regressions are reported in Appendix 7.1. Results of estimating regressions of *mass preferences* suggest that the instruments work reasonably well across the five issue areas. According to model goodness of fit statistics, the explanatory variables account for three-quarters or more of the variance in supporter positions. *R*-square statistics range from 0.73 for left-right positions to 0.86 for the globalization issue scale. Joint significance tests find that, with the exception of models for supporter positions on immigration, the significance of the group-level instruments are statistically significant at $p = 0.01$ or better. Results of estimating regressions of *elite preferences* on these instruments, plus a set of country fixed effects, also perform well. Model *R*-squared statistics are again acceptable, at values of 0.79 and above. And in all models, the joint effects of the instruments – party age, vote share, and party family – are statistically significant at $p < 0.01$.

7.3.2. Results

With exogenous indicators of public opinion and elite positions at hand, I estimate equations 7.1 and 7.2 using two-stage least squares. Table 7.1 shows that, for each of the five issue dimensions, the effect of supporter position on elite position, $\hat{\alpha}_1$, is positive and statistically significant. Table 7.2 reveals much the same thing: In each case, the effect of elite position on supporter positions, as captured by $\hat{\beta}_1$, is positive and precisely estimated. Supporter preferences

[10] I expect that older, larger, and more mainstream parties will be more positively inclined toward globalization than younger, smaller parties with more consensual (democratic) forms of internal governance. At the same time, these variables should be suitably independent from supporter preferences, the dependent variable: there is no *a priori* reason to believe that a party's age, vote share, or long-held party family membership status should impact the preferences of its supporters. Each is determined exogenously from the system.

TABLE 7.2. *Assessing elite-to-mass communication flows, 2SLS estimates*

	Left-right	Tax-spend	Immigration	Trade	Globalization
Estimated elite Position ($\hat{\beta}_1$)	0.70***	0.49***	0.44***	0.28***	0.26***
	(0.06)	(0.06)	(0.08)	(0.06)	(0.07)
Constant ($\hat{\beta}_0$)	1.64***	0.58	3.31***	4.00***	4.59***
	(0.34)	(0.37)	(0.31)	(0.36)	(0.49)
R-squared	0.84	0.86	0.81	0.70	0.80
N	35	35	35	35	35

Notes: Cells report two-stage least squares estimates with Huber-White robust standard errors in parentheses. All models include country fixed effects. *** $p < .01$, ** $p < .05$, * $p < .10$, two tailed test. First stage regressions reported in Table 7.A2 in Appendix 7.1.

help explain variation in the position-taking behavior of party elites. Likewise, elite positions help account for how party supporters place themselves on the issues.

Moreover, the relative magnitudes of these communication flows vary for mass-to-elite flows and elite-to-mass and do so in ways which comport with our theoretical expectations. First consider mass-to-elite flows. Estimates reported in Table 7.1 show that party positions are informed more strongly by supporter preferences on some issues than others. Comparing across models, the largest parameter estimate on *estimated supporter preference* is attached to the model for globalization preferences ($\hat{\alpha}_1 = 2.50$), followed by trade ($\hat{\alpha}_1 = 2.41$). In contrast, the influence of mass preferences on representatives' positions are comparatively small for the left-right divide ($\hat{\alpha}_1 = 1.27$) and tax-spend ($\hat{\alpha}_1 = 1.95$). Table 7.2 shows that the magnitude of elite-to-mass communication flows also varies across issues. But here relative magnitudes are very much different – in fact, the opposite – from what we observe in Table 7.1. Elite influence on supporters, or cueing effects, are strongest for the economic issues like left-right and tax-spend (with coefficients of $\hat{\beta}_1 = 0.70$ and $\hat{\beta}_1 = 0.49$) and weakest in models for trade ($\hat{\beta}_1 = 0.28$) and globalization ($\hat{\beta}_1 = 0.26$).

These differences in the relative importance of issue areas comport with expectations regarding representational linkages. Informed by room-to-maneuver considerations, I maintain that on cleavage-reinforcing, economics-related matters, communications should flow from elites to masses more so than from masses to elites. Evidence of this point is provided by comparing the coefficient estimates in Table 7.2, which are greatest in magnitude for left-right and tax-spend issues and weaker for immigration and, especially, trade and globalization. However, for position issues that cut across dominant cleavage lines, such as those related to globalization, theoretical expectations predict that mass preferences will have a relatively stronger effect on elite position-taking than the other way around. This too is supported by the 2SLS results, as indicated by a comparison of coefficients in Table 7.1. When it comes to mass-to-elite linkages, the weakest effects are for left-right ideology, followed by tax-spend, with supporter preferences on trade and globalization exerting the strongest influence on party elite positions. The progression of effects is nearly the opposite for cue-taking by party supporters.

These analyses indicate that while communication flows are reciprocal between party elites and their supporters, the strength of these ties varies by issue. On certain issues, elites find it to their advantage to align their positions, at least partially, with those of their supporters. These tend to be only weakly related to dominant cleavage lines. In western democracies, these cross-cutting issues include those associated with open markets, such as immigration, international trade, and globalization. Elite attitudes are less susceptible to the views of their supporters when it comes to economic issues related to taxes and spending, redistribution, and the government's role in the economy. The opposite is true of elite-to-mass flows. Although public opinion appears to be shaped by messages from in-group elites, the strength of this connection varies by issue. With respect to issues related to the economy, I find strong evidence that party constituencies receive cues. Indeed, these issues, such as the left-right divide and questions of tax versus spend, are those for which most parties' positions are well-defined. Evidence for cue-taking is much weaker for issues on which party positions are, generally, less well-established.

These findings resonate with this book's broader arguments about how globalization alters electoral politics. With respect to economic issues, widely shared perceptions of constrained policy room to maneuver serve to weaken elite incentives to update their policy stances to align with those of their supporters. The need to align positions with the demands of the world economy, and not those of the electorate, dominates. Recognizing this reduced room to maneuver on the economy, citizens will thus compensate for their lack of influence and increase efforts to sway policymaker action in alternative, non-economic, policy matters. I return to these points at the end of this chapter. But first, I build a more solid foundation for these conclusions by investigating the dynamics of representational linkages within a single party system. By drawing on a novel set of longitudinal data on elite and mass preferences on different issues, I test claims about mass-to-elite and elite-to-mass linkages over time in the context of party politics in Denmark.

7.4. The Dynamics of Elite-Mass Communications: A Danish Case Study

The Danish case is useful for examining the push and pull of mass-elite ties. In terms of the electorate, the Danish public has been characterized as relatively prospective and issue-oriented (Borre 2001; Paldam and Nannestad 1997). Compared to neighboring democracies, party attachments are strongly related to positions on the issues (Bengtsson et al. 2014, chapter 3). And on the elite side, perhaps reflecting this issue-based party system, party politics has been characterized by a good deal of change. In the past twenty years, the electoral fortunes of some parties have dropped precipitously while others' have risen rapidly. This electoral change has played out in the shape of governing coalitions which have shifted from the center-right in the late 1980s to one led by Denmark's traditional party of government, the Social Democrats, for much of the 1990s and back once again to a bourgeois coalition between 2001 and 2011.

In what follows, I consider how voters and political elites have responded to one another on the two policy issues of great importance to Danish politics in the past twenty years: public spending and immigration.[11] Public spending closely approximates an economic issue in that it is eminently familiar to voters, deals with policy ends in terms of the size and allocations of budgets, and aligns closely with the traditional, identity-shaping cleavage in Denmark.[12] Issues pertaining to refugees and migrants approximate more closely a noneconomic issue.[13]

7.4.1. *Public Spending*

As in many industrial democracies, the 1970s brought economic hard times for Denmark. Rising inflation and an expanding balance of payments deficit contributed to the "earthquake" election of 1973 in which the number of parties represented in the Folketing, the Danish parliament, jumped from six to ten. While all parties agreed on the need to address these problems, inter-party fragmentation led to policy inaction. Protracted economic difficulties led to the resignation of the Social Democrat-led government in late 1982. Although successful in controlling prices, the center-right coalition governments that followed failed to stabilize economic growth and, especially, at lowering unemployment.

A new Social Democrat-led government came to power in 1993 with a mandate to solve the unemployment problem. In line with its core constituency on the center-left, the government's strategy at first centered on growing the economy through a set of expansionary macroeconomic policies. Over time, however, government policies were redirected at reforming the labor market and tax system to make them more flexible and efficient. These policy changes amounted to a departure from the party's traditional positions on social spending. By prioritizing public-private partnerships, unemployment protections at the expense of job protection initiatives, and knowledge-based value-added

[11] Benoit and Laver's (2006, 257) survey of experts from 2003–2004 identifies immigration as the most important issue in Denmark, followed by public spending.

[12] Bengtsson et al. (2014, 36) claim that attitudes toward the size of the public sector "can be regarded as a concrete reflection of the underlying left-right orientation."

[13] This is not to say that immigration does not have an economic component. However, opinions of foreigners tend to cut across dominant economic- and class-based divisions in Danish politics (Stubager 2010). Further, the motives for foreigners residing in Denmark are multifaceted, as are the political and economic implications for native-born citizens.

industries, the government co-opted many of the bourgeois parties' neoliberal prescriptions. On economic grounds, the policy shift appeared successful. The balance of payments deficit was reversed and unemployment declined from near 13 percent in 1994 to less than 6 percent in 1999.

The impetus for these reforms, however, came less from the demands of government supporters than from perceptions of a diminished policy room to maneuver. Indeed, for much of the 1990s, while the government was moving right, the Social Democratic Party supporter in the electorate, if anything, became more leftist in orientation. In 1994, nearly two-thirds of party identifiers maintained that the size of the public sector should stay the same or be increased; only 36 percent believed cuts were in order. In 1998, 84 percent voiced a preference for maintaining or increasing expenditures to the public budgets against only 16 percent claiming budget cuts were the right thing to do.[14] Rather than reflecting public preferences, the party leaders were driven by beliefs in the possible within the boundaries of the world economy. Reflecting on the economic recovery, a member of the center-left government admitted that "it would have been impossible for our government in the 1990s to make this economic boost without a good world economy." "If you compare the Danish economy with Germany or France," he noted to me, "you see that we did changes and reforms they would never be able to do ... We [were] forced to do it." Recalling this period, another party spokesperson told me, "we decided to work more directly on the structural capacity of the economy ... we also decided to modernize the economy." Tellingly, he added that it was widely believed that "it is ok if old industries leave."[15]

Opposition parties also realigned their positions on social spending during the 1990s. Since the beginning of the decade, the center-right Liberals had launched unusually strong attacks on the welfare state. However, its failure to bring voters on board meant that by the end of the decade the party had abandoned neo-liberal rhetoric and instead declared its support for the welfare state. Whereas the party's 1994 program only made mention of the need to limit social spending, its 1998 and 2001 platforms called for the need to maintain and introduce new social welfare measures, such as improved maternity and paternity leave, and for larger budgets for hospitals (Andersen 2003, 190).

More generally, an elite consensus emerged during the 1990s that tax reform was essential. In order to compete in a world economy, and in order to remain solvent in the face of vast structural pressures – demographic shifts, the decline of manufacturing, the rise of service industries, the changing nature of work, and the like – some form of tax relief was deemed necessary. Yet while this view was shared broadly among party elites across the political spectrum, the same was not the case for public opinion. Across the 1990s and 2000s, opinion

[14] Figures are taken from the Danish National Election Studies program (DNES, www.valgprojektet.dk).

[15] Personal interviews, Copenhagen, March 2003.

surveys consistently showed that the public, center-right partisans included, was in favor of maintaining or even improving welfare services compared with the option of greater tax relief (Andersen 2006).

Two reasons lay behind the electorate's distaste for tax reductions. First, the public associated tax revenue with their highly valued social services, and few were willing to make such a sacrifice. Second, there existed a credibility deficit: since taxes had only crept upward over the years, few actually believed it possible that the government could reduce tax levels. The following from a Liberal Party member of the Folketing in 2003 describes this well:

> We've reached a point where [both the center-right and the center-left] want to reduce taxes on income. You don't have to go back any further than three years and we didn't discuss taxes. Any government that stressed this as a campaign issue, they lost. Not because people didn't want tax reductions, they just didn't believe it. The population had never experienced tax reductions in the past 30 years. Not one. Maybe the politicians made a reduction in one place, but they had financed in at another. That's why our campaign was on tax stop. And people [could] believe that.[16]

Thus, rather than reducing taxes, the Liberals – the largest party in Parliament since 2001 – engineered a set of reforms to freeze all taxes at present levels.

The center-right governments of the 2000s sought to justify their social policy reforms in terms of the pressures exerted from outside on this small, open welfare state. A clear indication of this was Prime Minister Anders Fogh Rasmussen's 2004 endorsement of Denmark's a policy of 'flexicurity' in labor markets and broad-based general-training education as remedies for the challenge of globalization (Andersen 2006, 394). One should not interpret the advancement of market-oriented reforms to mean that the bourgeois government adopted policies without consideration of their electoral consequences. Indeed, rather than put liberalizing reforms as a center-right alternative to expanding social protections, Rasmussen's government delivered the reform proposal as a more moderate option to all-out welfare retrenchment. A member of Rasmussen's Liberal Party conveyed the issues the party had to confront, rhetorically asking, "Can we still have the highest taxes when people more and more notice that you get a better salary after taxes if you move to London? Our social security system, can it survive? It gets harder with globalization. [Our party] has had big discussions on how we are influenced by politics abroad."[17]

The center-right's continued ability to stay in power arguably owed more to fostering a belief in a limited room to maneuver than it did to any penchant for parties to (re)align proposals to the positional sentiment of the electorate. A 2005 public opinion survey found that 46 percent of Danes, and 62 percent among center-right party supporters, believed that globalization forced policymakers

[16] Personal interview, Copenhagen, March 2003.
[17] Personal interview, Copenhagen, March 2003.

to reduce taxes and welfare spending. Given such room-to-maneuver concerns, it appears the Liberal-Conservative coalition's ability to stay in power during the 2000s – winning elections in 2005 and 2007 – owed much to its perceived advantage over the Social Democrats with respect to their ability to manage globalization. Indeed, Danish Election Studies data from 2005 and 2007 show that while the Social Democrats were viewed as most competent on a whole host of issues, including jobs, taxes, healthcare, education, and the environment, the bourgeois parties held a two-to-one margin over the center-left as the best at meeting the challenges posed by globalization.

This overview of the politics of public spending in Denmark suggests that the positions of party elites guided, rather than responded to, popular sentiment. This is consistent with the argument that for those traditional, party-defining issues related to the economy, the direction of representational linkages runs chiefly from the political elites to their supporters in the electorate rather than vice-versa. These findings are consistent with the evidence from the analyses of the cross-sectional data with respect to the left-right and tax-spend issues (see Models 1 and 2 in Tables 7.1 and 7.2). Later in this chapter I present similar statistical analyses using Danish survey data. But first let us consider the direction of elite-mass communications in another issue, immigration.

7.4.2. Immigration

Where spending on social services approximates an economic issue, the issue of "foreigners" in Denmark is more multifaceted, encompassing a range of considerations. Among these considerations is a strong noneconomic element associated with cultural and ethnic differences. This was perhaps most infamously illustrated by the fervor represented by racist and blasphemous depictions of Muhammad in a Danish newspaper in 2006, an event that challenged Danish liberalism on social matters.[18] Given differences in its relative complexity and its relationship to the main cleavage lines, the immigration issue should be characterized by a different sort of communication flows. If arguments from the opening of this chapter are correct, then we should expect less-constrained party elites to be free to respond to the shifting preferences of their supporters. Indeed, except for the Danish People's Party, a relatively recent addition to the party system, party identity has not traditionally been closely wed to a particular position on the immigration issue. Evidence of elites informing the view of the masses should be weak to nonexistent. Rather, parties should be willing to be guided by their supporters in the electorate, and we should find evidence that the preferences of the masses inform those of party elites.

Since the mid-1990s, the immigration issue has been rapidly rising in salience in Denmark. According to the Danish National Election Surveys, in the first part of the 1990s, less than 10 percent of the Danish public considered immigration

[18] Dan Bilefsky, "Cartoon Dispute Prompts Identity Crisis for Liberal Denmark." *International Herald Tribune*, February 12, 2006.

an important issue requiring politicians' attention. By the 2000s, however, more than half believed this to be the case. The immigration issue appears to have first registered on the public's agenda during the September 1994 election campaign. Public concerns with immigration in the face of rising unemployment produced changes in the traditionally pro-foreigner Social Democratic government. Opposition parties on the right pressed for more restrictive measures to slow the flow of immigrants and refugees (Thomsen 1995).

But were these crystallizing elite views on immigration, this relatively "new" issue, driven by voter preferences? Or were they crafted independently? While the answer is not clear-cut, observed changes to the Danish party system suggest that party elites have reacted to mass opinion on immigration rather than shaped it. Here, the role of the Danish People's Party (*Dansk Folkpartei*, DF) is informative. The DF emerged from a split in the Progress Party in 1995. The Progress Party's positional identity was rooted in position-taking on economic issues, specifically with respect to tax cuts and liberal economic policies. The DF, however, made its mark as a party by staking out a position – and a clearly restrictionist one at that – on the noneconomic matter of immigration and foreigners. Even before it was a force in the Folketing, the DF's growing clout registered an effect on the center-left government. By 1997, the DF had gained support in opinion polls to such a degree that Poul Nyrup Rasmussen, the Social Democratic prime minister, was moved to replace the minister of the interior with a person thought to have a stricter position on foreigners (Elklit 1999). In the 1998 election, the DF, along with the remaining members of the Progress Party, fared better in all constituencies than the Progress Party alone had in the previous election. Unlike in the 1980s, when the issue attracted high but only short-lived attention, in the 1990s, immigration had become salient among Danish voters (Andersen 2003).

The political importance of immigration, refugees, and foreigners in general persisted into the 2000s. The 2001 election campaign was something of a watershed with respect to immigration. Opinion polls showed the immigration issue to be the most important concern – more important than any other – in the minds of the voters (Andersen et al. 2002). Yet many political parties failed to capitalize on this growing concern. As they had in previous elections, all center parties (Radicals, Center Democrats, and Christian People's Party) as well as the left-wing parties (Unity List and Socialist People's Party) could be characterized as moderately liberal on immigration, resistant to calls for tighter rules. On the center-left, Social Democratic members of parliament were divided and somewhat ambivalent on the issue (Andersen 2003, 189). However, the rhetoric of the two center-right parties, the Liberals and the Conservatives, had become more extreme by the 2001 campaign. Hoping to pre-emptively contain the issue, the Social Democrats reacted by making unspecified promises about tightening rules on immigration and on admittance of asylum seekers. The bourgeois parties quickly responded by stating more extreme positions. The right's calculated hardline stance was a success. The Liberal and Conservative

Parties gained in strength and were able to form the first center-right government since 1993. With the exception of the small Radical Party, all so-called immigration-friendly parties lost voters during the campaign.[19]

This shift toward the center-right and away from the center-left can best be attributed to the parties' relative ability to align their policy proposals with those of their supporters. Most voters favored tighter restrictions on immigration as proposed by the parties on the center-right (Andersen 2003, 189). By the time of their rightward shift, bourgeois party supporters had already come out strongly against more liberal immigration policies. For example, a 1998 poll showed that 70 percent of Liberal and Conservative Party partisans were of the belief that Denmark must receive fewer foreigners, a share that remained high at 76 percent in 2001. In contrast, Social Democratic supporters in the electorate sent muted signals to their political representatives. This stemmed from a split on the issue: half of the parties' supporters favored cutting back on the allowance of refugees while the other half maintained that levels should hold constant or even increase. The strength of the signal from bourgeois supporters, and the ambivalence observed on the part of center-left voters, provides an explanation for the success of the Liberal-Conservative coalition.

This brief account of the electoral politics of immigration in Denmark paints a picture whereby political elites follow rather than lead public opinion. In some cases, this is demonstrated through shifting positions on the parts of parties. In other cases, this is demonstrated by the emergence of a new force on the party landscape embodying the issue (the DF).

7.4.3. Regression Analysis

To better assess the direction of communication flows, I turn to a statistical analysis of the association between elite and mass positions on the social spending issue. Data are from post-election surveys from the Danish National Election Studies program (DNES, www.valgprojektet.dk) from six election years between 1994 and 2011.[20] As with the analyses of cross-sectional data, I use these individual survey data to construct party-level variables for elite and mass policy preferences. But where the previous analysis pooled parties over ten countries, here I pool parties in the same country over election cycles. This longitudinal set-up leads to a slight change in the models of representational linkages. To assess mass-to-elite communications, I specify a model as

$$elite\_position_{jt} = \alpha_0 + \alpha_1 supporter\_preference_{jt-1} + u_{jt}, \qquad (7.3)$$

[19] This changing voter sentiment was also apparent in the vote gains by the Danish People's Party. Having received 13 seats in the 179-seat parliament in 1998, its size increased considerably to 22 following the 2001 election, a level it has retained in subsequent votes. The party received 24 seats following the 2005 election, 25 in 2007, and 22 in 2011, indicating its support has plateaued at around 13 percent of the electorate.

[20] I thank Rune Stubager and Kasper Hansen for assistance with these data.

and for elite-to-mass flows, the specification is

$$supporter\_preference_{jt} = \beta_0 + \beta_1 elite\_position_{jt-1} + v_{jt}. \tag{7.4}$$

Equations 7.3 and 7.4 are the same as equations 7.1 and 7.2 with one important exception: t designates election year. The longitudinal nature of the election studies data makes it possible to examine the effect of previous supporter preferences on current elite positions (7.3) and previous elite positions on current supporter preferences (7.4). This provides us with an additional means to address endogeneity concerns in the study of representational linkages.

Mirroring the earlier discussion, I statistically examine these relationships for two issue-areas: the size of the public sector and the question of refugees. To measure attitudes toward the public sector, the DNES has since 1994 posed the following question: "The parties disagree how large the public sector should be. Some parties say we should cut public revenues and expenditures. Others say that we must face increasing public revenues and expenditures. Where about would you place [party]: cut deep, cut a little, stay the same, increase a little, increase strongly." This item is asked with reference to each of the main Danish parties. I take the survey mean for each party to create a measure of its position on social spending in the given election year. Since surveys also ask respondents to self-identify on the same five-point scale, I am able to pair party issue positions with mass opinion by using of party supporters, where supporter positions are taken as the average position among those identifying with the party.[21]

For preferences pertaining to immigration and refugees, I make use of a series of survey items, also appearing continuously in DNES surveys since 1994: "The parties disagree on how many refugees we can receive. Some think we receive far too many. Others say we easily can take more refugees. Where about would you place [party]: far fewer refugees, somewhat fewer, same as now, somewhat more, far more."[22] I use mean responses to these items to construct measures, on a five-point scale, for party elite positions on refugees such that low values are for preferences for fewer refugees and higher values are for allowing more. I again use responses to the self-placement versions of the

[21] The partisan identification item from the DNES is worded in English as "Do you consider yourself as, for example, a Social Democrat, a Conservative, a Liberal, a People's Socialist or something else, or don't you feel as an adherent of any party?" In order to capture as may identifiers as possible, those not initially identifying with a party receive the follow-up "All the same, is there a party which you feel you are closer to than to other parties?"

[22] The words "refugee" and "immigrant" function more or less as synonyms in the Danish debate and correlations between items using either word are usually high. I therefore take results of these analyses to indicate communication flows between parties and citizens on the issue of refugees, immigrants, and "foreigners" in general. This assumption is particularly innocuous given our interest in relative positions over time. I thank Rune Stubager for clarification on this point.

TABLE 7.3. *Assessing mass-to-elite communication flows, Denmark 1994–2011*

	Public expenditure	Refugees
Supporter preference$_{jt-1}$ (α_1)	0.34*	0.45***
	(0.17)	(0.12)
Constant (α_0)	2.60***	2.10***
	(0.58)	(0.32)
Adj R^2	0.90	0.98
N	30	30

Notes: Cells report ordinary least squares estimates with standard errors in parentheses. All models include party-fixed effects. *** $p < .01$, ** $p < .05$, * $p < .10$, two-tailed test.
Source: Danish National Election Study.

identically worded survey question, in tandem with the partisanship items, to construct measures of party supporters' preferences on the issue.

Both sets of analyses include measures for the six largest Danish Parties over this period, the Social Democrats, the Liberals, the Conservatives, the Radical Left, the Socialist People's Party, and the Danish People's Party.[23] Lagging the right-hand side variable one period means that model dependent variables are taken from five of the six post-election surveys, for a total of thirty observations, or six parties over five elections. Finally, models include party-fixed effects in order to isolate the effects produced by over-time change in party and supporter positions.

First consider the influence of supporter preferences on party elite positions, as reported in Table 7.3. Model 1 examines preferences on public spending. The estimate on $supporter\_preference_{jt-1}$ is 0.34, marginally statistically significant at $p = 0.06$. Additional analyses, however, show this estimate to be sensitive to the presence of the Danish People's Party.[24] Evidence of mass-to-elite linkages is far more robust on the issue of refugees, as shown in Model 2. Here, the effect of supporter preferences on elite positions is a substantively significant 0.45. For each one-unit shift by party identifiers, elite positions move by about one half of a unit. For example, if Social Democratic party *supporters* change their position from allowing "far more" refugees to preferring a status quo "stay the same" policy, the model predicts that Social Democratic party *elites* would change their views from a "far more" position to "somewhat

[23] The next largest party, the Red-Green Unity List, is considerably smaller and lacks sufficient number of identifiers in the dataset to construct the supporter mean position. That said, results reported here do not change substantively when smaller parties are included. Note that the Danish People's Party was created in 1995 as a faction of the Progress Party. Thus, for 1994 I use the Progress Party's elite and supporter positions.

[24] When the DF is removed, $\alpha_1 = 0.16$ with standard error 0.13.

TABLE 7.4. *Assessing elite-to-mass communication flows, Denmark 1994–2011*

	Public expenditure	Refugees
Elite position$_{jt-1}$ (β_1)	0.48***	0.39
	(0.15)	(0.25)
Constant (β_0)	1.65***	1.37
	(0.55)	(0.83)
Adj R^2	0.80	0.91
N	30	30

Notes: Cells report ordinary least squares estimates with standard errors in parentheses. All models include party-fixed effects. ** $p < .05$, * $p < .10$, two-tailed test.
Source: Danish National Election Study.

more." Thus, on the issue of immigration, Danish parties appear responsive to the views of their constituencies. On the issue of public spending, however, the capacity of supporters to influence the views of parties is weak.

Table 7.4 takes up the reverse relationship, examining the effect of elite positions from the previous election on the views of their supporters. The first model shows that elite views have a strong and precisely estimated influence on mass preferences on public spending. This result is robust to iteratively removing individual parties from the analysis.[25] The second model, however, shows no evidence for such an elite-to-mass communication flow with respect to the refugee issue. When it comes to such matters, mass preferences appear unaffected by the views of their preferred parties. Just as results displayed in Table 7.2 are the mirror image of those in Table 7.1, results reported in Table 7.4 for the case of Denmark are the opposite of those displayed in Table 7.3.

7.5. Discussion: Representational Linkages in Globalized Democracies

This chapter has sought to understand the direction and magnitude of representational linkages between elites and their supporters. The goal here is to consider the influence of a globalized economic context. In today's postindustrial societies, do vote-seeking political elites react to the preferences of their constituencies in the electorate by updating their own positions in kind? Or does globalization and notions of a limited room to maneuver serve to weaken

[25] Noting Bengtsson et al.'s (2014, 36) assertion that attitudes toward the public sector reflect left-right positions, I re-estimated Table 7.4 Model 1 using the more general 11-point left-right scale in place of the more specific public expenditures item. Results showed evidence for elite-to-mass linkages (β_1, estimated at 0.27, $p < 0.10$).

policymaker incentives to incorporate their supporters' wishes in their own stated positions on the issues of the day? And what of mass preferences? Are they formed independently from the views of elites themselves? The answers to these questions speak to the performance of representative democracy more generally. If linkages are mass-to-elite, then there is the possibility of a responsive political leadership. But if communications are predominantly elite-to-mass, we then have an opening for party elites to impart their views on a mass public eager to use elite messages to crystallize their preferences.

But the point is not that representation exists or that it does not. The general argument in this book is that forces associated with the opening up of national economies have altered mass politics. By complicating the structure of issue politics and reducing political control, signals from the world economy upset the bases of mass politics post industrial democracies. Placing limits on the policy room to maneuver and deepening bonds across what were once largely national markets shifts the bases of mass politics by reducing the salience of those economic issues that, for most of the postwar era, have defined the issue-bases of party identity and, therefore, political competition. Insomuch as these issues have declined in relative terms, other issues have played a larger role in affecting how voters decide and policymakers act. Globalization, I have argued, grants impetus to citizens to "balance demands" of politicians in one area against those in another.

With respect to representational linkages, this means that the strength and direction of these communication flows should vary as a consequence. Chapter 6 showed that the issue space in post industrial democracies is multidimensional. This chapter has shown how this dimensionality matters for the strength and direction of mass-elite communication flows. For those non-economic issues on which party competitors have yet to develop fully crystallized issue stances, a pair of data analyses provides evidence of a positive and robust mass-to-elite connection. When it comes to issues like immigration, refugees, international trade, and globalization, the positions of party elites are informed in part by the views of their supporters. However, for economics-based concerns, the record is mixed at best. On issues like left-right and tax-spend, political parties are as or more likely to shape public opinion then they are to respond to it. The reason, I suggest, is that politicians' credible claims of a limited policy capacity reduce incentives to do so. On these economic issues, the story is somewhat pessimistic from the perspective of a delegate model of democracy. These empirical findings are consistent with research on representational linkages across issue domains (Carmines and Stimson 1989; Hill and Hurley 1999) as well as with this book's broader argument on balancing demands in globalized economies.

I continue to examine the supply side of mass politics in the next chapter. I examine elite responsiveness to public opinion in greater detail by incorporating signals from the world economy directly. Reasoning from its influence on issue politics and policy capacity, the argument in Chapter 8 is that globalization weakens party responsiveness to the preferences of the median voter by constraining the policy space in which parties can maneuver.

Appendix 7.1. Instrumental Variables Regressions

TABLE 7.A1. *Instrumental variables regression for supporter positions*
Dependent variable: supporter position on issue scale

	Left-right	Tax-spend	Cultural issues	Immigration	Trade	Globalization
Age	0.27	0.19	0.07	0.15	0.08	0.12
	(0.08)	(0.06)	(0.05)	(0.07)	(0.04)	(0.04)
Female	3.29	1.47	2.26	1.02	0.79	−0.72
	(3.31)	(2.79)	(2.06)	(3.14)	(1.76)	(1.81)
Income	18.16	7.56	4.10	4.51	7.58	1.86
	(4.99)	(4.20)	(3.11)	(4.74)	(2.66)	(2.73)
Professional	7.20	1.64	2.98	−1.95	8.10	0.83
	(6.37)	(5.36)	(3.96)	(6.05)	(3.39)	(3.49)
Services	8.20	2.47	1.81	−3.89	8.45	4.76
	(6.95)	(5.86)	(4.33)	(6.61)	(3.70)	(3.81)
Manual	7.28	−0.66	7.46	−0.21	9.41	−1.34
	(9.78)	(8.23)	(6.09)	(9.29)	(5.21)	(5.36)
Political information	−2.81	0.47	0.80	−1.41	0.14	1.08
	(1.94)	(1.63)	(1.21)	(1.84)	(1.03)	(1.06)
Constant	−24.03	−11.53	−6.79	−2.62	-9.30	−1.65
	(8.77)	(7.38)	(5.45)	(8.32)	(4.67)	(4.80)
Country fixed effects	Yes	Yes	Yes	Yes	Yes	Yes
Joint significance instruments[a]	6.35 p=0.001	3.46 p=0.016	1.68 p=0.178	1.98 p=0.114	4.07 p=0.008	3.64 p=0.013
R2	0.73	0.75	0.86	0.74	0.81	0.86
N	35	35	35	35	35	35

Cells report OLS coefficients with robust standard errors reported in parentheses.
[a] Reports F-statistic to test for joint significance of all party-level covariates.

TABLE 7.A2. *Instrumental variables regression for party positions*
Dependent variable: party position on issue scale

	Left-right	Tax-spend	Cultural issues	Immigration	Trade	Globalization
Ln party age	−0.21	−0.10	−0.03	−0.36	0.05	−0.20
	(0.29)	(0.32)	(0.38)	(0.32)	(0.32)	(0.27)
Party vote	0.54	1.81	0.69	−1.65	6.73	5.44
share	(2.22)	(2.46)	(3.11)	(2.46)	(2.45)	(2.07)
Party family	−0.65	−0.56	0.74	1.92	−1.89	−0.93
Communist	(1.00)	(1.10)	(0.70)	(1.10)	(1.10)	(0.93)
Party family	1.27	0.70	0.82	3.34	−0.66	0.73
Social Dem.	(1.10)	(1.12)	(1.23)	(1.13)	(1.12)	(0.95)
Party family	3.69	3.12	0.58	4.24	0.17	3.05
Liberal	(0.97)	(1.08)	(1.26)	(1.08)	(1.26)	(0.91)
Party family	3.28	2.18	2.71	4.00	0.17	1.48
Chr. Dem	(1.14)	(1.26)	(1.47)	(1.26)	(1.26)	(1.07)
Party family	4.66	4.14	3.73	5.88	1.13	2.35
Conservative	(0.94)	(1.04)	(1.17)	(1.04)	(1.04)	(0.87)
Party family	3.87	3.73	3.13	5.79	0.80	0.57
ethnic	(1.08)	(1.20)	(1.35)	(1.20)	(1.19)	(1.01)
Constant	2.92	2.71	2.35	2.57	2.67	3.57
	(1.22)	(1.35)	(1.51)	(1.35)	(1.35)	(1.14)
Country fixed effects	Yes	Yes	Yes	Yes	Yes	Yes
Joint significance	12.40	9.02	4.33	8.02	6.33	10.73
instruments[a]	$p<0.001$	$p<0.001$	$p=0.006$	$p<0.001$	$p<0.001$	$p<0.001$
R2	0.87	0.82	0.80	0.84	0.80	0.86
N	35	35	35	35	35	35

Cells report OLS coefficients with robust standard errors reported in parentheses.
[a] Reports *F*-statistic to test for joint significance of all party-level covariates.

8

Credible Responses: Globalization, Political Parties, and the Supply Side

Representative democracy means that voters choose leaders to represent them in substantive terms (Pitkin 1967). In recent years, several studies have put this evaluative standard to the test. Many examine the extent to which political parties respond to public preferences. On this point, many find that parties in industrialized democracies are responsive to the public's preferences (Powell 2000; McDonald and Budge 2005; Soroka and Wlezien 2010). And while the penchant of representatives to respond to public demands may be shaped in part by electoral rules, party system polarization, party type, and so on, most studies conclude that, ultimately, democracy works.

Though edifying, this conclusion may ring hollow for citizens in many advanced capitalist democracies today. As then-Shadow Chancellor Harold Wilson's disparaging reference to financiers as "gnomes of Zurich," implies, politicians in western democracies both *in* and (as in Wilson's case) *out* of government have long struggled with how to balance public demands with the pressures of the market. In the 1970s, for instance, financial markets were hedging against sterling as the British economy fell into recession. Torn between fulfilling campaign promises to increase spending and requirements for receiving loans from the International Monetary Fund, the government chose the latter. In France, the Socialist Party was swept to power in the 1980s with a mandate for nationalization and redistribution. Yet less than two years later, President Mitterrand backtracked on the policies preferred by the public and embarked on a policy regime of *rigueur* to bring the economy in line with global capitalism. Since the 1970s and 1980s, market dependencies have multiplied and deepened. In Greece, a Socialist-led government in 2009 began a process of rolling back the generous welfare state protections and entitlements popular with most of the electorate. In Ireland, the implosion of an asset bubble has required politicians to become attentive to bond ratings – and arguably so against the wishes of the median voter. And in Italy, attempts to dismiss the government were initially stymied. At the time, observers credited Prime Minister Berlusconi's temporary survival not to the popularity of his policies with Italian voters but to fears of speculation by globally minded financial market actors. These examples and many others highlight instances where politicians face a choice between responding to voters and responding to markets.

The political implications of market dependence have not gone unnoticed. As discussed in the introduction to this book, the globalization literature is replete with studies of whether and how openness ties the government's hands. Many studies examine the consequences for policy outcomes, such as taxes, interest rates, or spending. Others pertain to economic performance outcomes, such as income levels, or to policy preferences. But few consider how globalization affects political parties.[1] As with Chapter 7, this chapter focuses on the supply side, or elite end, of mass politics. But while the previous chapter examined the extent to which party positions are informed by the preferences of their supporters (and vice-versa), this chapter is concerned with the dynamics of party behavior. Specifically, the objective is to examine globalization's consequences for parties' policy orientations, conceived here as changes in political parties' position-taking strategies.

I start from the premise that parties in democracies have many incentives to change their orientations to better approximate the views of the electorate. However, these incentives are altered in a context of increasingly globalized economies. On the one hand, exposure to global markets undermines elite incentives to align their policy statements with the preferences of the electorate. This is the case for those issue areas on which globalization is viewed as exerting downward pressure on national governments' policy room to maneuver. Therefore, in these economic areas – including the provision of jobs, income redistribution, regulation of industry, and so on – globalization weakens party responsiveness to mass preferences. At the same time, office-seeking parties will find a way to curry favor with the voters. To do so, they will be ever more attentive to public pressures in alternative, noneconomic policy domains. As introduced in Chapter 2, these areas include quality of life issues, education, healthcare, crime, level of public corruption, and the environment. In these areas, globalization-induced pressures on the policy room to maneuver are not readily apparent. Citizen demands appear not to be compromised by globalization in noneconomic domains. Chapter 3 showed that openness in fact *increases* popular sentiment for policies to address in these areas. If we extend this compensation or "balancing demands" reasoning, it follows that globalization matters for elite behavior, not only in economic

[1] Those that connect shifts in party policy positions to globalization include Haupt (2010), Adams, Haupt, and Stoll (2009), and Ward, Ezrow, and Dorussen (2011). Yet none of these studies examine whether and how global economic ties influence party responsiveness to changes in voter preferences.

areas, by weakening incentives to respond to public preferences, but also, in a compensatory fashion, in noneconomic policy domains, by increasing incentives to be *more* responsive.

In the next section, I develop this argument in more detail. I review the factors driving elite incentives to respond to public opinion and lay out the rationale for why the integration of national markets should affect these incentives. This leads to a pair of hypotheses. The Policy Constraints Hypothesis states that economic openness depresses party responsiveness to public opinion on economic issues. The Balancing Demands Hypothesis predicts that openness increases responsiveness on noneconomic issues. Hypotheses are tested on two data sets. The first set of analyses is performed on a cross-national panel of elections between 1977 and 2009. Statistical models examine the determinants of party position shifts in terms of the economic left-right dimension. The second set of analyses is performed on data from a single country, Sweden. The richness of the Swedish data makes it possible to test both research hypotheses, for economic and noneconomic policy domains alike. Evidence from both data sets shows that, in terms of economic policy preferences, parties in less open contexts are systematically more responsive to shifts in public opinion than parties competing in more open economies. Analyses conducted on the Swedish data further show that economic openness increases the responsiveness of parties to public opinion on noneconomic issues.

8.1. Globalization, Policy Constraints, and Party Responsiveness to Public Opinion

Since Downs (1957), research on political party competition has emphasized the primacy of the median voter's policy preference as the starting point for democratic representation. Regardless of whether they are motivated by votes, office, or policy, political parties have incentives to react to changes in the preferences of the median voter. The literature regularly finds parties to be vote-maximizing and center-oriented (e.g., Huber and Powell 1994; McDonald and Budge 2005; Powell 2000; and Stimson et al. 1995). Even in cases for which it does not constitute the end goal in itself, vote share maximization remains an efficient strategy for office- and policy-seeking parties. In the former case, increasing vote share *ceteris paribus* enhances the party's position for post-election coalition negotiations. In the latter case, a credible assumption is that, as a policy-seeking party's electoral strength increases, it gains leverage to pull the governing coalition's policy in its preferred direction.[2] In short, be it for reasons of power, policy, or both, elections provide parties with incentives to

[2] For example, Adams and Merrill (2009) show that parties in multiparty systems are motivated to adjust their policies in response to their beliefs about the median voter's position, rather than in response to the diversity of voter ideologies.

respond to changes in the preferences of the median voter. Party adherence to this strategy was apparent in western democracies over the postwar era. Whereas parties previously succeeded by appealing to the narrower wishes of their core constituencies, this so-called catch-all strategy prescribed broad-based appeals (Katz and Mair 1995). These appeals could largely be met by delivering policies in response to the preferences of the median voter.

The effectiveness of this median voter strategy, however, rests on a degree of separation between the domestic and world economies. With globalization, we get complications. The complications not only impinge on government policymakers, a point already made, but also affect the incentives of individual party actors. Consider parties' policy, office, and vote-based motivations in closed and open economy settings. In the former, each of these motivations provides parties with incentives to respond to voter preferences. But in the case of the latter, standard motivations of policy, office, and vote are no longer mutually reinforcing. Responding in kind to the preferences of the median voter may remain an effective vote maximizing strategy, but only in the short term or on a limited set of issues. Globalization requires party actors to look beyond the electorate's demands to consider the preferences of an expanded number of actors in a less certain policy environment. Economic interdependence prods political elites to seek the knowledge and expertise of market elites with respect to issues like the construction of bilateral investment treaties, the workings of financial market regulations, or shifts in the location of production centers. As a consequence, market integration increases the relevance of transnationally mobile market actors – credit rating agencies, pension fund managers, financial actors, and the like – and distracts political elites from their electorates.

The influence accorded to market actors might be of little consequence if they held preferences identical to those of the median voter, but the weight of the evidence suggests otherwise. Unelected technocrats, such as those governing central banks, tend to prefer policies that privilege stability over short-term growth. Multinational corporations identify taxes and regulation as the greatest perceived obstacles to operating in industrial economies (Batra, Kaufmann, and Stone 2004; Broz, Frieden, and Weymouth 2008). Mosley (2003) demonstrates that the investment behavior of financial market participants is guided by a narrow range of indicators, chiefly public deficits and inflation rates. Issues that many voters care about, such as public spending and labor market performance, are widely viewed by these actors as unimportant. In their cross-national study of mass and elite opinion, Sanders and Tóka (2013) find that while the public at large favors a more social model for Europe, economic elites prefer an environment structured by market competition. In short, while elections motivate parties to respond to shifts in the mean voter position, economic interdependence distracts parties from their electorates toward market actors, adding uncertainty to the political landscape. Hence, currying favor with markets likely weakens party incentives to respond to shifting public preferences.

The upshot is that globalization may reduce party incentives to the preferences of the median voter.

This should only be the case, however, for issues in those economic issue domains for which globalization places downward pressure on the policy room to maneuver. In regards to noneconomic issues, parties face no such pressure. Globalization does not preclude parties from incorporating voter preferences when developing or updating their positions on the issues. Rather, *parties make promises in the areas where these promises remain credible*. On economic matters, parties may be hesitant to react to the wishes of the median voter, preferring instead a strategy of "competing over less" (Blyth and Katz 2005), but on noneconomic issue areas, they should continue to align positions with the preferences of the electorate.

The use of different strategies for different issue areas was depicted by the policy supply and demand curves in Figure 2.3. In this simplified political economy, you will recall, there are two types of policy outputs, economic (m) and noneconomic (n). Although it pertains to the policy outputs of governments, the figure could be recast in terms of the positions taken by competing parties in these two policy domains. In closed economies, parties strive to respond to voter demands in both areas. In globalized economies, however, voters will come to expect less from their representatives in the economic domain. And elites, accordingly, react by reducing their responses to voter preferences. Voters, however, *shift demands* onto other, noneconomic issues to which they expect their representatives to respond. As the pressures increase for parties to deliver in these noneconomic areas, parties necessarily become more attentive to voter preferences and, as a consequence, more responsive in how they craft their policy positions.

In sum, the incentives parties face in globalized economies differ from those they confront in more sheltered ones. When the policy space has been compromised, incentives shift away from a median voter strategy (in relatively closed economies) and toward a strategy of reducing expectations about how much policy change is credible (in more globalized ones). Prompting this divergence from the wishes of the public is the constraint globalization exerts on credible policy action. Balancing demands reasoning, however, implies that globalization will have a different effect on party incentives in noneconomic areas. Given constraints in the economy, parties are limited in demonstrating their responsiveness to the public to other, noneconomic areas. This leads to a pair of hypotheses:

Policy Constraints Hypothesis: In economic issue domains, the responsiveness of political parties to the preferences of the median voter is weaker as national economies become more exposed to world markets.

Balancing Demands Hypothesis: In noneconomic issue domains, the responsiveness of political parties to the preferences of the median voter is greater as national economies become more exposed to world markets.

8.2. Party Position Shifts in Eighteen Countries, 1977–2009[3]

8.2.1. Model, Data and Measures

Hypotheses are evaluated by estimating a series of models examining the determinants of party behavior. If parties respond to the preferences of the mean (or median) voter, they should adjust their positions on the issues as a function of shifting voter preferences. Levels of globalization, however, should mediate this relationship. Accordingly we specify a basic model:

$$Party\ Shift_{jkt} = \beta_0 + \beta_1 Public\ Opinion\ Shift_{kt} + \beta_2 Globalization_{kt} \\ \beta_3 Public\ Opinion\ Shift_{kt} * Globalization_{kt} + \varepsilon_{jkt} \quad (8.1)$$

where $Party\ Shift_{jkt}$ is the change in the position of party j in country k at the current election t compared with its position at the previous election $t-1$. $Public\ Opinion\ Shift_{kt}$ is the change in the position of the mean voter in country k at election t compared with its position at election $t-1$. $Globalization_{kt}$ is a measure of country k's exposure to the international economy at time t, ε_{jkt} is a disturbance, and the βs are parameters to be estimated.[4]

The first analysis employs data from party statements and public opinion for eighteen countries in elections taking place between 1977 and 2009. Hypotheses require measures for party position shifts and public opinion shifts. In this analysis, both are measured using left-right placements. The left-right dimension is useful because it is the one issue dimension for which comparable data on parties and public opinion exist overtime and across a wide range of countries.[5] However, the left-right divide is also substantively appropriate as a proxy for party positions on economic matters like taxation, public spending, income redistribution, and regulation of industry. Economics-related issues have been shown to account for the key source of variation in the left-right super-dimension. This enables us to test the Policy Constraints Hypothesis on globalization and reduced party responsiveness on economic issue positions.

Measures of party positions are constructed using data from the Comparative Manifesto Project (CMP, Budge et al. 2001; Klingemann et al. 2006). The CMP data provide the only cross-national and, especially, longitudinal estimates of party policies.[6] I measure left-right positions using Laver and Budge's (1992)

[3] Section 8.2 draws on Ezrow and Hellwig (2014). I thank Lawrence Ezrow for allowing its inclusion.

[4] Note that while this specification assumes a particular causal pathway, implications of plausible alternative (endogenous) relationships are also considered in the online appendix.

[5] While the Comparative Manifesto Project data are flexible enough to construct measures of party positions in several different policy domains, the public opinion data – taken here mainly from the Eurobarometer survey series – are limited to the left-right scale.

[6] Measures produced from the CMP are generally consistent with those produced from other methods, such as those based on expert placements, citizen perceptions of parties' positions, and parliamentary voting analyses (Hearl 2001; McDonald and Mendes 2001; Laver et al. 2003; Marks 2007).

additive measure that combines party statements in twenty-six policy areas. The measure has a possible maximum value of +100 (extreme right) and a minimum of −100 (extreme left), which I rescale onto a 0–10 scale. The dependent variable, *Party Shift*$_{jkt}$, is measured as the change in party *j*'s position in country k from election $t-1$ to t.

The left-right position of the median voter comes from a public opinion survey item that asks respondents to place themselves on a left-right scale running from 1 (left) to 10 (right).[7] The mean of respondents' self-placements on the scale is taken as the expected value of the preferences of the median voter, given that the distribution of self-placements is generally unimodal and relatively symmetric. Data for most of the cases are from the Eurobarometer surveys: Austria, Belgium, Denmark, Finland, France, Germany, Greece, Ireland, Italy, Luxembourg, the Netherlands, Portugal, Spain, Sweden, and the United Kingdom.[8] I supplement this sample with public opinion data for three other established democracies, Australia, New Zealand, and Norway, for which appropriate measures on left-right self-placement exist.[9] Appendix 8.1 lists the elections and parties included in the analysis.[10]

For economic globalization, I rely mainly on a general measure of country exposure to the world economy, which we subsequently substitute with other, narrower, measures. The measure comes from the KOF Economic Globalization Index and combines two aspects of economic globalization: actual flows and the absence of restrictions (Dreher 2006). As previous chapters noted, public support for policy has been shown to be pro-cyclical. Accordingly, I control for the domestic economy by including the election-to-election change annual per capita growth rate from election, provided by the World Development Indicators database. Finally, I control for the role of parties' past behavior on their current policy shifts. Inclusion of *Party Shift*$_{jkt-1}$ on the right-hand-side accounts for the possibility of policy alternation (Budge 1994).[11]

[7] I recalibrated public opinion measures to fit on a 0–10 scale.

[8] The first elections covered by the Eurobarometer survey series were in 1973. For each, country data from these first ($t-1$) election years are used to create *Party Shift*$_{jkt}$ and *Public Opinion Shift*$_{kt}$ variables and thus do not make up an observation in the data set. The first election year included is 1976. Spain and Portugal were not included in the Eurobarometer surveys until 1981 and 1986, respectively, and Austria, Finland and Sweden were not until 1995.

[9] The Australian data come from the Australian Election Studies data from 1987 to 2004. The New Zealand data are from the New Zealand Elections Study program for elections from 1990 to 2002. The Norwegian data in the analysis are based on Norwegian Election Studies, 1973–2005. Because of a lack of recurrent public opinion surveys with the left-right placement measure, our sample does not include Canada, Japan, Switzerland, or the United States.

[10] Overall, shifts by elites and masses alike are fairly symmetrical. The measure for elite shifts, *Party Shift*$_{jkt}$, has an in-sample mean of −0.01 and a standard deviation of 0.78. Forty-five percent of the shifts are to the right, 43 percent to the left, and 12 percent exhibit no change. As for the mean voter, *Public Opinion Shift*$_{kt}$ has a mean of −0.02 with standard deviation 0.23; 57 percent leftward shifts, 42 percent rightward, and 1 percent no change

[11] The inclusion of *Party Shift*$_{jkt-1}$ also has implications for inference. Given the structure of the data, serially correlated errors within countries is also a possibility. The lagged dependent

8.2.2. Results

Models are estimated using OLS. By nesting parties within country-elections, the structure of the data set gives rise to two additional considerations that, if left unaddressed, could lead to biased and inefficient parameter estimates. I therefore take two precautions. First, to eliminate bias from unmeasured country-level factors that are not uncorrelated with the other explanatory variables, models are estimated with a full set of country-fixed effects. Second, it is likely that election-specific factors could affect all parties' policy shifts, and this would produce correlated errors among parties competing in the election. I address this concern by estimating heteroskedastic robust standard errors clustered by election period.

Table 8.1 reports model estimates. Model 1 reports results of estimating this interactive specification for all party shifts in our sample. The estimate on $PublicOpinionShift_{kt}$, which indicates the influence of public opinion on party shifts in a completely closed economy ($Globalization_{kt} = 0$), is positive but imprecisely estimated. The estimate on the interaction term, $PublicOpinionShift_{kt} * Globalization_{kt}$, though carrying the expected negative sign, is also not distinguishable from zero at conventional levels. These results do not provide definitive support for the claim that parties systematically respond to public opinion, nor do they show that globalization mediates the relationship between left-right shifts in public opinion and shifts in all parties' positions.

Model 1 results are nonetheless illuminating and suggest a more refined specification may be in order, particularly with respect to heterogeneity in party attributes. For certain parties, globalization may not matter to their strategies – or in the same way – as for others. In multiparty democracies, many of the smaller and newer parties exist to appeal to narrower segments of the electorate rather than to the mean voter, and many such parties have never had the responsibility of making actual policy. External constraints on policy room to maneuver, such as those arising from the world economy, are therefore less likely to play much role in the strategies of these parties. By contrast, for parties that have been saddled with the responsibility of governing, constraints should be palpable. It may be that only after being in a position of leadership do party actors come to grips with the need to balance the preferences of the electorate with those of other actors.[12]

variable addresses this possibility (Beck and Katz 2009). While some caution against inclusion of lagged dependent variables in fixed effects models (Plümper et al. 2005), including it in the specification yields more conservative estimates. Results are as strong or stronger when $Party\ Shift_{jkt-1}$ is omitted.

[12] For example, reflecting on the implications of never rising to governing party status until 1981, a member of the mainstream French Socialist Party noted that "after 23 years in the minority, [we] had lost contact with the reality of how to exercise power with pragmatism" (interview, Paris, March 3, 2003).

TABLE 8.1. *Multivariate analyses of parties' left-right policy shifts in eighteen democracies, 1977–2009*

	All Parties (1)	Governing experience[a] (2)	No Governing experience (3) (4)
Public opinion shift$_{kt}$	0.60	3.65**	−1.42
	(1.13)	(1.31)	(1.08)
Globalization$_{kt}$	−1.45*	−1.66	−1.47
	(0.84)	(1.03)	(0.93)
Public opinion shift$_{kt}$ x Globalization$_{kt}$	−0.77	−4.55**	1.75
	(1.44)	(1.60)	(1.39)
ΔGrowth$_{kt}$	0.03**	0.02	0.03**
	(0.01)	(0.02)	(0.01)
Party shift$_{jkt-1}$	−0.45**	−0.39**	−0.50**
	(0.05)	(0.07)	(0.07)
Constant	0.75	0.47	−0.14
	(0.60)	(0.91)	(0.81)
N	580	252	328
R^2	.23	.24	.29

Notes: Dependent variable is *Party shift*$_{jkt}$. Robust standard errors clustered by election are in parentheses. * p < .10, ** p < .05, two-tailed test (unconditional estimates). The estimates of public opinion and party position have been recalibrated to a 0–10 scale. The models are estimated with country-specific intercepts.

[a] "Governing experience" refers to those parties in the dataset that have experience as the largest partner in a governing coalition or have governed with a single party majority or minority.

I therefore examine whether globalization conditions the strategies of parties that have played a leading role in policy formation. By "leading role" I mean those parties with experience as the largest partner in a governing coalition or as the sole member of a single-party majority or minority government. Results of estimating the model on this subset of parties appear in the Model 2 of Table 8.1. Estimates reveal the importance of governing experience. The coefficient on *PublicOpinionShift*$_{kt}$ is positive and, now, precisely estimated (β_1 = 3.65).[13] The negative estimate on *PublicOpinionShift*$_{kt}$ * *Globalization*$_{kt}$ (−4.55) indicates that the positive effect of public opinion on party behavior decreases with exposure to the global economy. Thus, for parties having experienced the rigors of governing, their tendency to be responsive to the mean voter is tempered by the broader economic environment. For completeness, Model 3 results show that parties that have not governed are neither

[13] This means that in the hypothetical case of a closed economy a one unit shift in the mean voter's left-right position is predicted to cause the party's position to shift over three units in the same direction.

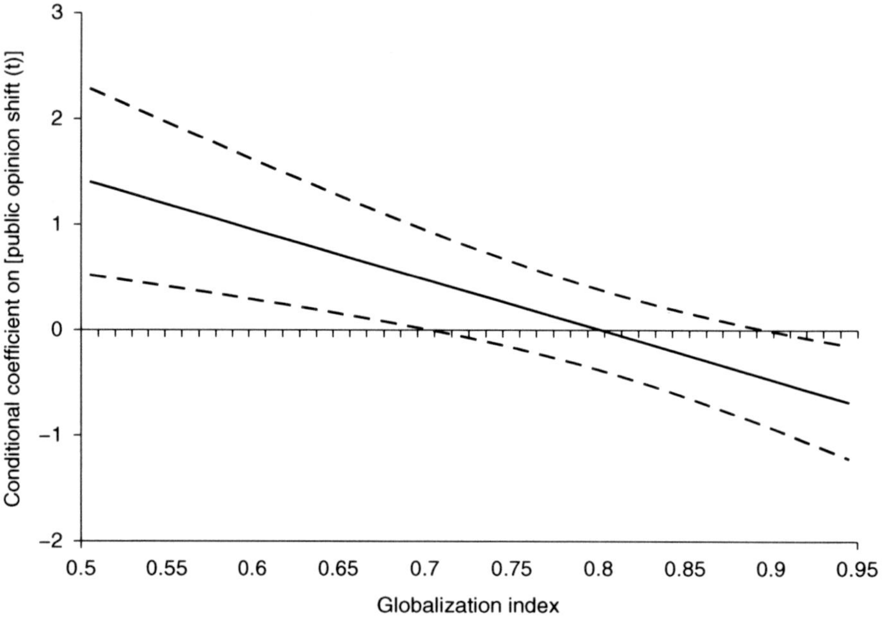

FIGURE 8.1. Effect of public opinion shift on party shift conditional on economic globalization for parties with governing experience.

Notes: Figure charts the estimated coefficient on public opinion shift on party position shifts over values of the economic globalization index, as provided by Table 8.1 Model 2 estimates. The globalization index is rescaled from 0–100 to 0–1. Dashed lines report 90 percent confidence intervals.

responsive to public opinion nor are their position-taking strategies affected by globalization.

Figure 8.1 uses estimates from Model 2 to chart the marginal effects of public opinion shifts on party shift across the sample range of values for economic globalization. The negative slope indicates that, as globalization increases, the estimate of party responsiveness to the mean voter position decreases. The coefficient on $PublicOpinionShift_{kt}$ attains statistical significance when $Globalization_{kt}$ is below 0.70 on the 0–1 index. In the remainder of cases – those more exposed to trade, capital flows and employing more liberal policies – our model estimates that changes in public opinion, as represented by the mean voter, have no statistically significant influence on party shifts.

Regression estimates shed light on particular country experiences. Take France, a country that has grappled considerably with the wider political effects of globalization. In 1988, the French economy was relatively closed from international trade and capital flows. At this time, France's KOF Globalization index equaled 0.57. At such a level of globalization, in terms of Model 2 estimates, the conditional coefficient on the $PublicOpinionShift_{kt}$ variable is 1.06

([(1*3.65)–(.57*4.55)] = +1.06), suggesting a near one-to-one relationship between median voter shifts and party shifts. By the time of the 2007 election, the economy had opened up considerably, rating a 0.75 on the globalization index. At this level of integration, the model predicts no systematic relationship between shifts in public opinion and shifts in the positions of such parties with governing experience.

In sum, analyses of data from eighteen countries for more than thirty years shows that globalization reduces the responsiveness of the main, experienced party competitors to public opinion on left-right, economics-oriented issues. This supports the Policy Constraints Hypothesis. The interested reader is referred to Appendix 8.2, which discusses several additional analyses that were performed to establish the robustness of this finding. These results demonstrate that the main finding is not sensitive to alternative specifications or measures.

8.3. Party Position Shifts in Sweden, 1976–2010

We have seen that economic globalization has a robust *negative* impact on party responsiveness to the preferences of the mean voter in advanced capitalist democracies – at least with respect to the left-right divide. This appears as a troubling collateral political effect attached to any welfare gains associated with liberal market economies. Does this imply that parties will eventually cease crafting policies to respond to the median voter in favor of doing whatever it takes to "respond" to more mobile market actors? Perhaps. But before drawing this conclusion, we should consider other issues on which parties take positions. As we have seen, globalization exerts heterogeneous effects on mass politics, and these effects are shaped by issue domain. If in some issue areas market integration reduces popular demands, responsibility attributions, or policy-based voting, mass publics compensate by allotting greater importance to other issues. This section examines the logic of this compensational reasoning for political elites through a test of the Balancing Demands Hypothesis, which states that in noneconomic issue domains, party responsiveness to the preferences of median voter *increases* with exposure to world markets.

Assessing this claim requires information on the preferences of parties and voters on a noneconomic dimension. For parties, this requirement poses no particular barrier. The flexibility of the comparative manifesto data makes it possible to construct longitudinal measures of parties' positions on a range of issues, economic and noneconomic alike (e.g., Tavits 2007). However, construction of mass preferences on noneconomic matters presents a challenge. Since survey items tapping public attitudes on noneconomic issues appear infrequently, it is difficult to match party shifts with appropriate indicators of public opinion over a large set of democracies.[14] It is, however, possible to examine elite

[14] The Eurobarometer survey series does allow for longitudinal analysis of opinions on one area: European integration (Carrubba 2001; Steenbergen et al. 2007). I do not conduct such

responsiveness to the mean voter on such issues within a single national context. This is the approach taken here. This is appropriate because the theories tested in this chapter deal with over-time changes – that is the effect of changing exposure to the world economy on changes in party behavior.

The case is Sweden from 1976 to 2010. The analysis is made possible by the presence of high quality public opinion data. But the Swedish case is appropriate for reasons apart from data considerations. In terms of politics, Sweden's multiparty parliamentary democracy includes a range of party actors reflective of the dominant party families existing in most European democracies (Bengtsson et al. 2014). In terms of economics, Sweden has long been an active player in the international economy. Indeed, trade politics and the issue of the tariff sharply divided Swedish constituencies as far back as the nineteenth century (Gourevitch 1986). In spite of this history and the relatively small size of its domestic economy, Sweden ranks as a middling case in terms of its exposure flows from abroad. Relative to other advanced industrial economies of Europe, Japan, and North America, Sweden in the 1970s ranked somewhat below the mean in terms of exposure to trade, capital markets, and foreign investment. By the 2000s, Sweden rated somewhat above average on these terms. So while no single case is truly representative, Sweden from the 1970s to 2010 arguably comes close.

8.3.1. Data and Measures

The empirical analysis proceeds similarly to the pooled analysis in examining the impact of public opinion on party behavior. The difference is, for the Swedish case, I examine party responsiveness to public opinion on two policy dimensions, an economic dimension and a noneconomic dimension. I again use the left-right scale as a proxy for preferences over economic policy. As in many other countries, left-right placements align closely with more expressly economic considerations in Sweden. For example, evidence from surveys of party experts finds that positions on the tax-spend issue and on the deregulation issue are both highly correlated with locations on the left-right continuum positions.[15] For party positions, I again use the additive left-right measure from the comparative manifesto project dataset (Laver and Budge 1992). And for mean voter positions I again use mean values of respondent self-placements on the 0–10 left-right scale. Survey data are provided by the Swedish National Election Studies (SNES).[16]

analyses, however, since it is not clear whether the issue of Europe is "economic" or "social," or, as Bakker et al. (2012) argue, a distinct dimension unto itself. And, in any event, the issue of Europeanization is not easily extracted from globalization more broadly. Apart from European integration, the one use of Eurobarometer series data to construct an index of mass positions on noneconomic policies is Tavits (2007). Data availability, however, restrict her analyses to a limited number of surveys from the 1980s.

[15] Analysis of party expert data from Benoit and Laver (2006) shows that for both tax-spend and deregulation, Pearson correlations with left-right are +0.98.

[16] I thank Henrik Oscarsson, Per Oleskog Tryggvasan, and Michele Coldrey for assistance with data collection. Neither they nor the Swedish National Election Studies bears responsibility for the findings reported here.

For noneconomic areas, I use items held in common from the CMP codes and SNES surveys to construct similar issue-based indices. Noneconomic policy items selected include immigration, defense, pornography, foreign aid, the environment, technology, Christian values, technology, law and order, family, Swedish values, and refugees. The measure for party positions is constructed by adopting the Laver-Budge additive index to this set of noneconomic areas. For the mean voter's position on noneconomic policies, I create a summary index from a large set of issue preference items included in the SNES surveys. I first catalogued the available items in each survey. I then selected items for inclusion in a noneconomic policy preferences index based on the frequency of their appearance in the surveys. This produced a list of eleven survey items. Items are coded such that high values indicate more conservative noneconomic positions, and low values more liberal ones.[17] Items were standardized on a 0–1 scale and were combined additively. The resulting index was rescaled from 0 to 10 to match up to the party data. Finally, taking the mean across all respondent values on the scale for a given year provides us with the position of the mean voter at time *t*. Appendix 8.3 provides more information on the procedures and items used to create the noneconomic measures for parties and voters.

Figure 8.2 displays the Swedish mean voter position for the left-right and noneconomic dimensions from 1976 to 2010. With respect to left-right, we observe a sharp but temporary shift to the right in 1991, the year in which a four-party center-right coalition government rose to power after a decade of center-left governments. The figure also captures a growing liberalization of Swedish attitudes on noneconomic and cultural areas, beginning in 1998 and continuing through 2010. To what extent do parties respond in kind to these shifts in mass sentiment? And does globalization condition the response of Sweden's political parties to public opinion?

8.3.2. Results

To answer these questions, we re-estimate the model described in equation 8.1 using the Swedish data. Table 8.2 displays results. I again limit the sample to those parties with governing experience.[18] Since factors specific to each election could affect all parties' policy shifts, models are estimated with heteroskedastic

[17] Not all items were asked in all surveys; missing data were filled in via linear regression. As an example, the item on attitudes toward pornography was not asked in the 1988 election survey. Using a dataset that pooled across the ten election surveys, I regressed the pornography item (which was available in the remaining ten surveys) on a set of eleven other policy items, including left-right self-placement. From this regression I retained out of sample linear predictions, which I then used to replace the missing values for 1988. The effects of any errors or excessive uncertainty produced by such procedure are likely ameliorated by summing respondents and taking mean values as the final measure of *Public opinion noneconomic shift* (see Table 8.2).

[18] For Sweden, parties with governing experience include the Social Democrats, the Liberal People's Party, the Center Party, and the Moderates. However, restricting the analyses to these parties has no substantive bearing on the results. Estimates are similar to those reported in Table 8.2 when we estimate the model for all parties.

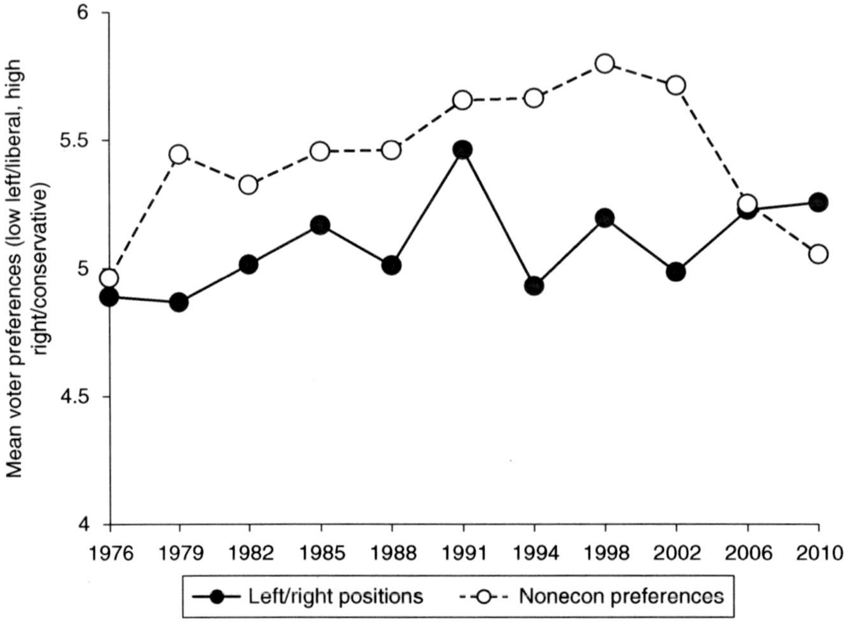

FIGURE 8.2. Mean voter positions on left-right and noneconomic policy dimensions, Sweden 1976–2010.

Note: Figure displays mean voter positions on left-right and noneconomic policy dimensions. Higher values reflect more right-leaning or conservative positions; lower values are more left/liberal.

Source: Swedish National Election Studies, 1976–2010.

robust standard errors clustered by election period. The first pair of models examines the conditioning effects of the KOF general economic globalization index on shifts in party policy positions. Model 1 looks at left-right shifts. As with the analyses of the eighteen-country pooled model in Table 8.1, we find that the coefficient estimate on *Public opinion shift*$_t$ is positive while the estimate on its interaction with *Globalization*$_t$ is negative; the policy statements of Swedish parties respond in kind to the shifting views of the mean voter – conveyed in terms of left-right ideology – but this responsiveness is tempered by the extent to which the Swedish economy is exposed to (or dependent on) global markets. Figure 8.3 graphs the conditional effects across the range of the globalization index. It shows that the effect of public opinion shifts on party left-right shifts is positive and precisely estimated, as long as globalization levels are sufficiently low. Once globalization levels exceed the in-sample mean value, this effect is no longer statistically significant. This conditional finding is consistent with the Policy Constraints Hypothesis.[19]

[19] Substantive results do not change when election year fixed effects are included.

TABLE 8.2. *Multivariate analyses of Swedish parties' left-right and noneconomic policy shifts, 1976–2010*

Parties with governing experience[a]

Dependent variable:	**Left-right** (1)	**Noneconomic** (2)
Public opinion shift$_t$	17.14**	–1.67
	(6.78)	(1.99)
Globalization index$_t$	–0.24	0.26
	(0.96)	(1.41)
Public opinion shift$_t$ x Globalization index$_t$	–21.01**	1.95
	(8.29)	(2.34)
ΔGrowth$_t$	0.05**	0.04**
	(0.02)	(0.01)
Party shift$_{jt-1}$	–0.17	–0.32**
	(0.21)	(0.13)
Constant	0.12	–0.21
	(0.65)	(1.17)
N	35	35
R^2	.25	.19

Notes: Dependent variable is *left-right shift$_{jt}$* for Model 1 and *Noneconomic shift$_{jt}$* for Model 2. Robust standard errors clustered by election are in parentheses. * p < .10, ** p < .05, two-tailed test (unconditional estimates). The estimates of public opinion and party position have been recalibrated to a 0–10 scale.

[a] "Governing experience" refers to those parties that have experience as the largest partner in a governing coalition or have governed with a single party majority or minority. For Sweden, this is the Social Democrats and the Center Party (entire sample), the Liberal People's Party (from 1979), and the Moderates (from 1994).

Model 2 in Table 8.2 models noneconomic shifts. The estimate on the interaction term, *Public opinion shift$_t$ x Globalization$_t$*, carries a positive sign. This appears in line with the prediction of the Balancing Demands Hypothesis; that is, mean-voter responsiveness in noneconomic issue domains is sharpened in more globalized political economies. The precision of the estimate, however, is poor. The unconditional parameter estimate of 1.95 is smaller than its unconditional standard error of 2.34. And examination of the conditional effects shows parties are not responsive to shifts in mean-voter preferences on the noneconomic dimension, regardless of degree of globalization.

Together, the pair of models reported in Table 8.2 demonstrates where globalization matters and where it does not with respect to party strategies. When it comes to the position-taking behavior on the economic left-right dimension, Swedish parties are less responsive to mean voter shifts when the economy has been more globalized. Globalization, however, has no such influence on party

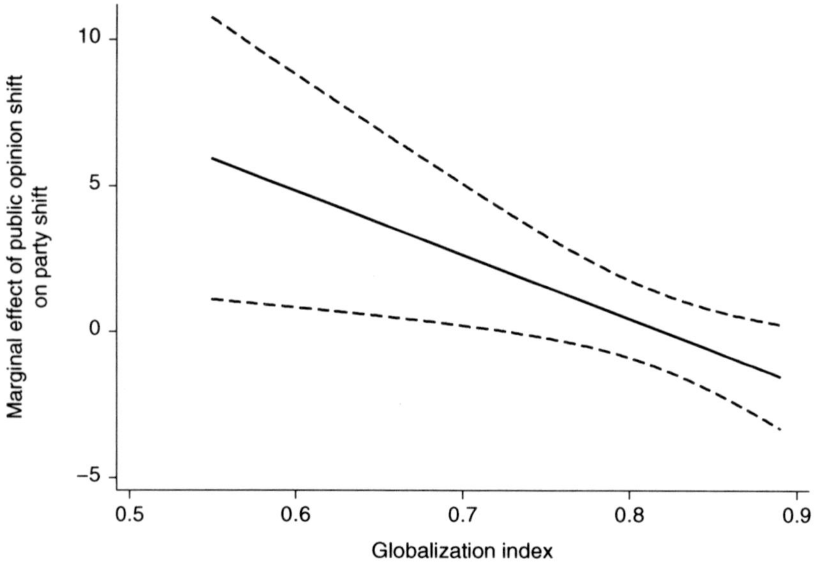

FIGURE 8.3. Effect of left-right public opinion shift on left-right party shift conditional on economic globalization, Sweden 1976–2010.

Notes: Figure charts the estimated coefficient on public opinion shift on party position shifts on the left-right dimension over values of the economic globalization index, as provided by Table 8.2 Model 1 estimates. The globalization index is rescaled from 0–100 to 0–1. Dashed lines report 90 percent confidence intervals.

behavior on noneconomic issues, as gauged by evidence from the Swedish National Election Studies data. To probe these relationships further, I briefly consider different components of economic globalization, provided by parsing the general KOF index into objective flows (trade and capital movements) and policies (the *removal* of restrictions on trade and capital movements). Figure 8.4 displays these series for Sweden. In terms of flows, the opening of the Swedish economy over the past forty years was, compared to many of its neighbors, fairly constant in its growth. Policy adaptation, however, proceeded in less monotonic fashion. Under the aegis of the Rehn-Meidner model of economic management, the Swedish economy through the 1970s was fairly regulated. Such stasis reflected the stable policy regime over much of the 1970s (Figure 8.4 grey line). During the 1980s, however, Sweden undertook a series of liberalizing reforms as part of the Social Democratic government's "Third Road" (*den tredje vägen*) strategy, an important component of which was a 16 percent devaluation aimed to encourage international competitiveness. Finally, the figure shows that by the end of the century, limits on liberalizing tendencies had set in.

These components of globalization – flows and policies – may bear differently on party responsiveness to public opinion. Models reported in Table 8.3

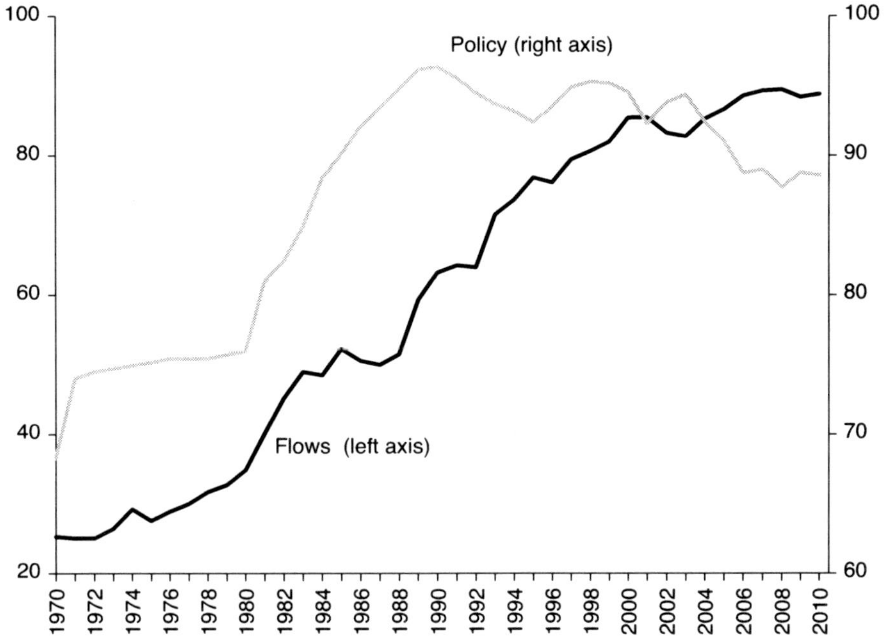

FIGURE 8.4. Economic globalization trends, Sweden 1970–2010.
Notes: Graph reports values on the KOF Economic Globalization index for Sweden 1970–2010. Index parsed into flows (left-hand axis) and policy (right-hand axis) components.

examine whether this is the case. Models 1 and 2 examine the conditioning effects of flows for left-right and noneconomic shifts, respectively. The results are substantively similar to those reported in Table 8.2. Models 3 and 4 consider the effects of policy liberalization. Estimates show that policy liberalization has a strong conditioning positive effect on party responsiveness in the noneconomic policy arena (see also Figure 8.5). The more liberal the policies adopted by Swedish governments, the more responsive parties become in the non-material, or noneconomic, domain.

The Swedish case study suggests that parties do, it turns out, respond to the preferences of the mean voter, even when faced with a reduced room to maneuver. However, their incentives to do so depend in part on ties to the world economy. When the economy is sheltered from international business cycles, party behavior is guided by the public's views on economic matters. But when susceptibility toward the world economy is greater, parties become less responsive to citizen preferences on matters economic and, in compensating fashion, more attentive to the electorate's preferences on other, noneconomic issues. Results from the analysis of the Swedish case nonetheless support the predictions of the Balancing Demands Hypothesis. In noneconomic issue domains,

TABLE 8.3. *Multivariate analyses of Swedish parties' left-right and noneconomic policy shifts, 1976–2010*

Parties with governing experience[a], alternative globalization indicators

Dependent variable:	**Left-right (1)**	**Noneconomic (2)**	**Left-right (3)**	**Noneconomic (4)**
Public opinion shift	8.32**	–0.79	–16.33	–16.14**
	(3.14)	(1.21)	(23.37)	(4.83)
Globalization flows$_t$	–0.22	0.44		
	(0.59)	(0.99)		
Public opinion shift$_t$ x Globalization flows$_t$	–11.87**	1.11		
	(4.54)	(1.36)		
Globalization policy$_t$			–0.40	–4.59**
			(2.10)	(1.97)
Public opinion shift$_t$ x Globalization policy$_t$			17.13	18.42**
			(25.10)	(5.61)
ΔGrowth$_t$	0.05**	0.04**	0.04	0.06**
	(0.02)	(0.01)	(0.02)	(0.01)
Party shift$_{jt-1}$	–0.19	–0.33**	–0.35	–0.25*
	(0.22)	(0.14)	(1.84)	(0.12)
Constant	0.10	–0.31	0.35	4.17*
	(0.30)	(0.74)	(1.84)	(1.74)
N	35	35	35	35
R^2	.30	.20	.10	.29

Notes: Dependent variable is *Left-right shift$_{jt}$* for Models 1 and 3 and *Noneconomic shift$_{jt}$* for Models 2 and 4. Robust standard errors clustered by election are in parentheses. * $p < .10$, ** $p < .05$, two-tailed test (unconditional estimates). The estimates of public opinion and party position have been recalibrated to a 0–10 scale.

[a] "Governing experience" refers to those parties that have experience as the largest partner in a governing coalition or have governed with a single party majority or minority. For Sweden, this is the Social Democrats and the Center Party (entire sample), the Liberal People's Party (from 1979), and the Moderates (from 1994).

political parties become more attentive to the preferences of the median voter as national economies become more exposed to world markets.

8.4. Globalization and the Supply Side of Mass Politics

For some time now, the political consequences of ever-closer degrees of economic interdependence have held the interest of researchers and policymakers. Much research has addressed whether national governments have the capacity for policy action. Initial concerns about the race-to-the-bottom in tax competition and public spending levels gave way to more optimistic arguments suggesting that, despite globalization, policymakers can still possess a measure of discretionary control. More recently, the central questions addressed in the IPE/

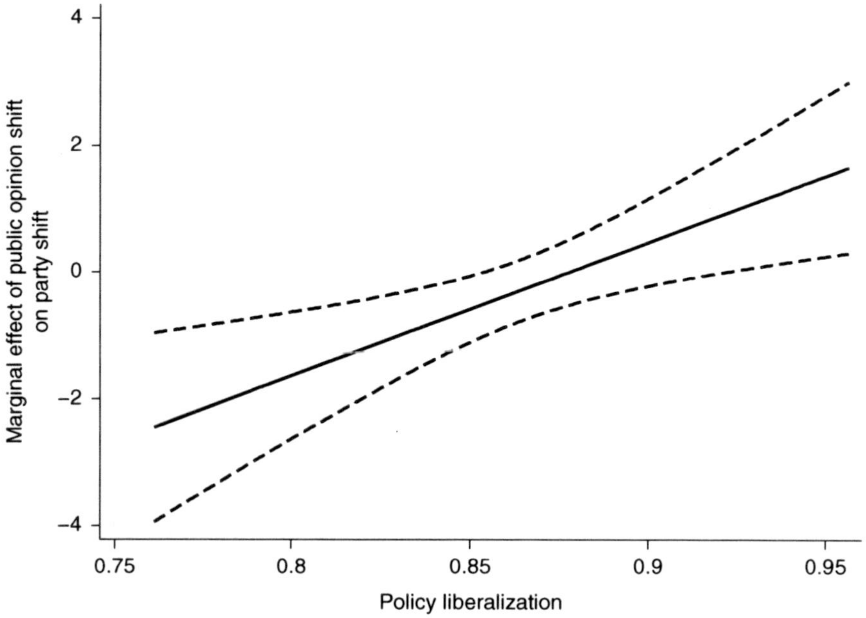

FIGURE 8.5. Effect of noneconomic public opinion shift on noneconomic party shift conditional on policy liberalization, Sweden 1976–2010.

Notes: Figure charts the estimated coefficient on public opinion shift on party position shifts in the noneconomic policy dimension over values of the economic globalization policy index, as provided by Table 8.3 Model 4 estimates. The index is rescaled from 0–100 to 0–1. Dashed lines report 90 percent confidence intervals.

CPE literature have migrated from debates about policy divergence/convergence toward efforts to explain the diffusion of economic liberalism (Simmons and Elkins 2004; Simmons et al. 2006). While earlier research viewed the task of managing globalization as one of working in tandem with domestic interests to respond to exogenous forces, recent research on diffusion, networks, and strategic interaction places government choices at the center of the analysis. This chapter shares with the diffusion literature an interest in actor choices under the globalization of economic liberalism. But rather than probing the bases of government reform decisions, I have examined the effects of globalization on party actors competing for office. While I share with the diffusion literature an interest in actor motivations, my emphasis is not on how individual governments emulate, compete with, or learn from others but instead is on how signals from the world economy shape parties' incentives and behavior.

Parties have incentives to respond to public opinion, be it for reasons of office, policy, or votes. Through an examination of party shifts and mean voter preferences, results reported in this chapter support this conclusion, if the economy is sheltered from world markets. As globalization increases, things get more complicated. With respect to the kind of distributional and regulatory issues that have shaped politics in western democracies for much of the postwar era, globalization weakens party-voter ties. As countries become integrated into world markets, globalization's constraining influence on domestic politics is such that party representatives appear less and less responsive to citizen preferences. Yet all hope for representative democracy is not lost. Globalization's adverse influence on party responsiveness is not present across all issues over which parties compete. Evidence from the Swedish case study suggests that with globalization parties become not less but more attentive to voter preferences on noneconomic areas. As in previous chapters on mass policy preferences, political accountability, issue voting, and political communications, findings reported in this chapter underline the importance of issue heterogeneity of the policy room to maneuver for understanding how economic globalization is altering mass politics.

Appendix 8.1. Countries, Elections, and Parties Included in Table 8.1

Country	Election(s) at *t*	Parties
Australia	1990, 1993, 1996, 1998, 2001, 2004, 2007	Labor Party (ALP), Democrats (AD), Liberal Party, (LPA), National Party (NPA), Greens
Austria	1999, 2003, 2006, 2008	Austrian Peoples' Party (OVP), Freedom Movement (VdU/FPO), Social Democratic Party (SPO), Green Alternative (GA), Bundnis Zukunft Ostrerreich
Belgium	1978, 1979, 1981, 1985, 1987, 1991, 1995, 1999, 2003, 2007	Christian Social Party (PSC), Christian People's Party (CVP), Liberal Reformation Party (PRL), Liberal Reformation Party – Francophone Democratic Front (PRL-FDF), Flemish Liberals and Democrats (VLD), Francophone Socialist Party (PS), AGALEV, ECOLA, Flemish Block (VB)
Denmark	1979, 1981, 1984 1987, 1988, 1990, 1994, 1998, 2001, 2005, 2007	Conservative People's Party (KF), Radical Party (RV), Liberals (V), Social Democratic Party (SD), Center Democrats (CD), Socialist People's Party (SF), Progress Party (FP), Red-Green Unity List (EL)
Finland	1999, 2003, 2007	National Rally (KOK), Finnish Center (KESK), Finnish Social Democrats (SSDP), Left Wing Alliance (VL), Green Union (VL), Christian Democrats, True Finns, Swedish People's Party

Country	Election(s) at *t*	Parties
France	1978, 1981, 1986, 1988, 1993, 1997, 2002, 2007	Rally for the Republic / Union for a Popular Movement (RPR / UMP), Union for French Democracy (UDF), Socialist Party (PS), French Communist Party (PCF), National Front (FN)
Germany	1980, 1983, 1987, 1990, 1994, 1998, 2002, 2005, 2009	Christian Democratic Party/Christian Social Union (CDU/CSU), Free Democratic Party (FDP), Social Democratic Party (SDP), Party of German Socialism (PDS) / the Left Party
Greece	1985, 1989 (Jun), 1989 (Nov), 1990, 1993, 1996, 2000	New Democracy (ND), Panhellenic Socialist Movement (PASOK), Communist Party of Greece (KKE), Progressive Left Coalition (SAP)
Ireland	1977, 1981, 1982 (Feb), 1982 (Nov), 1987, 1989, 1992, 1997, 2002, 2007	Fianna Fail, Fine Gail, Progressive Democrats (PD), Labour Party (LP), Greens, Sinn Fein
Italy	1979, 1983, 1987, 1992, 1994, 1996, 2001, 2006, 2008	Italian Social Movement (AN), Northern League (LN), Go Italy (FI), Italian People's Party (PPI), Republican Party (PRI), Italian Democratic Socialist Party (PSDI), Socialist Party (PSI), Newly Founded Communists (RC), Democrats of the Left (DS)
Luxembourg	1984, 1989, 1994, 1999, 2004, 2009	Christian Social People's Party (PCS/CSV), Patriotic and Democratic Group (PD/DP), Socialist Workers' Party (POSL/LSAP), Communist Party (PCL/KPL)
Netherlands	1981, 1982, 1986, 1989, 1994, 1998, 2002, 2003, 2006	Christian Democratic Appeal (CDA), People's Party for Freedom and Democracy (VVD), Labour Party (PvdA), Democrats 66 (D'66), Green Left (GL), Christian Union (CU), List Pim Fortuyn (LPF)
New Zealand	1993, 1996, 1999, 2002, 2005, 2008	Labour Party, Alliance, ACT, National Party (NP), New Zealand First Party (NZFP), Greens, Maori
Norway	1989, 1993, 1997, 2001[20]	Left Socialists (SV), Labour (DNA), Liberals (V), Christian People's Party (KrF), Conservatives, Centre Party (SP), Progress Party (FrP)
Portugal	1987, 1991, 1995, 1999, 2002, 2005	Center Social Democrats (CDS/PP), Popular Democrat Party (PPD/PSD), Portuguese Socialist Party (PSP), Unified Democratic Coalition (CDU), Left Bloc (BE)

[20] Manifesto codes are missing for the 2005 Norwegian election.

Country	Election(s) at *t*	Parties
Spain	1989, 1993, 1996, 1996, 2000, 2004, 2008	Popular Alliance (AP/PP), Convergence and Union (CiU), Spanish Socialist Workers' Party (PSOE), Communist Party (IU), Basque National Party, Catalan Re-public, Canarian Coalition, Galego Nationalist Bloc
Sweden	2002, 2006	Moderate Coalition Party (MSP), Christian Democratic Community Party (KdS), People's Party (FP), Center Party (CP), Social Democratic Labour Party (SdsP), Communist Party (VP), Green Party
United Kingdom	1983, 1987, 1992, 1997, 2001, 2005	Conservative Party, Liberal Democrats (LD), Labour, Scottish Nationalist Party, Democratic Unionist Party, Ulster Unionist Party, Sinn Fein

Note: Measuring shifts in party and public opinion requires data from the current election *t* and the previous election *t–1*. Election dates listed here pertain to time *t* only.
Sources: Eurobarometer trendfile (Schmitt and Scholz 2005), supplemented with data from individual Eurobarometer surveys and from the Australian Election Studies, New Zealand Election Studies, and Norwegian Election Studies (Valen et al. 2010). The Norwegian data are based on "Norwegian Election Studies, 1973–2005." The survey was financed by The Research Council of Norway. Data are provided by Henry Valen, Bernt Aadral, Institute for Social Research (ISF) and Statistics Norway (SSB) and prepared and made available by Norwegian Social Science Data Services (NSD). Henry Valen, Bernt Aardal, ISF, SSB, and NSD are not responsible for the analysis/interpretation of the data presented here.

Appendix 8.2. Sensitivity Analyses for the Cross-National Study of Party left-right Shifts

I explored several alternative contingencies and measures to establish the robustness of our statistical results. One distinction that has received much attention is the behavior of niche parties, that is, parties that limit their issue appeals and do not face a trade-off between advocating their preferred policy beliefs and moderating policies to maximize electoral support (Adams et al. 2006; Meguid 2008). It may be that the governing experience effect shown in Table 8.1 is picking up a "mainstream" effect, that is, globalization may only affect parties belonging to the Social Democratic, Conservative, Christian Democratic, or Liberal party families.[21] I examine this conjecture by estimating

[21] Mainstream and governing experience classifications are not synonymous; while nearly all parties with executive experience are mainstream, 48 percent of mainstream parties in our sample have no experience heading up governments.

models to test whether the parameters on the interaction term β_3 in equation 8.1, is statistically different for mainstream and niche parties. Unlike the governing experience distinction, the mainstream-niche distinction is found to have no effect. I also examined whether results were driven by left- and right-of-center parties and by centrists relative to extremist parties. None of these distinctions matter to the degree that governing experience does.[22] These non-findings bolster the argument that politicians who have headed governments are more distracted by market integration than politicians of other parties.

Second, I consider the direct effects of globalization on party behavior. We might expect increasing globalization to shift parties to the right, to more neoliberal policy positions. A definitive test of this claim would require us to incorporate measures of economic elites' preferences into our model. Unfortunately, such data are unavailable for a sufficient number of cases. But it is possible to examine whether increasing globalization influences party shifts directly. Model 1 in Table 8.A1 presents these results by including the inter-election shift in globalization on the right-hand side ($\Delta Globalization_{kt}$). The parameter estimate is positive, indicating that parties tend to shift to the right when market integration increases. Substantive results, however, remain unchanged. This result is consistent with the argument that if increasing globalization motivates political elites to place greater weight on economic elites' policy preferences at the expense of the voters', and if the preferences of economic elites are to the right of the mass public, then increasing globalization should motivate parties to shift to the right.

Third, I consider alternative globalization indicators. Different components of globalization may have different effects on political outcomes. Is this the case for party responsiveness? To investigate this issue, I re-estimated Table 8.1 Model 2 separating out Dreher's indices of flows and restrictions. *Flows* incorporate information on imports and exports of goods and services, foreign direct investment, portfolio investment, and income payments to foreign nationals. *Restrictions* includes information on hidden import barriers, mean tariff rates, import and export duties and other taxes on international trade, and capital account restrictions.[23] Models 2 and 3 of Table 8.A1 report estimates for flows and restrictions. Substituting these series for the more general globalization measure produces no change in the relationship of interest. Model 4 further narrows the focus by looking at trade openness alone. Results

22 In none of these cases do the F tests of the joint significance of public opinion shift, globalization, and party type achieve statistical significance. For the interactive model distinguishing mainstream parties from niche parties, $F = 0.98$, $p = 0.40$; for left parties versus non-left, $F = 2.04$, $p = 0.11$; for right parties versus non-right, $F = 1.46$, $p = 0.23$; and for center versus extreme, $F = 1.11$, $p = 0.40$.

23 Lower values on these restrictions contribute to higher values on the index, reflecting greater liberalization.

TABLE 8.A1. *Multivariate analyses of left-right policy shifts for parties with governing experience, additional models*

	Shifts in globalization	KOF flows	KOF restrictions	Trade	Election year control	Detrended globalization	EU member States	Significant Shifts
	(1)	(2)	(3)	(4)	(5)	(6)	(7)	(8)
Public opinion $shift_{kt}$	3.62**	1.95**	6.76**	0.78	3.48**	0.03	4.23**	4.85**
	(1.40)	(0.89)	(1.91)	(0.53)	(1.30)	(0.26)	(1.23)	(1.92)
$Globalization_{kt}$	−1.79*	−1.28*	−0.92	−0.37	0.77	−0.17	−1.49	−1.93
	(0.99)	(0.70)	(1.18)	(0.40)	(1.89)	(2.07)	(1.01)	(1.61)
Public opinion $shift_{kt}$ x $Globalization_{kt}$	−4.57**	−2.65**	−7.79**	−0.88*	−4.37**	−4.05*	−4.97**	−6.30**
	(1.71)	(1.14)	(2.22)	(0.47)	(1.59)	(2.28)	(1.50)	(2.69)
$\Delta Growth_{kt}$	0.02	0.02	0.02	0.02	0.01	0.02	0.01	0.04
	(0.02)	(0.02)	(0.02)	(0.02)	(0.02)	(0.02)	(0.02)	(0.03)
Party $shift_{jkt-1}$	−0.39**	−0.39**	−0.38**	−0.41**	−0.40**	−0.39**	−0.35**	−0.54**
	(0.07)	(0.07)	(0.07)	(0.07)	(0.07)	(0.07)	(0.08)	(0.09)
Δ $Globalization_{kt}$	3.57*							
	(2.07)							
$Year_{kt}$					−0.02*			
					(0.01)			
Constant	1.73*	0.09	−0.16	−0.60	38.59*	−0.98**	0.34	1.69
	(0.97)	(0.59)	(1.08)	(0.54)	(20.08)	(0.16)	(0.88)	(1.31)
N	252	252	252	270	252	252	218	156
R^2	.25	.24	.24	.19	.25	.22	.23	.33

Notes: Dependent variable is *Party* $shift_{jkt}$. Robust standard errors clustered by election are in parentheses. All models estimated with country-specific intercepts.
* $p < .10$, ** $p < .05$, two-tailed test, unconditional coefficients.

again confirm our initial findings. Our substantive conclusions again remain unchanged.

A fourth consideration pertains to over-time trends. Exposure of national economies to flows from abroad has generally, though not always, increased with time. Thus, we might be concerned that what appears as a globalization effect may simply be capturing a secular decline in parties' tendencies to respond to public opinion.[24] To address this concern, I performed a pair of supplemental analyses. I re-estimated the parameters of the basic model specification including an election year variable to control for time. I also purged the globalization index of the time element by regressing it on election year. The residuals from this model were then used as a "de-trended" measure of economic globalization in the basic specification. In both cases, results support the same conclusions as earlier (Table 8.A1 Models 5 and 6).

Fifth, results might not be due to globalization but to the fact that in many European Union member states, political parties in government are formally bound to a more limited set of credible policy options. By including in the dataset countries that are in and outside of the EU, we have in part already diffused this concern. However, if it can be shown that economic globalization reduces party tendencies to shift positions in response to public opinion within EU member states, we can take this as evidence that, despite limits on their jurisdictional competence, variation with respect to economic globalization is driving weaker responsiveness rather than "Europeanization." Hence, Table 8. A1 Model 7 reports model estimates for EU members only. Results do not change from those produced by the entire sample.

Finally, there is the question of concept measurement. One historical problem with measuring party positions using the CMP data is that the estimates of party position have not been published with corresponding estimates of uncertainty. If a party "shifts" two units based on the CMP estimates, for example, but the uncertainty around the estimate is five units, then it is possible that the party did not shift position at all. One way to address this concern, and consider the implications of uncertainty, is to estimate the parameters of the model specification for Table 8.1 Model 2 for only party shifts greater than the bootstrapped standard errors published by Benoit et al. (2009). Table 8.A1 Model 8 reports estimates for only significant party shifts. The estimates based on a limited number of observations (156 from 252) support our substantive results.

[24] For example, the professionalization of election campaigns may cause parties to downplay their responsiveness on policy grounds in favor of emphasizing other qualities with respect to party image or candidates for office.

Appendix 8.3. Measuring Survey Noneconomic Preferences for Parties and Public Opinion, Sweden 1976–2010

Party Positions

Party positions on noneconomic issues are measured using the issue domain codes from the Comparative Manifesto Project. The measure is

$$\text{Non-Economic Position} = \begin{pmatrix} \text{per}104 + \text{per}109 + \text{per}305 + \text{per}507 + \text{per}601 \\ +\textbf{per603} + \text{per}605 + \textbf{per606} + \text{per}608 \end{pmatrix} - \begin{pmatrix} \text{per}105 + \textbf{per107} + \textbf{per411} + \text{per}501 + \text{per}503 \\ +\text{per}506 + \text{per}607 + \text{per}705 + \text{per}706 \end{pmatrix}$$

This yields a measure with a theoretical minimum value of –100 and maximum +100. The measure is rescaled onto a 0–10 scale.

Conservative		Liberal
Military: positive (104)	minus	Military: negative (105)
Internationalism: negative (109)		Peace (106)
Political authority (305)		Internationalism: positive (107)
Education limitation (507)		Technology and infrastructure (411)
National way of life: positive (601)		Environmental protection (501)
Traditional morality: positive (603)		Social justice (503)
Law and order (605)		Education expansion (506)
Social harmony (606)		Multiculturalism: positive (607)
Multiculturalism: negative (608)		Underprivileged minorities (705)
		Noneconomic dem. groups (706)

Note: Headings and numbers refer to (quasi-)sentence codes of party manifestos as provided by Klingemann et al. (2006).

Mean Voter Positions

Mean voter positions on noneconomic issues are measured using individual responses from the Swedish National Election Studies (SNES) files. To develop a measure for the mean voter's position on noneconomic policies, I make use of a large set of issue preference items included in the SNES surveys to create a summary index. For each of the eleven available election surveys (1976–2010), I first catalogued the available items. I then selected items for inclusion in a noneconomic policy preferences index based on the frequency of their appearance in the surveys. This yielded a list of eleven items. Items are coded such that high values indicate more conservative noneconomic positions, and low values more liberal ones. Missing data were filled in using regression analyses. Items were standardized on a 0–1 scale and were combined additively. The resulting index was rescaled from 0 to 10 to match up to the party data. Finally, taking the mean across all respondent values on the scale for a given year provides us with the position of the mean voter at time *t*.

Item name	Question wording	Missing surveys
Immigration	What is your opinion about the proposal to increase support to immigrants so that they can keep their own culture? (very/fairly good, neither good nor bad, fairly/very bad)	None
Defense	What is your opinion about the proposal to reduce defense expenditure? (very/fairly good, neither good nor bad, fairly/very bad)	None
Pornography	What is your opinion about the proposal to prohibit all forms of pornography? (very/fairly good, neither good nor bad, fairly/very bad)	1988
Foreign aid	What is your opinion about the proposal to reduce third world aid? (very/fairly good, neither good nor bad, fairly/very bad)	1976, 1991
Environment	What do you think about the proposal to work towards an environmentally friendly society even if it means little or no economic growth? (11-point scale from very bad proposal to very good proposal)	1976, 1979
Technology	What do you think about the proposal to work towards a society which utilizes advanced techniques such as computers and industrial robots to make production effective? (11-point scale from very bad proposal to very good proposal)	1976, 1979, 2006
Christian values	What do you think about the proposal to work towards a society where Christian values are more important? (11-point scale from very bad proposal to very good proposal)	1976, 1979, 1988
Law and order	What do you think about the proposal to work towards a society with more law and order? (11-point scale from very bad proposal to very good proposal)	1976, 1979, 1982, 1985, 1988
Family	What do you think about the proposal to work towards a society that strengthens the position of the family? (11-point scale from very bad proposal to very good proposal)	1976, 1979, 1982, 1985, 1988
Swedish values	What do you think about the proposal to work towards a society that protects traditional Swedish values? (11-point scale from very bad proposal to very good proposal)	1976, 1979, 1982, 1985, 1988
Refugees	What is your opinion about the proposal to accept fewer refugees into Sweden? (very/fairly good, neither good nor bad, fairly/very bad)	1976, 1979, 1982, 1985, 1991

Source: Swedish National Election Studies surveys, 1976, 1979, 1982, 1985, 1988, 1991, 1994, 1998, 2002, 2006, 2010.

9

Conclusion

This book has been motivated by the need to understand globalization's consequences for representative democracy in those countries – the industrialized west – where both these processes have functioned the longest. Distinguished from other work in the field, our concern has not been on globalization's effects on government composition or policy outcomes, *per se*, but on citizens and their representatives. This focus on globalization's "downstream" effects makes for a timely contribution. Judged in terms of the removal of restrictions on capital movements and attendant increases in international finance, economic globalization took off in the 1990s. Increases in international trade and in foreign direct and portfolio investment, as well as increased harmonization of financial markets and national business cycles, set off a wave of research. Would globalization push governments to adopt more market-friendly neoliberal policies? Would it lead to a race to the bottom in social policy protections? Would we see the emergence of new classes of "winners" and "losers" in re-structured post industrial economies? By the 2000s, it was clear that globalization's effects were not limited solely to questions of government policy. Globalization became a rallying cry for protest activity. This was realized both as movements against unpopular government reforms at home (many times in the form of strikes by producers) and as rallies against international institutions charged with assisting the world's economies, such as the World Trade Organization and the International Monetary Fund. The Occupy Wall Street movement of 2011 is, in this sense, just the most recent in a succession of rallies against the inequities associated with unfettered markets.

The recurrence of financial crises – which begin in one country but spread quickly to others – have called our attention to just how interconnected the world's economies are. The current crisis, the full effects of which will not be known for some time, has only underlined the depth of country dependence on world markets. The crisis is notable in many respects. Three of these, however, stand out with respect to globalization and mass politics. First, unlike the 1980s debt crisis in Latin America or even the Asian financial crisis of the late 1990s, this current crisis originated in and has disproportionately affected the economies of the industrialized west. No longer can citizens of these rich democracies credibly think that their financial systems can shield them from the volatility of world financial markets. Second, fueled by a lack of financial market regulation and by increased harmonization of national practices, the crisis spread rapidly from country to country. And third, the crisis has evolved rapidly in form. Relegated initially to financial markets, it quickly affected the "real" economy of industry and employment and, in the course, has put increased pressure on sovereign debt.

These events provide reason to revisit old questions. Can governments effectively manage economies in the face of highly integrated and extremely dense market transactions? Can they continue to make globalization politically palpable by constructing policies to compensate the losers? Will the eventual response to economic stagnation in the world's established industrialized democracies – particularly in Europe – lead to a permanent harmonization of monetary, fiscal, and regulatory regimes, thereby undermining democracy within the confines of the nation-state? In an effort to manage financial globalization, will new institutions be constructed, or existing ones strengthened, in a way to (further) supplant national authority? Or, alternatively, will the crisis have in the end disintegrative effects, leading nations to turn inward rather than make the compromises necessary to produce common solutions?

These questions are each important, to be sure. Yet, in a way, they miss an important intermediate step linking globalization and democratic outcomes. Before we can prognosticate on the status of democracy in globalized markets, we must develop a better understanding of how globalization influences the players in democracy's game – the voters and their representatives. That's where this book comes in. I have argued that the forces of globalization – in times both good and bad – reshape the incentives of self-interested citizens and vote-seeking politicians, alternating their behavior in the process. International integration, I claim, impinges on mass politics via two channels: the capacity of governments to shape outcomes and the effect of issue positions on political behavior. By highlighting these linkages, this book has shown that internationalization matters for democracy, does so in systematic fashion, and affects both the "demand" and "supply" sides of the equation.

In the remainder of this concluding chapter, I summarize the book's main findings for the demand and supply sides of mass politics and discuss the study's implications for the study of political economy and political behavior.

9.1. Globalization and the Demand Side of Mass Politics

Globalization matters for the demands citizens exert on national policymakers, for how they assign responsibility for past outcomes, and for whether and how they hold policymakers to account in elections. These shifts in policy demands and performance evaluations constitute a clear break from the economics-based, materialist type of politics that characterized mass politics in western societies for the second half of the twentieth century. Consider policy preferences. As we saw in Chapter 3, increases in the level of commercial and financial integration have led publics to temper demands in those areas in which their governments can no longer credibly deliver and expand demands in those areas where they still can. The first category includes policies for managing the economy and for delivering aid to industry and the unemployed. The second set of policies pertains to issues that are not explicitly economic, such as the environment, education, and healthcare. In short, citizens balance demands, trading pressures in one set of policy domains for those in another.

Chapter 4 showed how globalization complicates the task – essential to evaluating governments in democracies – of assigning responsibility for policy outcomes. In modern democracies, assignment of credit and blame is never as simple as Keysian (Key 1966) conceptions of accountability make it out to be. Political institutions designed to diffuse power also have the effect of diffusing responsibility (Hellwig and Samuels 2008; Powell and Whitten 1993). National economies with porous borders play a similarly diffusing role when it comes to responsibility attributions. Globalization decreases the likelihood that citizens hold their governments responsible for economic conditions. In place of attributing outcomes to governments, citizens in more exposed economies associate national economic conditions with fluctuations in international business cycles. This shift in responsibility attributions is further realized in retrospective voting. As shown in Chapter 5, the balancing demands logic of trading demands in economic areas for noneconomic ones finds its way into performance-based voting. While globalization suppresses economic voting (Duch and Stevenson 2008; Hellwig 2001; Hellwig and Samuels 2007), it also *amplifies* the relevance of noneconomic performance for incumbent support.

Completing politics on the demand side, we have seen that globalization also matters for prospective, issue-oriented voting. With the help of an original data set of mass and elite positions, I demonstrated how issues pertaining to globalization are reshaping how voters relate to and choose among political parties in elections. The analysis of position issues in Chapter 6 showed that the policy space for political competition in western democracies is today multidimensional. The first dimension is informed chiefly by the old issues of "left" and "right." The second is anchored by immigration, trade, and economic globalization more broadly defined. Further, while "old politics" issues still matter, they do not dominate. Lastly, I showed that the extent to which voter-party proximity on these globalization-related issues structures voter decisions is shaped in part by objective and elite-crafted signals from the world economy.

9.2. Globalization and the Supply Side of Mass Politics

With the fallout from the financial crisis, the line blurring the domestic from the international has been further blurred, if not altogether erased. It is thus important that we understand how globalization impinges on the behavior of strategic political parties. The balancing demands logic also proves a useful framework for understanding globalization's influence on the supply side. Globalization affects the set of issues on which elections are decided in advanced capitalist democracies. The evolution of issue preferences and issue salience is, in part, already well-known by observers of electoral politics in these countries (e.g., Dalton et al. 1984; Kriesi et al. 2008). However, this study is novel in that it links these changes explicitly to issues related to the world economy. Just as globalization has led voters to rethink how they incorporate economic concerns into their calculus, so too has it affected elite behavior.

When it comes to communications between elites and the masses, globalization-related issues are distinct from economic issues. The latter are dominated by elite-to-mass flows (see Chapter 7). On these "left-right" issues, the position-taking behavior of party elite positions strongly affects the preferences of their supporters in the electorate. The reason, I suggest, is that, on matters such as taxes and spending, party positions are well-known, fairly stable, and easily communicated to voters. However, when it comes to such concerns as immigration, trade, and preferences for globalization, elite positions are not strongly anchored. Thus, mass-to-elite flows dominate communications with respect to policy positions on these "new politics" issues and issues for which the notion of a limited room to maneuver is not well established. This conclusion was supported by a cross-sectional analysis of parties and voters in ten countries and a case study of the dynamics of representational linkages in Denmark.

This yields an important implication: Parties are *more* attentive to the wishes of their constituents on globalization-related issues than they are to the traditional issues structuring political competition in western societies. On the one hand, this is a positive result; political elites appear relatively more responsive to – rather than manipulative of – public opinion on issues that promise to become more and more salient as societies become more and more entwined in world markets. On the other hand, there are reasons to value dominant elite-to-mass flows as essential for exercising policy leadership. We might be concerned that parties are slow to adapt, if not lead, on issues pertaining to the world economy. The case of immigration in Denmark in the 1990s and 2000s provides a case in point; on this issue the mainstream parties were slow to lead. As a consequence, space opened up for a new party, the Danish People's Party, to take advantage. Established parties on the left and right alike remained in a reactive, rather than proactive, position.[1] National policy responses – or the lack thereof – to the euro crisis of 2010–2012 provide another example of parties' inability to control the policy debate on a new, globalization-related issue.

The heterogeneous nature of globalization for mass politics is also evident with respect to whether parties respond to shifting public preferences. The conventional wisdom has it that parties in industrialized democracies are responsive to the public's preferences (Adams and Somer-Topcu 2009; Ezrow 2010; McDonald and Budge 2005; Powell 2000). Even if parties are motivated mainly by electoral concerns, it is in their long-term interest to adhere to shifts in voter preferences. A consideration of globalization, however, might give us reason to rethink whether and how parties respond to public opinion. We say in Chapter 8 that party responsiveness in terms of "left" and "right" is weaker in more globalized economies. As evidence from elite interviews and from the expert surveys indicates, parties confront the realities of globalization by reducing voters' expectations and competing over less. Elites recognize that crafting responses to economic problems in a globalized economy runs the risk of appearing non-credible. Incentives to respond to public opinion are weakened. But, once again, the balancing demands argument finds support, this time on the supply side. For, like voters, parties adapt, trading responsive behavior in one set of issues for another. Evidence from a study of voter and party shifts in Sweden shows that while economic globalization weakens mean-voter responsiveness on the left-right dimension, it strengthens responsiveness on the alternative noneconomic dimension of policy contestation.

9.3. Implications for International and Comparative Political Economy

In addition to making and testing an argument about globalization and mass politics, this book was motivated by a need to better connect international and comparative political economy (IPE/CPE) scholarship with insights from political behavior. IPE/CPE scholars have been concerned for some time with the question of the room to maneuver, broadly conceived. Questions have focused in the main on whether and how government partisanship, the organization of domestic interests, and institutions for aggregating preferences mediate globalization's influence on domestic politics (see Figure 1.1). This work has done much to explicate the conditions under which the effects of economic interdependence are greater or weaker.

This book also revolves around questions of the policy room to maneuver. As with mainstream IPE/CPE, the force driving relationships is the interaction

[1] Meguid's (2008, chapter 6) discussion of immigration, the National Front, and party politics in France shares many characteristics with the Danish case. See also Givens' (2005) comparative study of radical right-wing parties.

of national economies with global markets. I approach the question from a different angle, however. Where the unit of analysis in IPE/CPE typically is the nation state, I examine individuals. Drawing further distinction, I examine individual behavior not with respect to economic interests as, say, determined by skill levels or positions in national labor markets (e.g., Iversen and Soskice 2001), but rather, individuals in this story are viewed expressly in the roles they play in representative democracy, as citizens and their elected representatives.[2] Hence, where IPE/CPE research is concerned with domestic politics in terms of policy (e.g., public spending, taxes, regulations, and the like), the outcomes of interest here are public preferences, voter choice, and the behavior of political elites.

Viewing globalization politics through the lens of voters and their representatives uncovers a new set of puzzles for the field of IPE/CPE. Take, for instance, the efficiency thesis. It contends that transnational markets undermine the capacity of national politicians to adopt autonomous policies. Spatial models of party competition, however, would predict this conclusion applies only if market integration creates incentives for elite proposals to diverge from the preferences of the median voter. Or take the compensation perspective. Arguments that globalization serves to reinforce preexisting organizational comparative advantages imply that open markets, if anything, facilitate policy autonomy and foster responsive policymaking. A consideration of voter opinions suggests this logic is contingent on the public's support for government redistribution of wealth in the first place (see Chapter 3).

This mass politics approach yields a more nuanced view of how globalization affects politics. It paints a less rosy picture of the prospects for democracy in a globalized world. But while mainstream IPE/CPE is less sanguine about globalization's consequences today than in years past, many still subscribe to the compensational logic that market dependence puts pressure on governments to respond with redistributive policies. Politicians who fail to deliver policies to shield vulnerable voters, the reasoning goes, will soon find themselves out of a job. While there is some truth to this argument, findings from this book indicate that standard compensation arguments underestimate the capacity of voters to reason about the pressures globalization exerts on their policymakers. Again, popular reactions to the economic crisis in Europe are illustrative. In some countries, painful reforms deemed essential by the troika (European Commission, European Central Bank, and International Monetary Fund) have been met with violent protest. Greece comes to mind. Yet elsewhere, cuts to public spending on pensions, education, and the like have been met largely with quiescence. This has been the case, for example, in Ireland

[2] This is not to say that there is anything wrong with examining individual behavior with respect to their economic interests. I only wish to draw a point of distinction between the "mass politics" approach adopted here and the more prevalent "interests" based approach employed in contemporary political economy research.

and Spain, where popular resentment has only occasionally flared up in the form of protest behavior. This suggests that, rather than being myopic and self-centered, citizens of these countries recognize that the options facing national policymakers are limited.

9.4. Implications for Political Behavior

This study also carries implications for work on mass political behavior. Where the IPE/CPE globalization research has pivoted on the question of the room to maneuver, public opinion research has focused on a pair of related questions: 1) How much do voters know, and does it matter? 2) Where do mass preferences come from? This book speaks to both of these larger questions. First, take knowledge about politics. While most acknowledge that voters, on average, know little about politics, students of public opinion debate whether this matters for representative democracy. Many argue that voters' lack of knowledge impedes democracy insomuch as voters fail to process the (non-) effects of policymaker actions on their own personal welfare. If, for instance, the voter's capacity to process political issues is shallow and short-lived (e.g., Achen and Bartels 2008; Campbell et al. 1960, Zaller 1992), then we should not be optimistic that citizens can adequately assign credit or blame to elected and unelected actors in complex, globalized environments. Results reported here, however, provide some hope. Citizens are capable of assigning responsibility to a variety of factors, including fluctuations in the world economy (see also Alcañiz and Hellwig 2011). These attributions are driven by the signals they receive about globalization's reach, both from objective sources (flows) and subjective ones (elite messages). This capacity to hold actors other than the government accountable is in turn reflected in their electoral behavior. With regard to debates about what voters know, this research contributes to an alternative body of scholarship that argues voters are sufficiently able to work through complex environments to make reasonable decisions (Alesina and Rosenthal 1995; Duch and Stevenson 2008; Kedar 2009).

This study also speaks to wider debates about mass preference formation. On the question of where preferences come from, some argue that individual preferences are driven by self-interest considerations. According to this view, citizens act in their own best interests as producers – given, say, their position in national and international labor markets – or consumers of goods and services (Iversen and Soskice 2001; Scheve and Slaughter 2001; 2004; see also Baker 2005). Others argue that preferences on matters of policy come instead from above, via elite discourse from politicians. This perspective maintains that persuasion by political elites is a key determinant of public opinion formation (Berinsky 2007; Zaller 1992). While not providing a test of these contending perspectives, results presented here lend some support to the second perspective. By drawing on an original set of expert surveys, I show that the amount and consistency of elite messages on globalization can have an effect on how the masses assign responsibility (Chapter 4), whether they hold incumbents accountable (Chapter 5), and the relative salience of globalization as a position issue (Chapter 6).

9.5. Retaining the Room to Maneuver?

Even before the financial crisis of 2008, the belief was widespread that globalization had reduced the policy room to maneuver. Interviews I conducted some years ago indicated as much. "There is an interaction between globalization and policy decisions," asserted a member of the Danish Folketing. Another Danish politician noted that "most national parliamentarians think that many of the laws we make nationally have no chance to cope with issues which are structured by economic globalization."[3] British politicians held similar views. "Globalization has inevitably infringed on the capacity of individual parliaments," noted a Conservative member of parliament (MP). Another MP noted that "one has to assess the broader economic effects of any decision you might take for domestic reasons." "World markets create a 'straightjacket,'" added a member of the Liberal Democratic leadership, taking a page out of Friedman's book (1999).[4] And in France, globalization has long been associated with a sense of ineffectiveness. As a former Socialist minister told me, "we effectively no longer have a French state, in the sense that we have a government having the weight it once did."[5]

When it comes to delivering policies in advanced capitalist democracies, globalization is recasting the boundaries between the possible and the unattainable. As voters and their representatives in these economies confront the fallout of the worst downturn since the 1930s, the fate of mass democracy may hang in the balance. Economic hardship may lead to wide-scale protests as publics vent their frustrations and politicians prove unable or unwilling to respond. Taking the findings from this book to heart, however, we arrive at a different conclusion. Recognizing the dense connections that weave together national economies, citizens may react differently to crisis, tempering their demands in light of constrained policymakers. The result will likely be a different sort of representative democracy for the twenty-first century.

[3] Interviews in Copenhagen, March 18–20, 2003.
[4] Interviews in London, February 4, 5, and 10, 2003.
[5] Interviews in Paris, February 26 and March 3, 2003.

Bibliography

Achen, Christopher H., and Larry M. Bartels. 2006. It Feels Like We're Thinking: The Rationalizing Voter and Electoral Democracy. In *Annual Meeting of the American Political Science Association*. Philadelphia, PA.

2008. *Myopic Retrospection and Party Realignment in the Great Depression*. Princeton, NJ: Princeton University Press.

Adams, James, Michael Clark, Lawrence Ezrow, and Garrett Glasgow. 2006. "Are Niche Parties Fundamentally Different from Mainstream Parties? The Causes and the Electoral Consequences of Western European Parties' Policy Shifts, 1976–1998." *American Journal of Political Science* **50** (3): 513–529.

Adams, James, Andrea B. Haupt, and Heather Stoll. 2009. "What Moves Parties?" *Comparative Political Studies* **42** (5): 611–639.

Adams, James, and Samuel Merrill III. 2009. "Policy-Seeking Parties in a Parliamentary Democracy with Proportional Representation: A Valence-Uncertainty Model." *British Journal of Political Science* **39** (3): 539–558.

Adams, James, Samuel Merrill, and Bernard Grofman. 2005. *A Unified Theory of Party Competition: A Cross-National Analysis Integrating Spatial and Behavioral Factors*. New York: Cambridge University Press.

Adams, James, and Zeynep Somer-Topcu. 2009. "Policy Adjustment by Parties in Response to Rival Parties' Policy Shifts: Spatial Theory and the Dynamics of Party Competition in Twenty-Five Post-War Democracies." *British Journal of Political Science* **39** (4): 825–846.

Adams, James, Catherine E. De Vries, and Debra Leiter. 2012. "Subconstituency Reactions to Elite Depolarization in the Netherlands: An Analysis of the Dutch Public's Policy Beliefs and Partisan Loyalties, 1986–98." *British Journal of Political Science* **42** (1): 81–105.

Adams, James, Jane Green, and Caitlin Milazzo. 2012. "Has the British Public Depolarized Along With Political Elites? An American Perspective on British Public Opinion." *Comparative Political Studies* **45** (4): 507–530.

Adserà, Alicia, and Carles Boix. 2002. "Trade, Democracy, and the Size of the Public Sector: The Political Underpinnings of Openness." *International Organization* **56** (2): 229–262.

Ai, Chunrong, and Edward C. Norton. 2003. "Interaction Terms in Logit and Probit Models." *Economics Letters* **80** (1): 123–129.

Alcañiz, Isabella, and Timothy Hellwig. 2011. "Who's to Blame? The Distribution of Responsibility in Developing Democracies." *British Journal of Political Science* **41** (2): 389–411.

Alesina, A., A. Devleeschauwer, W. Easterly, S. Kurlat, and R. Wacziarg. 2003. "Fractionalization." *Journal of Economic Growth* **8** (2): 155–194.

Alesina, Alberto, and Howard Rosenthal. 1995. *Partisan Politics, Divided Government, and the Economy*. New York: Cambridge University Press.

Alt, James E. 1985. "Political Parties, World Demand, and Unemployment: Domestic and International Sources of Economic Activity." *American Political Science Review* **79** (4): 1016–1040.

Andersen, Jørgen Goul. 2003. "The General Election in Denmark, November 2001." *Electoral Studies* **22** (1): 153–193.

Andersen, Jørgen Goul. 2006. "The Parliamentary Election in Denmark, February 2005." *Electoral Studies* **25** (3): 393–415.

Andersen, Jørgen Goul, Jakob Rathlev, Claus Hansen, Henrik Jørgensen, and Gregers Lehrmann Bruun. 2002. *Danish National Elections Study 2001*. Copenhagen: Dansk Data Archive.

Anderson, Christopher. 1995. *Blaming the Government: Citizens and the Economy in Five European Democracies*, Comparative Politics Series. Armonk, NY: M.E. Sharpe.

Anderson, Christopher J., and Jason D. Hecht. 2012. "Voting When the Economy Goes Bad, Everyone is in Charge, and No One is to Blame: The Case of the 2009 German Election." *Electoral Studies* **31** (1): 5–19.

Andrews, Josephine T., and Jeannette Money. 2009. "The Spatial Structure of Party Competition: Party Dispersion within a Finite Policy Space." *British Journal of Political Science* **39** (4): 805–824.

Arceneaux, Kevin. 2006. "The Federal Face of Voting: Are Elected Officials Held Accountable for the Functions Relevant to Their Office?" *Political Psychology* **27** (5): 731–754.

Bailey, Michael A., and David Brady. 1998. "Heterogeneity and Representation: The Senate and Free Trade." *American Journal of Political Science* **42** (2): 524–544.

Baker, Andy. 2005. "Who Wants to Globalize? Consumer Taste and Labor Markets in a Theory of Trade Policy Beliefs." *American Journal of Political Science* **49** (4): 924–938.

Bakker, Ryan, Seth Jolly, and Jonathan Polk. 2012. "Complexity in the European Party Space: Exploring Dimensionality with Experts." *European Union Politics* **13** (2): 219–245.

Barnes, Samuel H., and Max Kaase. 1979. *Political Action: Mass Participation in Five Western Democracies*. Beverly Hills, CA: Sage Publications.

Bartels, Larry M. 2002. "Beyond the Running Tally: Partisan Bias in Political Perceptions." *Political Behavior* **24** (2): 117–150.

Beck, Nathaniel, and Jonathan N. Katz. 2009. Modeling Dynamics in Time-Series Cross-Section Political Economy Data. California Institute of Technology Social Science Working Paper 1304.

Bélanger, Éric, Jean Chiche, Michael S. Lewis-Beck, and Vincent Tiberj. 2006. "Party, Ideology, and Vote Intentions: Dynamics from the 2002 French Electoral Panel." *Political Research Quarterly* **59** (4): 503–515.

Bengtsson, Åsa, Kasper Hansen, Ólafur Þ Harðarson, Hanne Marthe Narud, and Henrik Oscarsson. 2014. *The Nordic Voter: Myths of Exceptionalism*. Colchester, UK: ECPR Press.

Benoit, Kenneth and Michael Laver. 2006. *Party Policy in Modern Democracies*. London: Routledge.

Benoit, Kenneth, Michael Laver, and Slava Mikhaylov. 2009. "Treating Words as Data with Error: Uncertainty in Text Statements of Policy Positions." *American Journal of Political Science* **53** (2): 495–513.

Berinsky, Adam J. 2007. "Assuming the Costs of War: Events, Elites, and American Public Support for Military Conflict." *Journal of Politics* **69** (4): 975–997.

Berman, Sheri. 2009. "The Primacy of Economics versus the Primacy of Politics: Understanding the Ideological Dynamics of the Twentieth Century." *Perspectives on Politics* 7 (3): 561–578.

Bernhard, William, and David Leblang. 2006. *Democratic Processes and Financial Markets*. New York: Cambridge University Press.

Blyth, Mark, and Richard Katz. 2005. "From Catch-all Politics to Cartelisation: The Political Economy of the Cartel Party." *West European Politics* **28** (1): 33–60.

Boix, Carles. 1998. *Political Parties, Growth, and Equality: Conservative and Social Democratic Strategies in the World Economy*. New York: Cambridge University Press.

2000. "Partisan Governments, the International Economy, and Macroeconomic Policies in Advanced Nations, 1960–93." *World Politics* no. **53** (1): 38–73.

Borre, Ole. 2001. *Issue voting: an introduction*. Aarhus; Oakville, CT: Aarhus University Press.

Brooks, Clem, and Jeff Manza. 2006. "Why Do Welfare States Persist?" *Journal of Politics* **68** (4): 816–827.

2007. *Why Welfare States Persist: The Importance of Public Opinion in Democracies, Studies in Communication, Media, and Public Opinion*. Chicago: University of Chicago Press.

Broz, J. Lawrence, and Michael Brewster Hawes. 2006. "Congressional Politics of Financing the International Monetary Fund." *International Organization* **60** (2): 367–399.

Brune, Nancy, and Geoffrey Garrett. 2005. "The Globalization Rorschach Test: International Economic Integration, Inequality, and the Role of Government." *Annual Review of Political Science* **8** (1): 399–423.

Budge, Ian. 1996. *The New Challenge of Direct Democracy*. Cambridge, MA: Polity Press.

Budge, Ian, and Dennis Farlie. 1983. *Explaining and Predicting Elections: Issue Effects and Party Strategies in Twenty-three Democracies*. London; Boston: Allen & Unwin.

Budge, Ian, Hans-Dieter Klingemann, Andrea Volkens, and Judith Bara. 2001. *Mapping Policy Preferences: Estimates for Parties, Electors, and Governments, 1945–1998*. Oxford; New York: Oxford University Press.

Busemeyer, Marius R. 2009. "From Myth to Reality: Globalisation and Public Spending in OECD Countries Revisited." *European Journal of Political Research* n**48** (4): 455–482.

Butler, David, and Donald Stokes. 1969. *Political Change in Britain*. New York: St. Martin's Press.

Cameron, David R. 1978. "The Expansion of the Public Economy: A Comparative Analysis." *The American Political Science Review* **72** (4): 1243–1261.

Campbell, Angus, Philip E. Converse, Warren E. Miller, and Donald Stokes. 1960. *The American Voter*. New York: Wiley.

Carmines, Edward G., and James A. Stimson. 1989. *Issue Evolution: Race and the Transformation of American Politics*. Princeton, NJ: Princeton University Press.

Carrubba, Clifford J. 2001. "The Electoral Connection in European Union Politics." *Journal of Politics* **63** (1): 141–158.

Ceobanu, Alin M., and Xavier Escandell. 2010. "Comparative Analyses of Public Attitudes Toward Immigrants and Immigration Using Multinational Survey Data: A Review of Theories and Research." *Annual Review of Sociology* **36**: 309–328.

Centre d'Etudes de al Vie Politique Française (CEVIPOF), Centre d'Informatisation des Donnéés Socio-Politiques (CIDSP) and Politiques et Sociales (CRAPS) Centre de Recherches Administratives. 2001. French National Election Study, 1997 [Computer File] ICPSR Version. Ann Arbor, MI: ICPSR.

Christensen, Thomas. 2001. *Eurobarometer 55.1: Globalization and Humanitarian Aid, April-May 2001*. Inter-university Consortium for Political and Social Research (ICPSR). Ann Arbor, MI.

2003. *Eurobarometer 59.0: Lifelong Learning, Health, and Partners and Fertility, January-February 2003*. Cologne, Germany: Zentralarchiv fur Empirische Sozialforschung/Ann Arbor, MI: Inter-University Consortium for Political and Social Research.

Clark, William Roberts. 2003. *Capitalism, Not Globalism: Capital Mobility, Central Bank Independence, and the Political Control of the Economy, Michigan Studies in International Political Economy*. Ann Arbor: University of Michigan Press.

Clark, William Roberts, and Mark Hallerberg. 2000. "Mobile Capital, Domestic Institutions, and Electorally Induced Monetary and Fiscal Policy." *The American Political Science Review* **94** (2): 323–346.

Cnudde, Charles F., and Donald J. McCrone. 1966. "The Linkage Between Constituency Attitudes and Congressional Voting Behavior: A Causal Model." *American Political Science Review* **60** (1): 66–72.

Cohen, B.J. 1965. "Capital Controls and the United States Balance of Payments – Comment." *American Economic Review* **55** (1): 172–176.

Cohen, Benjamin J. 1993. "The Triad and the Unholy Trinity: Lessons for the Pacific Region." In *Pacific Economic Relations in the 1990s: Cooperation or Conflict?* ed. Richard Higgott, Richard Leaver, and John Ravenhill, 133–58. Boulder, CO: Lynne Rienner.

Converse, Philip E. 1964. "The Nature of Belief Systems in Mass Publics." In *Ideology and discontent*, ed. David E. Apter. London: Free Press of Glencoe.

Cutler, Fred. 2008. "Whodunnit? Canadian Voters, Intergovernmentalism, and Responsibility." *Canadian Journal of Political Science* **41** (3): 627–654.

Dalton, Russell J. 1985. "Political Parties and Political Representation: Party Supporters and Party Elites in Nine Nations." *Comparative Political Studies* **18** (3): 267–299.

2002. "Political Cleavages, Issues, and Electoral Change." In *Comparing Democracies 2: New Challenges in the Study of Elections and Voting*, ed. Lawrence LeDuc, Richard G. Niemi, and Pippa Norris. London: Sage.

2009. "Economics, Environmentalism and Party Alignments: A Research Note on Partisan Change in Advanced Industrial Democracies." *European Journal of Political Research* **48**(1): 161–175.

2014. *Citizen Politics: Public Opinion and Political Parties in Advanced Industrial Democracies*. 6th ed. Washington, DC: CQ Press.

Dalton, Russell J., Scott C. Flanagan, and Paul Allen Beck, eds. 1984. *Electoral Change in Advanced Industrial Democracies: Realignment or Dealignment?* Princeton, NJ: Princeton University Press.

De Boef, Suzanna. 2001. "Modeling Equilibrium Relationships: Error Correction Models with Strongly Autoregressive Data." *Political Analysis* **9** (1): 78–94.

De Boef, Suzanna, and Luke Keele. 2008. "Taking Time Seriously." *American Journal of Political Science* **52** (1): 184–200.

De Vries, Catherine E., and Gary Marks. 2012. "The Struggle Over Dimensionality: A Note on Theory and Empirics." *European Union Politics* **13** (2): 185–193.

De Vries, Catherine E., Armèn Hakhverdian, and Bram Lancee. 2013. "The Dynamics of Voters' Left/Right Identification: The Role of Economic and Cultural Issues." *Political Science Research and Methods* **1** (2): 223–238.

Destler, I.M. 2005. *American Trade Politics*. 4th ed. Washington, DC: Institute for International Economics.

Downs, Anthony. 1957. *An Economic Theory of Democracy*. New York: Harper.

Dreher, Axel. 2006. "Does Globalization Affect Growth? Evidence from a New Index of Globalization." *Applied Economics* **38** (10): 1091–1110.

Duch, Raymond M., and Randolph T. Stevenson. 2008. *The Economic Vote: How Political and Economic Institutions Condition Election Results, Political Economy of Institutions and Decisions*. New York: Cambridge University Press.

Duckett, Jane, and William L. Miller. 2006. *The Open Economy and its Enemies: Public Attitudes in East Asia and Eastern Europe*. Cambridge: Cambridge University Press.

Durr, Robert H. 1993. "What Moves Policy Sentiment?" *American Political Science Review* **87** (1): 158–170.

Elklit, Jørgen. 1999. "The Danish March 1998 Parliamentary Election." *Electoral Studies* **18** (1): 137–142.

Enelow, James M., and Melvin J. Hinich. 1984. *The Spatial Theory of Voting: An Introduction*. Cambridge; New York: Cambridge University Press.

Enns, Peter K., and Paul M. Kellstedt. 2008. "Policy Mood and Political Sophistication: Why Everyone Loves Mood." *British Journal of Political Science* **38** (3): 433–454.

Erikson, Robert S., Michael MacKuen, and James A. Stimson. 2002. *The Macro Polity, Cambridge Studies in Political Psychology and Public Opinion*. New York: Cambridge University Press.

European Commission. 2004. Eurobarometer 61.0: The European Union, Globalization, and the European Parliament, February-March 2004. Brussels: E.O.R. Group, ICPSR.

Evans, Geoffrey. 1998. "Euroscepticism and Conservative Electoral Support: How an Asset Became a Liability." *British Journal of Political Science* **28** (3): 573–590.

Evans, Geoffrey, and Robert Andersen. 2006. "The Political Conditioning of Economic Perceptions." *Journal of Politics* **68** (1): 194–207.

Evans, Geoffrey, and Mark Pickup. 2010. "Reversing the Causal Arrow: The Political Conditioning of Economic Perceptions in the 2000–2004 U.S. Presidential Election Cycle." *Journal of Politics* **72** (4): 1236–1251.

European Commission. 2009. *Eurobarometer 71.1: European Parliament and Elections, Economic Crisis, Climate Change, and Chemical Products, January-February 2009*. ICPSR28181-v3. Cologne, Germany: GESIS/Ann Arbor, MI: Inter-University Consortium for Political and Social Research.

Ezrow, Lawrence. 2010. *Linking Citizens and Parties: How Electoral Systems Matter for Political Representation, Comparative Politics*. Oxford; New York: ECPR: Oxford University Press.

Ezrow, Lawrence, and Timothy Hellwig. 2014 forthcoming. "Responding to Voters or Responding to Markets? Political Parties and Public Opinion in an Era of Globalization." *International Studies Quarterly*.

Feldman, Stanley. 1982. "Economic Self-Interest and Political Behavior." *American Journal of Political Science* **26** (3): 446–466.

Ferejohn, John. 1986. "Incumbent Performance and Electoral Control." *Public Choice* **50** (1): 5–25.

Fernández-Albertos, José. 2006. "Does Internationalization Blur Responsibility? Economic Voting and Economic Openness in 15 European Countries." *West European Politics* **29** (1): 28–46.

Fernández-Albertos, José, Alexander Kuo, and Laia Balcells. 2013. "Economic Crisis, Globalization, and Partisan Bias: Evidence from Spain." *International Studies Quarterly* **57** (4): 804–816.

Fiorina, Morris P. 1981. *Retrospective Voting in American National Elections*. New Haven, CT: Yale University Press.

Frank, Thomas. 2004. *What's the Matter with Kansas?: How Conservatives Won the Heart of America*. New York: Metropolitan Books.

Franzese, Robert J. 2002. *Macroeconomic Policies of Developed Democracies, Cambridge Studies in Comparative Politics*. Cambridge; New York: Cambridge University Press.

Freeman, John R. 1989. *Democracy and Markets: The Politics of Mixed Economies*. Ithaca, NY: Cornell University Press.

Friedman, Thomas L. 1999. *The Lexus and the Olive Tree*. 1st ed. New York: Farrar, Straus, Giroux.

Gabel, Matthew, and Kenneth Scheve. 2007. "Estimating the Effect of Elite Communications on Public Opinion Using Instrumental Variables." *American Journal of Political Science* **51** (4): 1013–1028.

Gaines, Brian J., James H. Kuklinski, Paul J. Quirk, Buddy Peyton, and Jay Verkuilen. 2007. "Interpreting Iraq: Partisanship and the Meaning of Facts." *Journal of Politics* **69** (4): 957–974.

Gallup International Association. 2006. *Voice of the People, 2006*. ICPSR study number 21380. Ann Arbor, MI: ICPSR.

Garrett, Geoffrey. 1998. *Partisan Politics in the Global Economy, Cambridge Studies in Comparative Politics*. Cambridge; New York: Cambridge University Press.

Garrett, Geoffrey, and Deborah Mitchell. 2001. "Globalization, Government Spending and Taxation in the OECD." *European Journal of Political Research* **39** (2): 145–177.

Givens, Terri. 2005. *Voting Radical Right in Western Europe*. New York: Cambridge University Press.

Gomez, Brad T., and J. Matthew Wilson. 2006. "Cognitive Heterogeneity and Economic Voting: A Comparative Analysis of Four Democratic Electorates." *American Journal of Political Science* **50** (1): 127–145.

Gourevitch, Peter Alexis. 1986. *Politics in Hard Times: Comparative Responses to International Economic Crises, Cornell Studies in Political Economy*. Ithaca, NY: Cornell University Press.

Green-Pedersen, Christoffer. 2007. "The Growing Importance of Issue Competition: The Changing Nature of Party Competition in Western Europe." *Political Studies* **55** (3): 607–628.

Greene, William H. 2000. *Econometric analysis*. 4th ed. Upper Saddle River, NJ: Prentice Hall.

Greider, William. 1999. *Fortress America: The American military and the Consequences of Peace*. New York: PublicAffairs.

Grofman, Bernard. 1985. "The Neglected Role of the Status Quo in Models of Issue Voting." *The Journal of Politics* **47** (1): 229–237.

Hall, Peter A. 1986. *Governing the Economy: The Politics of State Intervention in Britain and France, Europe and the International Order*. New York: Oxford University Press.

Hall, Peter A., and David Soskice, eds. 2001. *Varieties of Capitalism: The Institutional Foundations of Comparative Advantage*. New York: Oxford University Press.

Haupt, Andrea B. 2010. "Parties' Responses to Economic Globalization." *Party Politics* **16** (1): 5–27.

Hays, Jude C. 2009. *Globalization and the New Politics of Embedded Liberalism*. Oxford; New York: Oxford University Press.

Hays, Jude C., Sean Ehrlich, and Clint Peinhardt. 2005. "Government Spending and Public Support for Trade in the OECD: An Empirical Test of the Embedded Liberalism Thesis." *International Organization* **59** (2): 473–494.

Hearl, Derek. 2001. "Checking the Party Policy Estimates: Reliability." In *Mapping Policy Preferences: Estimates for Parties, Electors, and Governments 1945–1998*, eds. Ian Budge, Hans-Dieter Klingemann, Andrea Volkens, Judith Bara, and Eric Tanenbaum, 111–125. Oxford: Oxford University Press.

Heath, Anthony, Roger Jowell, and John Curtice. 2002. British Election Panel Study Data, 1997–2001; Waves 1 to 8 [computer file]. UK Data Archive version. University of Essex, Colchester.

Hellwig, Timothy. 2001. "Interdependence, Government Constraints, and Economic Voting." *The Journal of Politics* **63** (4): 1141–1162.

2008a. "Explaining the Salience of Left–Right Ideology in Postindustrial Democracies: The Role of Structural Economic Change." *European Journal of Political Research* **47** (6): 687–709.

2008b. "Globalization, Policy Constraints, and Vote Choice." *Journal of Politics* **70** (4): 1128–1141.

2011. Economic Globalization and Mass Politics Ten Country Study. V1: http://hdl.handle.net/1902.1/1698.

Hellwig, Timothy, and Eva Coffey. 2011. "Public Opinion, Party Messages, and Responsibility for the Financial Crisis in Britain." *Electoral Studies* **30** (3): 417–426.

Hellwig, Timothy T., Eve M. Ringsmuth, and John R. Freeman. 2008. "The American Public and the Room to Maneuver: Responsibility Attributions and Policy Efficacy in an Era of Globalization." *International Studies Quarterly* **52** (4): 855–880.

Hellwig, Timothy, and David Samuels. 2007. "Voting in Open Economies: The Electoral Consequences of Globalization." *Comparative Political Studies* **40** (3): 283–306.

2008. "Electoral Accountability and the Variety of Democratic Regimes." *British Journal of Political Science* **38** (1): 65–90.

Heston, Alan, Robert Summers and Bettina Aten. 2009. Penn World Table Version 6.3. edited by Income and Prices at the University of Pennsylvania Center for International Comparisons of Production. Philadelphia, PA.

Hibbs, Douglas A., Jr. 1977. "Political Parties and Macroeconomic Policy." *The American Political Science Review* **71** (4): 1467–1487.

Hill, Kim Quaile, and Patricia A. Hurley. 1999. "Dyadic Representation Reappraised." *American Journal of Political Science* **43** (1): 109–137.

Hobolt, Sara B., James R. Tilley, and Susan A. Banducci. 2013. "Clarity of Responsibility: How Government Cohesion Conditions Performance Voting." *European Journal of Political Research* **52**(2): 164–187.

Hobolt, Sara B., and James R. Tilley. 2014. "Who's in Charge? Voter Attribution of Responsibility in the European Union." *Comparative Political Studies*, forthcoming.

Hooghe, Liesbet, Gary Marks, and Carole J. Wilson. 2002. "Does Left/Right Structure Party Positions on European Integration?" *Comparative Political Studies* **35** (8): 965.

Huber, John D. 1989. "Values and Partisanship in Left-Right Orientations: Measuring Ideology." *European Journal of Political Research* **17** (5): 599–621.

1996. *Rationalizing Parliament: Legislative Institutions and Party Politics in France.* New York: Cambridge University Press.

Huber, John D., and G. Bingham Powell. Jr. 1994. "Congruences between Citizens and Policymakers in Two Visions of Liberal Democracy." *World Politics* no. 46 (3): 291.

Hurley, Patricia, and Kim Quaile Hill. 2003. "Beyond the Demand-Input Model: A Theory of Representational Linkages." *Journal of Politics* **65** (2): 304–326.

Iida, Takeshi, and Tetsuya Matsubayashi. 2010. "Constitutions and Public Support for Welfare Policies." *Social Science Quarterly (Blackwell Publishing Limited)* **91** (1): 42–62.

Inglehart, Ronald. 1977. *The Silent Revolution: Changing Values and Political Styles Among Western Publics.* Princeton, NJ: Princeton University Press.

1990. *Culture Shift in Advanced Industrial Society.* Princeton, NJ: Princeton University Press.

2008. "Changing Values among Western Publics from 1970 to 2006." *West European Politics* **31** (1–2): 130–146.

Israelewicz, Erik. 1995. "La Première Révolte contre la Mondialisation." *Le Monde*, 7 December.

ISSP Research Group. 2008. *International Social Survey Programme: Role of Government IV – ISSP 2006.* GESIS Data Archive, Cologne. ZA4700 Data file Version 1.0.0.

Iversen, Torben. 2005. *Capitalism, Democracy, and Welfare.* New York: Cambridge University Press.

Iversen, Torben, and Thomas R. Cusack. 2000. "The Causes of Welfare State Expansion: Deindustrialization or Globalization?" *World Politics* **52** (3): 313–349.

Iversen, Torben, and David Soskice. 2001. "An Asset Theory of Social Preferences." *American Political Science Review* **95** (4): 875.

Iversen, Torben, and Anne Wren. 1998. "Equality, Employment, and Budgetary Restraint: The Trilemma of the Service Economy." *World Politics* **50** (4): 507–546.

Jackman, Simon, and Paul M. Sniderman. 2002. "The Institutional Organization of Choice Spaces: A Political Conception of Political Psychology." In *Political Psychology*, ed. Kristen Monroe, 209–224. Mahwah, NJ: Lawrence Erlbaum.

Jahn, Detlef. 2006. "Globalization as 'Galton's Problem': The Missing Link in the Analysis of Diffusion Patterns in Welfare State Development." *International Organization* **60** (2): 401–431.

Jensen, Carsten. 2011a. "Conditional Contraction: Globalisation and Capitalist Systems." *European Journal of Political Research* **50** (2): 168–189.

Jensen, Carsten. 2011b. "Marketization via Compensation: Health Care and the Politics of the Right in Advanced Industrialized Nations." *British Journal of Political Science* **41** (3): 907–926.

2012. "Labour Market- versus Life Course-Related Social Policies: Understanding Cross-Programme Differences." *Journal of European Public Policy* **19** (2): 275–291.

Kaltenthaler, Karl C., Ronald D. Gelleny, and Stephen J. Ceccoli. 2004. "Explaining Citizen Support for Trade Liberalization." *International Studies Quarterly* **48** (4): 829–852.

Katz, Richard S., and Peter Mair. 1995. "Changing Models of Party Organization and Party Democracy." *Party Politics* **1** (1): 5–28.

Katzenstein, Peter J. 1985. *Small States in World Markets: Industrial Policy in Europe, Cornell Studies in Political Economy*. Ithaca, NY: Cornell University Press.

Kavanagh, Dennis, and Peter Morris. 1994. *Consensus Politics: From Attlee to Major*. 2nd ed. Cambridge, MA: Blackwell.

Kayser, Mark Andreas. 2007. "How Domestic Is Domestic Politics? Globalization and Elections." *Annual Review of Political Science* **10** (1): 341–362.

2009. "Partisan Waves: International Business Cycles and Electoral Choice." *American Journal of Political Science* **53** (4): 950–970.

Kayser, Mark Andreas, and Michael Peress. 2012. "Benchmarking across Borders: Electoral Accountability and the Necessity of Comparison." *American Political Science Review* **106**(3): 661–684.

Kedar, Orit. 2005. "When Moderate Voters Prefer Extreme Parties: Policy Balancing in Parliamentary Elections." *American Political Science Review* **99** (2): 185–199.

2009. *Voting for Policy, Not Parties: How Voters Compensate for Power Sharing*, New York: Cambridge University Press.

Keohane, Robert O., and Joseph S. Nye Jr. 2000. "Introduction." In *Governance in a Globalizing World*, eds. Joseph S. Nye Jr. and John D. Donahue, 1–41. Washington, DC: Brookings Institution Press.

Key, V.O., Jr. 1966. *The Responsible Electorate: Rationality in Presidential Voting 1936–60*. Cambridge, MA: The Belknap Press of Harvard University Press.

Kim, Jae-on, and Charles W. Mueller. 1978. *Factor Analysis: Statistical Methods and Practical Issues. Sage University Paper Series. Quantitative Applications in the Social Sciences*. Beverly Hills, CA: Sage Publications.

King, Gary, Michael Tomz, and Wittenberg Jason. 2000. "Making the Most of Statistical Analyses: Improving Interpretation and Presentation." *American Journal of Political Science* **44** (2): 347–361.

Kirchheimer, Otto. 1966. "The Transformation of the Western European Party Systems." In *Political Parties and Political Development*, eds. Peter Mair and Marcus Weiner, 177–200. Princeton, NJ: Princeton University Press.

Kitschelt, Herbert. 1994. *The Transformation of European Social Democracy, Cambridge Studies in Comparative Politics*. Cambridge; New York: Cambridge University Press.

Klingemann, Hans-Dieter, Andrea Volkens, Judith Bara, Ian Budge, and Michael McDonald. 2006. *Mapping Policy Preferences II: Estimates for Parties, Electors and Governments in Central and Eastern Europe, European Union and OECD 1990–2003*. Oxford: Oxford University Press.

Koopmans, Ruud. 2005. *Contested Citizenship: Immigration and Cultural Diversity in Europe, Social Movements, Protest, and Contention*. Minneapolis: University of Minnesota Press.

Korpi, Walter, and Joakim Palme. 2003. "New Politics and Class Politics in the Context of Austerity and Globalization: Welfare State Regress in 18 Countries, 1975–95." *American Political Science Review* **97** (3): 425–446.

Kriesi, Hanspeter, Edgar Grande, Romain Lachat, Martin Dolezal, Simon Bornschier, and Timotheos Frey. 2008. *West European Politics in the Age of Globalization*. Cambridge; New York: Cambridge University Press.

La Porta, R., F. Lopez-de-Silanes, A. Shleifer, and R. Vishny. 1999. "The Quality of Government." *Journal of Law, Economics, and Organization* **15** (1): 222–279.

Larsen, Christian Albrekt. 2008. "The Institutional Logic of Welfare Attitudes: How Welfare Regimes Influence Public Support." *Comparative Political Studies* **41** (2): 145–168.

Lau, Richard R., and David O. Sears. 1981. "Cognitive Links between Economic Grievances and Political Responses." *Political Behavior* **3** (4): 279–302.

Laver, Michael, and Ian Budge, eds. 1992. *Party Policy and Government Coalitions*. London: Macmillan.

Laver, Michael, Kenneth Benoit, and John Garry. 2003. "Extracting Policy Positions from Political Texts Using Words as Data." *American Political Science Review* **97** (2): 311–331.

Laver, Michael, and Norman Schofield. 1990. *Multiparty Government: The Politics of Coalition in Europe, Comparative European Politics*. Oxford England; New York: Oxford University Press.

Lewis-Beck, Michael S., and Marina Costa Lobo. 2011. "Anchoring the Portugese Voter: Panel Dynamics in a Newer Electorate." *Political Research Quartely* **64** (2): 293–308.

Lewis-Beck, Michael S., and Richard Nadeau. 2009. "Obama and the Economy in 2008." *PS: Political Science & Politics* **42** (3): 479–483.

Lewis-Beck, Michael S., Richard Nadeau, and Angelo Elias. 2008. "Economics, Party, and the Vote: Causality Issues and Panel Data." *American Journal of Political Science* **52** (1): 84–95.

Lipset, Seymour Martin. 1981. *Political Man: The Social Bases of Politics*. Expanded ed. Baltimore: Johns Hopkins University Press.

Lipset, Seymour Martin, and Stein Rokkan. 1967. *Party systems and voter alignments: cross-national perspectives. [Contributors: Robert R. Alford and others]*, *International Yearbook of Political Behavior Research*. New York: Free Press.

MacKuen, Michael B., Robert S. Erikson, and James A. Stimson. 1992. "Peasants or Bankers? The American Electorate and the U.S. Economy." *The American Political Science Review* **86** (3): 597–611.

Manin, Bernard, Adam Przeworski, and Susan Carol Stokes. 1999. "Elections and Representation." In *Democracy, Accountability, and Representation*, eds. Adam Przeworski, Susan Carol Stokes, and Bernard Manin, 29–54. Cambridge; New York: Cambridge University Press.

Mansbridge, Jane. 2003. "Rethinking Representation." *American Political Science Review* **97** (4): 515–527.

Mansfield, Edward D. Mutz Diana C. 2009. "Support for Free Trade: Self-Interest, Sociotropic Politics, and Out-Group Anxiety." *International Organization* **63** (3): 425–457.

Margalit, Yotam. 2011. "Costly Jobs: Trade-related Layoffs, Government Compensation, and Voting in U.S. Elections." *American Political Science Review* **105** (1): 166–188.

Marks, Gary (ed.). 2007. "Special Symposium: Comparing Measures of Party Positioning: Expert, Manifesto, and Survey Data." *Electoral Studies* **26**: 1–141.

Mayda, Anna Maria, and Dani Rodrik. 2005. "Why Are Some People (and Countries) More Protectionist Than Others?" *European Economic Review* **49** (6): 1393–1430.

McDonald, Michael D., and Ian Budge. 2005. *Elections, Parties, Democracy: Conferring the Median Mandate*, *Comparative Politics*. Oxford; New York: Oxford University Press.

McDonald, Michael D., and Silvia M. Mendes. 2001. "Checking the Party Policy Estimates: Convergent Validity." In *Mapping Policy Preferences: Estimates for Parties, Electors, and Governments 1945–1998*, eds. Ian Budge, Hans-Dieter Klingemann, Andrea Volkens, Judith Bara and Eric Tanenbaum, 127–142. Oxford: Oxford University Press.

Meguid, Bonnie M. 2008. *Party Competition between Unequals: Strategies and Electoral Fortunes in Western Europe*, *Cambridge Studies in Comparative Politics*. Cambridge; New York: Cambridge University Press.

Meltzer, Allan, and Scott Richard. 1981. "A Rational Theory of the Size of Government." *The Journal of Political Economy* **89** (5): 914–927.

Merrill, Samuel, and Bernard Grofman. 1999. *A Unified Theory of Voting: Directional and Proximity Spatial Models*. Cambridge; New York: Cambridge University Press.

Mishra, Ramesh. 1999. *Globalization and the Welfare State*. Cheltenham; Northampton, MA: Edward Elgar Publishing.

Moene, Karle Ove, and Michael Wallerstein. 2001. "Inequality, Social Insurance, and Redistribution." *American Political Science Review* **95** (4): 859–874.

Moses, Jonathon Wayne. 2000. *Open States in the Global Economy: The Political Economy of Small-State Macroeconomic Management*. New York: St. Martin's Press.

Mosley, Layna. 2003. *Global Capital and National Governments*. New York: Cambridge University Press.
Müller, Wolfgang C., and Kaare Strom. 2000. *Coalition Governments in Western Europe, Comparative Politics*. New York: Oxford University Press.
Mundell, R. A. 1960. "The Monetary Dynamics of International Adjustment under Fixed and Flexible Exchange-Rates." *Quarterly Journal of Economics* **74** (2): 227–257.
Nadeau, Richard, and Michael S. Lewis-Beck. 2001. "National Economic Voting in U.S. Presidential Elections." *The Journal of Politics* **63** (1): 159–181.
Nye, Joseph S., Jr., and John D. Donahue. 2000. *Governance in a Globalizing World*. Washington, DC: Brookings Institution Press.
Page, Benjamin I. 1994. "Democratic Responsiveness? Untangling the Links Between Public Opinion and Policy." *PS: Political Science and Politics* **27** (1): 17–21.
Paldam, Martin, and Peter Nannestad. 1997. "From the Pocketbook of the Welfare Man.: A Pooled Cross-Section Study of Economic Voting in Denmark, 1986–92." *British Journal of Political Science* **27** (1): 119–136.
Papacostas, Antonis. 2010. *Eurobarometer 61.0: The European Union, Globalization, and the European Parliament, February-March 2004*. Cologne, Germany: GESIS/Ann Arbor, MI: Inter-University Consortium for Political and Social Research.
Peffley, Mark A. 1984. "The Voter as Juror: Attributing Responsibility for Economic Problems." *Political Behavior* **6** (3): 275–294.
Pew Research Center, for the People & the Press. 2008. Early October 2008 Economic and Political Survey. www.people-press.org.
Pierson, Paul. 1994. *Dismantling the Welfare State? Reagan, Thatcher and the Politics of Retrenchment*. New York: Cambridge University Press.
2001. *The New Politics of the Welfare State*. Oxford; New York: Oxford University Press.
Pitkin, Hanna Fenichel. 1967. *The Concept of Representation*. Berkeley: University of California Press.
Plümper, Thomas, and Vera E. Troeger. 2007. "Efficient Estimation of Time-Invariant and Rarely Changing Variables in Finite Sample Panel Analyses with Unit Fixed Effects." *Political Analysis* **15** (2): 124–139.
Plümper, Thomas, Vera E. Troeger, and Philip Manow. 2005. "Panel Data Analysis in Comparative Politics: Linking Method to Theory." *European Journal of Political Research* **44** (2): 327–354.
Plümper, Thomas, Vera E. Troeger, and Hannes Winner. 2009. "Why is There No Race to the Bottom in Capital Taxation?" *International Studies Quarterly* **53** (3): 761–786.
Polanyi, Karl. 1944. *The Great Transformation: The Political and Economic Origins of Our Time*. Boston: Beacon Press.
Pontusson, Jonas. 1995. "Explaining the Decline of European Social Democracy: The Role of Structural Economic Change." *World Politics* **47** (4): 495–533.
Powell, G. Bingham, Jr. 2000. *Elections as Instruments of Democracy: Majoritarian and Proportional Visions*. New Haven, CT: Yale University Press.
Powell, G. Bingham, Jr., and Guy D. Whitten. 1993. "A Cross-National Analysis of Economic Voting: Taking Account of the Political Context." *American Journal of Political Science* **37** (2): 391–414.

Rattinger, H., S. Roßteutscher, R. Schmitt-Beck, B. Weßels et al. 2011. *Zwischen Langeweile und Extremen: Die Bundestagswahl 2009.* Nomos: Baden-Baden.

Ray, Leonard. 2003. "Reconsidering the Link between Incumbent Support and Pro-EU Opinion." *European Union Politics* **4** (3): 259–279.

Rehm, Philipp. 2011. "Social Policy by Popular Demand." *World Politics* **63** (2): 271–299.

Riker, William H. 1962. *The Theory of Political Coalitions.* New Haven, CT: Yale University Press.

Rodrik, Dani. 1997. *Has Globalization Gone Too Far?* Washington, DC: Institute for International Economics.

1998. "Why Do More Open Economies Have Bigger Governments?" *Journal of Political Economy* **106** (5): 997–1032.

2011. *The Globalization Paradox: Democracy and the Future of the World Economy.* New York: W. W. Norton & Co.

Rudolph, Thomas J. 2003. "Who's Responsible for the Economy? The Formation and Consequences of Responsibility Attributions." *American Journal of Political Science* **47** (4): 698–713.

Rudra, Nita. 2002. "Globalization and the Decline of the Welfare State in Less-Developed Countries." *International Organization* **56** (2): 411–455.

Rueda, David. 2005. "Insider–Outsider Politics in Industrialized Democracies: The Challenge to Social Democratic Parties." *American Political Science Review* **99** (1): 61–74.

Ruggie, John Gerard. 1982. "International Regimes, Transactions, and Change: Embedded Liberalism in the Postwar Economic Order." *International Organization* **36** (2): 379–415.

Samuels, David, and Timothy Hellwig. 2010. "Elections and Accountability for the Economy: A Conceptual and Empirical Reassessment." *Journal of Elections, Public Opinion & Parties* **20** (4): 393–419.

Samuels, David J., and Matthew S. Shugart. 2010. *Presidents, Parties, and Prime Ministers.* New York: Cambridge University Press.

Sartori, Giovanni. 1976. *Parties and Party Systems: A Framework for Analysis.* New York: Cambridge University Press.

Sattler, Thomas, John R. Freeman, and Patrick T. Brandt. 2008. "Political Accountability and the Room to Maneuver." *Comparative Political Studies* **41** (9): 1212–1239.

Sattler, Thomas, Patrick T. Brandt, and John R. Freeman. 2010. "Democratic Accountability in Open Economies." *Quarterly Journal of Political Science* **5** (1): 71–97.

Scheve, Kenneth F., and Matthew J. Slaughter. 2001. "What Determines Individual Trade-Policy Preferences?" *Journal of International Economics* **54** (2): 267–292.

2007. "A New Deal for Globalization." *Foreign Affairs* **86** (4): 34–47.

Scheve, Kenneth, and Matthew J. Slaughter. 2004. "Economic Insecurity and the Globalization of Production." *American Journal of Political Science* **48** (4): 662–674.

Schmitt, Hermann, and Evi Scholz. 2005. The Mannheim Eurobarometer Trend File, 1970–2002. edited by Zentralarchiv fur Empirische Sozialforschung. Cologne, Germany.

Shapiro, Virginia, and W. Phillips Shively. 2007. *Comparative Study of Electoral Systems Module* 2 [dataset]. Ann Arbor, MI: CSES.

Simmons, Beth A., Frank Dobbin, and Geoffrey Garrett. 2006. "Introduction: The International Diffusion of Liberalism." *International Organization* **60** (4): 781–810.

Simmons, Beth A., and Zachary Elkins. 2004. "The Globalization of Liberalization: Policy Diffusion in the International Political Economy." *American Political Science Review* **98** (1): 171–189.

Singer, Matthew M. 2011. "Who Says "It's the Economy"? Cross-National and Cross-Individual Variation in the Salience of Economic Performance." *Comparative Political Studies* **44** (3): 284–312.

2013. "The Global Economic Crisis and Domestic Political Agendas." *Electoral Studies* **32**(3): 404–410.

Singer, Matthew M., and Ryan E. Carlin. 2013. "Context Counts: The Election Cycle, Development, and the Nature of Economic Voting." *Journal of Politics* **75** (3): 730–742.

Sniderman, Paul M. 1993. "The New Look in Public Opinion Research." In *Political Science: The State of the Discipline II*, eds. Ada W. Finifter and American Political Science Association., 219–245. Washington, DC: American Political Science Association.

Sniderman, Paul M., Richard A. Brody, and Philip E. Tetlock. 1991. *Reasoning and Choice: Explorations in Political Psychology*. Cambridge: Cambridge University Press.

Sniderman, Paul M., and John Bullock. 2004. "A Consistency Theory of Public Opinion and Political Choice: The Hypothesis of Menu Dependence." In *Studies in Public Opinion: Attitudes, Nonattitudes, Measurement Error, and Change*, eds. Willem Saris and Paul M. Sniderman, 337–358. Princeton, NJ: Princeton University Press.

Sniderman, Paul M., Michael Gray Hagen, Philip E. Tetlock, and Henry E. Brady. 1986. "Reasoning Chains: Causal Models of Policy Reasoning in Mass Publics." *British Journal of Political Science* **16** (4): 405–430.

Solt, Frederick. 2009. "Standardizing the World Income Inequality Database." *Social Science Quarterly* **90**(2): 231–242.

Soroka, Stuart Neil, and Christopher Wlezien. 2010. *Degrees of Democracy: Politics, Public Opinion, and Policy*. New York: Cambridge University Press.

Steenbergen, Marco R., Erica E. Edwards, and Catherine E. de Vries. 2007. "Who's Cueing Whom? Mass-Elite Linkages and the Future of European Integration." *European Union Politics* **8** (1): 13–35.

Steiner, Nils D., and Christian W. Martin. 2012. "Economic Integration, Party Polarization, and Electoral Turnout: Testing for a Causal Chain." *West European Politics* **35** (2): 238–265.

Steinmo, Sven. 2002. "Globalization and Taxation." *Comparative Political Studies* **35** (7): 839–862.

2010. *The Evolution of Modern States: Sweden, Japan, and the United States*, New York: Cambridge University Press.

Stevenson, Randolph T. 2001. "The Economy and Policy Mood: A Fundamental Dynamic of Democratic Politics?" *American Journal of Political Science* **45** (3): 620–633.

Stevenson, Randolph T., and Raymond Duch. 2013. "The Meaning and Use of Subjective Perceptions in Studies of Economic Voting." *Electoral Studies* **32**: 305–320.

Stimson, James A. 1999. *Public Opinion in America: Moods, Cycles, and Swings*. 2nd ed. Boulder, CO: Westview Press.

Stimson, James A., Michael B. Mackuen, and Robert S. Erikson. 1995. "Dynamic Representation." *The American Political Science Review* **89** (3): 543–565.

Stokes, Donald E. 1963. "Spatial Models of Party Competition." *The American Political Science Review* **57** (2): 368–377.

Strøm, Kaare. 1990. "A Behavioral Theory of Competitive Political Parties." *American Journal of Political Science* **34** (2): 565–598.

Stubager, Rune. 2010. "The Development of the Education Cleavage: Denmark as a Critical Case." *West European Politics* **33** (3): 505–533.

Swank, Duane. 2002. *Global Capital, Political Institutions, and Policy Change in Developed Welfare States, Cambridge Studies in Comparative Politics*. Cambridge; New York: Cambridge University Press.

Tavits, Margit. 2007. "Principle vs. Pragmatism: Policy Shifts and Political Competition." *American Journal of Political Science* **51** (1): 151–165.

Thomsen, Soren Risbjerg. 1995. "The 1994 Parliamentary Election in Denmark." *Electoral Studies* **14** (3): 315–322.

Tomz, Michael, Joshua A. Tucker, and Jason Wittenberg. 2002. "An Easy and Accurate Regression Model for Multiparty Electoral Data." *Political Analysis* **10** (1): 66–83.

Tufte, Edward R. 1978. *Political Control of the Economy*. Princeton, NJ: Princeton University Press.

Vowles, Jack. 2008. "Does Globalization Affect Public Perceptions of 'Who in power Can Make a Difference'? Evidence from 40 Countries, 1996–2006." *Electoral Studies* **27** (1): 63–76.

Vowles, Jack, Timothy Hellwig, Georgios Xezonakis, and Eva Coffey. 2010. Survey of Experts on Political Parties and Globalization, January-April 2009. University of Exeter and Indiana University.

Walter, Stefanie. 2010. "Globalization and the Welfare State: Testing the Microfoundations of the Compensation Hypothesis." *International Studies Quarterly* **54** (2): 403–426.

Ward, Hugh, Lawrence Ezrow, and Han Dorussen. 2011. "Globalization, Party Positions, and the Median Voter." *World Politics* **63** (3): 509–547.

Warwick, Paul V. 2002. "Toward a Common Dimensionality in West European Policy Spaces." *Party Politics* **8** (1): 101–122.

Wibbels, Erik. 2006. "Dependency Revisited: International Markets, Business Cycles, and Social Spending in the Developing World." *International Organization* **60** (2): 433–468.

Wlezien, Christopher. 1995. "The Public as Thermostat: Dynamics of Preferences for Spending." *American Journal of Political Science* **39** (4): 981–1000.

2004. "Patterns of Representation: Dynamics of Public Preferences and Policy." *Journal of Politics* **66** (1): 1–24.

Wlezien, Christopher, Mark Franklin, and Daniel Twiggs. 1997. "Economic Perceptions and Vote Choice: Disentangling the Endogeneity." *Political Behavior* **19** (1): 7–17.

Wlezien, Christopher, and Stuart Neil Soroka. 2012. "Political Institutions and the Opinion-Policy Link." *West European Politics* **35** (6): 1407–1432.

Wooldridge, Jeffrey M. 2009. *Introductory Econometrics: A Modern Approach*. Mason, OH: Cengage.

Yergin, Daniel, and Joseph Stanislaw. 1998. *The Commanding Heights: The Battle between Government and the Marketplace that is Remaking the Modern World*. New York: Simon & Schuster.

Zaller, John. 1992. *The Nature and Origins of Mass Opinion*. New York: Cambridge University Press.

Zysman, John. 1983. *Governments, Markets, and Growth: Financial Systems and the Politics of Industrial Change*, Cornell Studies in Political Economy. Ithaca, NY: Cornell University Press.

Index

Books in the Series (*continued from page iii*)

Carles Boix, *Democracy and Redistribution*
Carles Boix, *Political Parties, Growth, and Equality: Conservative and Social Democratic Economic Strategies in the World Economy*
Catherine Boone, *Merchant Capital and the Roots of State Power in Senegal, 1930–1985*
Catherine Boone, *Political Topographies of the African State: Territorial Authority and Institutional Change*
Catherine Boone, *Property and Political Order in Africa: Land Rights and the Structure of Politics*
Michael Bratton, Robert Mattes, and E. Gyimah-Boadi, *Public Opinion, Democracy, and Market Reform in Africa*
Michael Bratton and Nicolas van de Walle, *Democratic Experiments in Africa: Regime Transitions in Comparative Perspective*
Valerie Bunce, *Leaving Socialism and Leaving the State: The End of Yugoslavia, the Soviet Union, and Czechoslovakia*
Daniele Caramani, *The Nationalization of Politics: The Formation of National Electorates and Party Systems in Europe*
John M. Carey, *Legislative Voting and Accountability*
Kanchan Chandra, *Why Ethnic Parties Succeed: Patronage and Ethnic Headcounts in India*
Eric C. C. Chang, Mark Andreas Kayser, Drew A. Linzer, and Ronald Rogowski, *Electoral Systems and the Balance of Consumer-Producer Power*
José Antonio Cheibub, *Presidentialism, Parliamentarism, and Democracy*
Ruth Berins Collier, *Paths toward Democracy: The Working Class and Elites in Western Europe and South America*
Pepper D. Culpepper, *Quiet Politics and Business Power: Corporate Control in Europe and Japan*
Rafaela M. Dancygier, *Immigration and Conflict in Europe*
Christian Davenport, *State Repression and the Domestic Democratic Peace*
Donatella della Porta, *Social Movements, Political Violence, and the State*
Alberto Diaz-Cayeros, *Federalism, Fiscal Authority, and Centralization in Latin America*
Thad Dunning, *Crude Democracy: Natural Resource Wealth and Political Regimes*
Gerald Easter, *Reconstructing the State: Personal Networks and Elite Identity*
Margarita Estevez-Abe, *Welfare and Capitalism in Postwar Japan: Party, Bureaucracy, and Business*

Henry Farrell, *The Political Economy of Trust: Institutions, Interests, and Inter-Firm Cooperation in Italy and Germany*
Karen E. Ferree, *Framing the Race in South Africa: The Political Origins of Racial Census Elections*
M. Steven Fish, *Democracy Derailed in Russia: The Failure of Open Politics*
Robert F. Franzese, *Macroeconomic Policies of Developed Democracies*
Roberto Franzosi, *The Puzzle of Strikes: Class and State Strategies in Postwar Italy*
Timothy Frye, *Building States and Markets After Communism: The Perils of Polarized Democracy*
Geoffrey Garrett, *Partisan Politics in the Global Economy*
Scott Gehlbach, *Representation through Taxation: Revenue, Politics, and Development in Postcommunist States*
Edward L. Gibson, *Boundary Control: Subnational Authoritarianism in Federal Democracies*
Jane R. Gingrich, *Making Markets in the Welfare State: The Politics of Varying Market Reforms*
Miriam Golden, *Heroic Defeats: The Politics of Job Loss*
Jeff Goodwin, *No Other Way Out: States and Revolutionary Movements*
Merilee Serrill Grindle, *Changing the State*
Anna Grzymala-Busse, *Rebuilding Leviathan: Party Competition and State Exploitation in Post-Communist Democracies*
Anna Grzymala-Busse, *Redeeming the Communist Past: The Regeneration of Communist Parties in East Central Europe*
Frances Hagopian, *Traditional Politics and Regime Change in Brazil*
Henry E. Hale, *The Foundations of Ethnic Politics: Separatism of States and Nations in Eurasia and the World*
Mark Hallerberg, Rolf Rainer Strauch, and Jürgen von Hagen, *Fiscal Governance in Europe*
Stephen E. Hanson, *Post-Imperial Democracies: Ideology and Party Formation in Third Republic France, Weimar Germany, and Post-Soviet Russia*
Silja Häusermann, *The Politics of Welfare State Reform in Continental Europe: Modernization in Hard Times*
Michael Hechter, *Alien Rule*
Timothy Hellwig, *Globalization and Mass Politics: Retaining the Room to Maneuver*
Gretchen Helmke, *Courts Under Constraints: Judges, Generals, and Presidents in Argentina*
Yoshiko Herrera, *Imagined Economies: The Sources of Russian Regionalism*
J. Rogers Hollingsworth and Robert Boyer, eds., *Contemporary Capitalism: The Embeddedness of Institutions*
John D. Huber and Charles R. Shipan, *Deliberate Discretion? The Institutional Foundations of Bureaucratic Autonomy*

Ellen Immergut, *Health Politics: Interests and Institutions in Western Europe*
Torben Iversen, *Capitalism, Democracy, and Welfare*
Torben Iversen, *Contested Economic Institutions*
Torben Iversen, Jonas Pontusson, and David Soskice, eds., *Unions, Employers, and Central Banks: Macroeconomic Coordination and Institutional Change in Social Market Economies*
Thomas Janoski and Alexander M. Hicks, eds., *The Comparative Political Economy of the Welfare State*
Joseph Jupille, *Procedural Politics: Issues, Influence, and Institutional Choice in the European Union*
Stathis Kalyvas, *The Logic of Violence in Civil War*
David C. Kang, *Crony Capitalism: Corruption and Capitalism in South Korea and the Philippines*
Stephen B. Kaplan, *Globalization and Austerity Politics in Latin America*
Junko Kato, *Regressive Taxation and the Welfare State*
Orit Kedar, *Voting for Policy, Not Parties: How Voters Compensate for Power Sharing*
Robert O. Keohane and Helen B. Milner, eds., *Internationalization and Domestic Politics*
Herbert Kitschelt, *The Transformation of European Social Democracy*
Herbert Kitschelt, Kirk A. Hawkins, Juan Pablo Luna, Guillermo Rosas, and Elizabeth J. Zechmeister, *Latin American Party Systems*
Herbert Kitschelt, Peter Lange, Gary Marks, and John D. Stephens, eds., *Continuity and Change in Contemporary Capitalism*
Herbert Kitschelt, Zdenka Mansfeldova, Radek Markowski, and Gabor Toka, *Post-Communist Party Systems*
David Knoke, Franz Urban Pappi, Jeffrey Broadbent, and Yutaka Tsujinaka, eds., *Comparing Policy Networks*
Allan Kornberg and Harold D. Clarke, *Citizens and Community: Political Support in a Representative Democracy*
Amie Kreppel, *The European Parliament and the Supranational Party System*
David D. Laitin, *Language Repertoires and State Construction in Africa*
Fabrice E. Lehoucq and Ivan Molina, *Stuffing the Ballot Box: Fraud, Electoral Reform, and Democratization in Costa Rica*
Mark Irving Lichbach and Alan S. Zuckerman, eds., *Comparative Politics: Rationality, Culture, and Structure*, 2nd Edition
Evan Lieberman, *Race and Regionalism in the Politics of Taxation in Brazil and South Africa*
Richard M. Locke, *Promoting Labor Standards in a Global Economy: The Promise and Limits of Private Power*
Pauline Jones Luong, *Institutional Change and Political Continuity in Post-Soviet Central Asia*
Pauline Jones Luong and Erika Weinthal, *Oil Is Not a Curse: Ownership Structure and Institutions in Soviet Successor States*

Julia Lynch, *Age in the Welfare State: The Origins of Social Spending on Pensioners, Workers, and Children*
Lauren M. MacLean, *Informal Institutions and Citizenship in Rural Africa: Risk and Reciprocity in Ghana and Côte d'Ivoire*
Beatriz Magaloni, *Voting for Autocracy: Hegemonic Party Survival and Its Demise in Mexico*
James Mahoney, *Colonialism and Postcolonial Development: Spanish America in Comparative Perspective*
James Mahoney and Dietrich Rueschemeyer, eds., *Comparative Historical Analysis in the Social Sciences*
Scott Mainwaring and Matthew Soberg Shugart, eds., *Presidentialism and Democracy in Latin America*
Isabela Mares, *The Politics of Social Risk: Business and Welfare State Development*
Isabela Mares, *Taxation, Wage Bargaining, and Unemployment*
Cathie Jo Martin and Duane Swank, *The Political Construction of Business Interests: Coordination, Growth, and Equality*
Anthony W. Marx, *Making Race, Making Nations: A Comparison of South Africa, the United States, and Brazil*
Doug McAdam, John McCarthy, and Mayer Zald, eds., *Comparative Perspectives on Social Movements*
Bonnie M. Meguid, *Party Competition between Unequals: Strategies and Electoral Fortunes in Western Europe*
Joel S. Migdal, *State in Society: Studying How States and Societies Constitute One Another*
Joel S. Migdal, Atul Kohli, and Vivienne Shue, eds., *State Power and Social Forces: Domination and Transformation in the Third World*
Scott Morgenstern and Benito Nacif, eds., *Legislative Politics in Latin America*
Kevin M. Morrison, *Nontaxation and Representation: The Fiscal Foundations of Political Stability*
Layna Mosley, *Global Capital and National Governments*
Layna Mosley, *Labor Rights and Multinational Production*
Wolfgang C. Müller and Kaare Strøm, *Policy, Office, or Votes?*
Maria Victoria Murillo, *Labor Unions, Partisan Coalitions, and Market Reforms in Latin America*
Maria Victoria Murillo, *Political Competition, Partisanship, and Policy Making in Latin American Public Utilities*
Monika Nalepa, *Skeletons in the Closet: Transitional Justice in Post-Communist Europe*
Ton Notermans, *Money, Markets, and the State: Social Democratic Economic Policies since 1918*
Eleonora Pasotti, *Political Branding in Cities: The Decline of Machine Politics in Bogotá, Naples, and Chicago*

Aníbal Pérez-Liñán, *Presidential Impeachment and the New Political Instability in Latin America*
Roger D. Petersen, *Understanding Ethnic Violence: Fear, Hatred, and Resentment in Twentieth-Century Eastern Europe*
Roger D. Petersen, *Western Intervention in the Balkans: The Strategic Use of Emotion in Conflict*
Simona Piattoni, ed., *Clientelism, Interests, and Democratic Representation*
Paul Pierson, *Dismantling the Welfare State? Reagan, Thatcher, and the Politics of Retrenchment*
Marino Regini, *Uncertain Boundaries: The Social and Political Construction of European Economies*
Kenneth M. Roberts, *Party Systems in Latin America's Neoliberal Era: Changing Course*
Marc Howard Ross, *Cultural Contestation in Ethnic Conflict*
Ben Ross Schneider, *Hierarchical Capitalism in Latin America: Business, Labor, and the Challenges of Equitable Development*
Lyle Scruggs, *Sustaining Abundance: Environmental Performance in Industrial Democracies*
Jefferey M. Sellers, *Governing from Below: Urban Regions and the Global Economy*
Yossi Shain and Juan Linz, eds., *Interim Governments and Democratic Transitions*
Beverly Silver, *Forces of Labor: Workers' Movements and Globalization since 1870*
Theda Skocpol, *Social Revolutions in the Modern World*
Dan Slater, *Ordering Power: Contentious Politics and Authoritarian Leviathans in Southeast Asia*
Regina Smyth, *Candidate Strategies and Electoral Competition in the Russian Federation: Democracy without Foundation*
Richard Snyder, *Politics after Neoliberalism: Reregulation in Mexico*
David Stark and László Bruszt, *Postsocialist Pathways: Transforming Politics and Property in East Central Europe*
Sven Steinmo, *The Evolution of Modern States: Sweden, Japan, and the United States*
Sven Steinmo, Kathleen Thelen, and Frank Longstreth, eds., *Structuring Politics: Historical Institutionalism in Comparative Analysis*
Susan C. Stokes, *Mandates and Democracy: Neoliberalism by Surprise in Latin America*
Susan C. Stokes, ed., *Public Support for Market Reforms in New Democracies*
Susan C. Stokes, Thad Hall, Marcelo Nazareno, and Valeria Brusco, *Brokers, Voters, and Clientelism: The Puzzle of Distributive Politics*
Duane Swank, *Global Capital, Political Institutions, and Policy Change in Developed Welfare States*

Sidney Tarrow, *Power in Movement: Social Movements and Contentious Politics*, Revised and Updated 3rd Edition

Tariq Thachil, *Elite Parties, Poor Voters: How Social Services Win Votes in India*

Kathleen Thelen, *How Institutions Evolve: The Political Economy of Skills in Germany, Britain, the United States, and Japan*

Kathleen Thelen, *Varieties of Liberalization and the New Politics of Social Solidarity*

Charles Tilly, *Trust and Rule*

Daniel Treisman, *The Architecture of Government: Rethinking Political Decentralization*

Guillermo Trejo, *Popular Movements in Autocracies: Religion, Repression, and Indigenous Collective Action in Mexico*

Lily Lee Tsai, *Accountability without Democracy: How Solidary Groups Provide Public Goods in Rural China*

Joshua Tucker, *Regional Economic Voting: Russia, Poland, Hungary, Slovakia, and the Czech Republic, 1990–1999*

Ashutosh Varshney, *Democracy, Development, and the Countryside*

Jeremy M. Weinstein, *Inside Rebellion: The Politics of Insurgent Violence*

Stephen I. Wilkinson, *Votes and Violence: Electoral Competition and Ethnic Riots in India*

Jason Wittenberg, *Crucibles of Political Loyalty: Church Institutions and Electoral Continuity in Hungary*

Elisabeth J. Wood, *Forging Democracy from Below: Insurgent Transitions in South Africa and El Salvador*

Elisabeth J. Wood, *Insurgent Collective Action and Civil War in El Salvador*

Lightning Source UK Ltd.
Milton Keynes UK
UKOW02f0618191016

285629UK00001B/153/P